School-Community Relations in Transition

by

Richard W. Saxe

University of Toledo

With Chapters by

David S. Rosenberger and Joseph C. Sommerville

McCutchan Publishing Corporation
2526 Grove Street
Berkeley, California 94704

ISBN 0-8211-1859-5
Library of Congress Catalog Number 83-62771

Typesetting composition by Al's Typesetting
Cover design by Terry Down, Griffin Graphics, Berkeley, Calif.
Book design and production editing by Kim Sharrar, MPC

CONTENTS

INTRODUCTION

In 1975 it seemed that the relationships between schools and their communities in this country were entering a new and significantly different phase. At that time there was debate and often political action about the proper relationship of schools and communities. Pressures for one reform or another were being brought at all levels of education. Critics and supporters alike were demanding that schools become more responsive—*to their particular agenda.*

At that time, educators were poorly prepared emotionally and professionally for the changing situation. The attacks on their expertise and authority were new, more frequent, and more forceful than ever before. In response to these phenomena, the senior author of this book wrote *School-Community Interaction* to provide information and suggest resources to help educators survive the changes and perhaps contribute to the improvement of the confusing, changing relations between schools and communities.

That was only nine years ago, but from our present perspective that time can be likened to the halcyon days of yore. Events have moved rapidly in response to powerful nationwide forces. Inflation has worsened and unemployment has spread. As a result, schools are faced with rising costs and a decreased public ability and will to provide resources at former levels, let alone to approve increases. Famous or infamous, depending upon one's point of view, propositions in California and elsewhere have legislated curbs on the main source of funding for schools, the property tax. Now, for the first time, the major share of the support of schools has shifted from local to state governments.

1

The influence of public schools has been eroded by poor press — accounts of declines in test scores and reports of the apparent inability of educators to cope with the new demands. In the midst of these vexing issues Congress passed legislation requiring *arithmetic* increases in funds and facilities and *geometric* increases in time and effort, adding to the inability of schools to address fully the concerns of other petitioners. And almost everything ended up in the courts.

In their wisdom, the courts found legal solutions without regard to financial obstacles. In their fashion, judges acted as Mark Twain is reputed to have solved the problem of the submarine menace during World War I: "Boil the water in the oceans," said Twain. When asked how to bring the oceans to 212 degrees Fahrenheit (100 degrees centigrade), Twain responded that it was his task to come up with a solution, someone else's to carry it out. So the courts ordered busing and special facilities and appointed financial supervisors and masters of desegregation — solutions for educators to implement.

As if these events were not trouble enough for weary educators (another development was the discovery of teacher/administrator "burnout"), other clients deserted schools in response to a newly felt need for a more moral, religious education. The crucial event in this litany was the election of a president who actively espoused alternatives to public schools and implemented campaign pledges to lessen the federal role in assisting education. Tuition-tax credits have become the bellwether of the future of public schools. The issue is in doubt for the first time since Horace Mann and others persuaded Americans that they must maintain free public education for all.

This is the context of this volume. It is radically changed from that in which schools were embedded in the seventies. That is why this book is titled *School-Community Relations in Transition*.

Happily, for purposes of motivation, there is a readiness among educators to attend more carefully to matters that fall within the realm of school-community relations. Unhappily, the crystal ball remains clouded, and future relationships can only be dimly perceived. Perhaps in the near future new and lasting accommodations will become apparent, but school is in session and we cannot wait. So readers are invited to join us in an ambitious attempt to contribute to the enhanced leadership of educators in associating with and serving their school communities.

We[1] shall begin in the traditional way—at the beginning—by identifying our understanding of the meanings of concepts to be explored. Part I explores phenomena that condition school-community relations; Part II deals with ways of influencing and responding to the phenomena explored.

The organization of education has shown remarkable rigidity over the years. There are aspects of this organization that are powerful barriers to school-community relations. Of equal importance in establishing barriers are some characteristics of professionalism. Our consideration of these concepts—organization and professionalism—will help suggest and define problem areas in school-community relations.

Attempts by parents and others to surmount these barriers have resulted in the creation of groups of like-minded persons who join together in pursuit of their shared objectives. Other unsuccessful petitioners of public education have sought and found the help of existing groups that work to secure the goals of some special interest. Interest groups and pressure groups of all types will be considered, especially as they operate to affect public education.

The new mix of special and changed interest groups in the communities as well as the long-established school-oriented organizations seek to identify and influence important decision makers. Such decision makers are not always elected officials or educational officers. There are several ways of identifying powerful persons in groups in a community. We will review and delineate ways of gathering data to discover whether such unofficial influentials exist and to consider their potential role in regard to the mission of public education.

The study of interest groups leads us to consider a new variable in the current educational scene—special and changing communities. Of course, there have always been subpopulations of school districts with particular concerns, but not with the transportation and education mandates that may result in uniquely complex parent and student groups in some schools. And, of course, there have always

---

[1]The senior author, convinced that "we" refers to reigning monarchs and Lindbergh and the Spirit of St. Louis, finds some comfort in noting that he is joined by two colleagues, making the first-person plural pronoun accurate.

been changing communities, but not in the ways and to the extent that they are now in the process of changing. These issues are the concern of a colleague who has been intimately involved in special and changing communities throughout his career. Dr. Joseph C. Sommerville prepared Chapter 6, Multiple and Changing School Communities.

As mentioned above when we likened jurists to Mark Twain, anything and everything can and all too often does end up in the courts. A line from Shakespeare concerning how to make a better world may occur to a superintendent or principal at the end of a six-hour session with seven assorted attorneys concerning an issue of less-than-monumental moment: "The first thing we do, let's kill all the lawyers" (*Henry VI*, Part II, act 4, scene 2). Since we cannot follow that advice, another colleague, a specialist in legal aspects of education, suggests how to live with and possibly influence the works of lawyers in a chapter on the impact of courts and legislatures on schools and communities. Dr. David S. Rosenberger wrote Chapter 7, Courts, Legislatures, and the School Community.

The second half of the book begins with the first of several chapters on practices in school-community relations: ways of assessing the needs and desires of a community. This is followed by suggestions on how to discover and employ community resources to accomplish educational objectives. Some of the resources will be human, some material. Some will be obvious, others unique and untapped.

Communication is the essence of school-community relations, and it deserves special attention in view of the confounding variables introduced in chapters on interest groups and changing and special communities. Will educators speaking in Esperanto be understood by all or mumble futilely from a tower of Babel? And how do parents and others send their incoming messages? A special type of communication is public relations, and we acknowledge its increased importance by devoting a chapter to it.

All these chapters are intended to serve as organizing elements, the better to approach the paramount issue of citizen participation in education. Ways of stimulating citizen involvement without damage to the valid prerogatives of educators will complete our study.

Ideally, the book will be read in the same order as the chapters are presented. However, it is possible for each chapter to stand alone so that it may be read according to the interests of various readers. Since each chapter deals with a different aspect of school-community relations, there is a separate body of literature for each topical area with a list of suggested readings at the end of each chapter.

Some readers will use this book with a group interested in school-community relations. They may wish to supplement or validate the central ideas of each chapter by performing some of the suggested activities listed at the end of each chapter. These are merely suggestive of countless ways of testing the authors' concepts against the real, specific school-community relations in the several areas available for study by readers.

An additional feature intended to help readers gain a more data-based understanding and appreciation of the concepts studied is provided by the exercises at the end of each chapter. These are activities that may be accomplished individually or in class with others studying school-community relations.

Where we have a bias—and we have a few—we try to identify it. (Perceptive readers will have gathered that at least one of the authors is not enamored of the new, extended role of the courts.) One of these biases, better, one of our assumptions, is that there will not be *one answer* for problems of school-community relations. There may be *many answers.* Some answers that seemed appropriate nine years ago do not seem to fit today. Similarly, answers that you, the readers, devise for today's problems may be worthless tomorrow. Hence, we commend the continuing study of school-community relations to educators everywhere.

Part I
School-Community Relations in Context

1

SCHOOL-COMMUNITY RELATIONS IN TRANSITION

"When I use a word," Humpty Dumpty said, in rather a scornful tone, "it means just what I choose it to mean—neither more nor less."

"The question is," said Alice, "whether you can make words mean so many different things."

"The question is," said Humpty Dumpty, "which is to be master—that's all."

(Lewis Carroll, *Alice Through the Looking Glass*)

As we noted in the Introduction, this book is about two dimensions of school-community relations. These are the conditions that affect community relations and suggested actions and reactions for educators. Conditions affecting community relations are qualitatively and quantitatively different than ever before. The challenge for educators to take appropriate action to anticipate and deal with rapidly changing events is formidable. There is no way of putting off the new demands and dealing with academic issues such as the teaching of reading or how to identify and obtain better instructional materials. If community relations are not attended to—properly attended to—educators will not be permitted to teach reading, and there will be no need to search for instructional materials. Some might think that we are dramatizing the situation, that the picture is not nearly so bleak as we have painted it. It is our perception that public education is in a crisis situation—a crisis directly related to tasks of school-community relations. Regaining and maintaining the confidence and support of the public are essential to maintaining free public education for all.

The National Education Association also perceives a crisis in public education, although their analysis stresses political forces more than social and economic influences. Members were "alert[ed] to the possibility (some are already saying probability) that our public schools are marked for extinction. . . . The Administration holds great disdain for our system of public education and is moving, step by planned step, to fund private school enterprises in its place" (McGuire, 1982).

For several years educators and their allies have assumed that there was a significant erosion of public confidence in education and have attempted to devise strategies to restore faith in and support for schools. (See, e.g., National Urban Coalition, 1979; note also that the National Association of Secondary School Principals received an award for its program to build confidence in education, *NASSP Newsleader,* September 1981.) Superintendent Alonzo Crim of Atlanta told elementary principals: "The public has lost its trust in education at a time when community support is needed more than ever, given the massive cuts in education being made from the federal level on down" (1982, p. 7). Writing in the journal of the Association for Supervision and Curriculum Development, Raywid compares previous criticism of education with the new context and concludes that "the only way that faith in public education is going to be restored to large segments of the American people is through a fundamental reworking and restructuring of the relationships between the home and the school, and/or the community and the school" (1979, p. 201).

Further support for the assertion that public education is at a crucial stage in a new context is found in a number of serious publications that question the continuance of education institutions as we know them. (See, e.g., Blumenfeld, 1981; Everhart, 1982; Seeley, 1981.) It is worth noting that these critics are from the philosophical/political right as contrasted to critics of the sixties and earlier seventies who were from the opposite pole. (See, e.g., Illich, 1972; Wasserman, 1970; Kohl, 1967.)

If conditions are as serious as we have described them, one would expect that there would be a steady stream of publications addressing issues of school-community relations. And, indeed, there is, but the publications are almost entirely addressed to parents and community groups. Furthermore, the literature generally assumes that educators are hostile to citizen participation and advocates an adversary stance toward educators. The general theme is to tell citizens how to demand and secure their rights from educators. (See, e.g., Buskin, 1975; Scribner and Stevens, 1975; Weinberg and Weinberg, 1979.) As we shall see in the next two chapters, there are elements of school organization and professional autonomy that are not conducive to school-community interaction. However, these are obstacles that can be overcome or changed and do not justify the implicit—often explicit—assumption that educators resent and resist any and all types of citizen participation.

The point here is that there is little guidance for educators to be found in the mass of writing about school-community relations. This is unfortunate, for most preparation programs give only minor attention to parent and community relations. Professional organizations have begun to address the new situation in workshops and publications, but these are optional and sometimes expensive.

The responsibility of effectively and efficiently addressing the crisis in confidence rests with individual districts and individual educators. We propose in these pages to identify some resources to assist them in their efforts. The first contribution we shall make is to issue a caveat about ambiguity in regard to all aspects of school-community relations. The quotation from Carroll with which this chapter begins is most appropriate. Few aspects of educational administration are defined in so many ways and used with so much ambiguity as *community relations.* Indeed, like words in Alice's Wonderland, *community relations* means what the user wishes it to mean. Unfortunately, only the user and a few of like mind may acknowledge any particular meaning. This lack of a common meaning often leads to misunderstanding and inhibits effective communication. So, we need to begin by considering some of the usages of *community relations.*

PUBLIC RELATIONS DEFINED

Many writers use the terms *community relations* and *public relations* as though they were interchangeable. In fact, some attempts to define community relations immediately become considerations of *public relations* (Hubbell, 1970). This would be all right for Humpty Dumpty and, as we shall maintain, sometimes it is all right for Alice and the rest of us as well. That is, in a sense, what is public relations at one level of an educational institution may be much like community relations at another level. This will take some explaining. If, for the moment, we mean by *community relations* all the communication that goes on between schools and their communities and by *public relations* we mean just those deliberate efforts by schools to influence the community's opinion, it is possible to make the case. At local school levels, relationships will predominantly fall in the general meaning taken for *community relations*. The community (and here readers should expect later difficulties with this term) is readily accessible. At the school district level, the community becomes more ephemeral, becomes the city, and the means of reaching it are more likely to be by *public relations*—news releases, television, radio, annual reports.

In this way, because the community of the city school administrator is so large and diverse, emphasis is given to ways of informing and persuading this broad community by means of public relations measures. Here we have made an important distinction. *Public relations* has become only one phase of the broader task of *community relations*. As such, a meaning for public relations will be more easily delineated. *Public relations will deal with practices initiated by educators and designed to influence the public; such things as news releases, displays, photography and audiovisual presentations, publications, speeches, and the like.* Kindred (1957) provides a definition that, although quite general, includes the essential elements of public relations. School public relations "is a process of communication between the school and community for the purpose of increasing citizen understanding of educational needs and practices and encouraging intelligent citizen interest and cooperation in the work of improving the school" (p. 16).

There is a nationwide organization, the National School Public Relations Association, that enrolls persons concerned with *public relations* as defined above; it is an affiliate of the National Education Association.[1]

Public relations originating with the schools and seeking to serve their purposes has been almost invariably favorable in its messages about schools. The notable exception is the bond issue campaign when shortcomings (usually physical) must be acknowledged to justify the requests for greatly increased resources.

Occasionally, public relations is used to denote a general level of

[1] 1201 Sixteenth Street, N.W., Washington, D.C. 20036.

public support for a district or a school superintendent. When used in this way, the assessment of "the superintendent's PR" does not refer to the practices used to inform and influence citizens but to an assessment of the degree of support or opposition for the administrator or district—a kind of popularity index.

The "grades" given to schools by respondents to the annual Gallup polls are examples of this usage of public relations. Data such as these are important to students of school-community relations. They not only reflect attitudes held by the sample population; because they are so widely disseminated they also influence unknown numbers of others as well. The problem for pollsters and for educators who subscribe to their services is complex. Even as the poll results report a global assessment of the perceived worthiness of the organization— its public relations rating—they are in themselves a PR process in action. Perhaps for some citizens the poll reports become their own opinion somewhat like the Will Rogers pleasantry: "All I know is what I read in the papers."

The polls are at any rate now part of the context of school-community relations, and we shall introduce their findings from time to time. The finding that is shared in Table 1.1 has to do with the general public relations rating of schools. One interpretation of these data is that the decline in confidence in education may have been arrested— like our economic recession it may have "bottomed out." We don't think so, but readers will have more recent polls so there is no point in conjecturing at this time. The cold facts will replace persuasive arguments. There is an important implication for educators in this connection. We need to question, as discreetly as possible, the sources of information used by friend and foe in arriving at their suggestions for the betterment of education. We need to introduce an acceptable translation of "Who says so?" And, even more important, we must be well grounded in the data that support our own positions. The time when pronouncements can be accepted *ex cathedra* is past.

Perhaps enough has been said to make clear our usage of the term *public relations.* It is one aspect of community relations. That a linguistic analysis could lead one to another conclusion is quite likely, for, after all, which is the greater, "public" or "community"? Nevertheless, we are dealing with the prevailing usage and, like Humpty Dumpty, the words *public relations* mean what we choose them to mean.

Table 1.1

Ratings of Public Schools

Students are often given the grades A, B, C, D, and Fail to denote the quality of
their work. Suppose the *public* schools themselves, in this community, were graded in
the same way. What grade would you give the public schools here—A, B, C, D, or Fail?

Ratings Given the Public Schools	National Totals (%)								
	1982	1981	1980	1979	1978	1977	1976	1975	1974
A	8	9	10	8	9	11	13	13	18
B	29	27	25	26	27	26	29	30	30
C	33	34	29	30	30	28	28	28	21
D	14	13	12	11	11	11	10	9	6
Fail	5	7	6	7	8	5	6	7	5
Don't know	11	10	18	18	15	19	14	13	20

Source: Gallup, 1982, p. 38.

MEANING OF SCHOOL-COMMUNITY RELATIONS

Our meaning of *community relations* may be somewhat more inclusive than other meanings. *Community relations will include all the interactions between any element of the school and any element of the community.*

What we really wish to focus on is the participation of citizens in
affairs of mutual concern to school people and the community. This
participation will run the gamut from the annual open house to
community control, from show and tell to paid community aides. The
term *community* itself will generally refer to any and all elements of the
society (neighborhood, district, town, city) involved with the school
for any purpose. When we depart from this global definition of
community, we will attempt to be more specific. Generally this will be
necessary when discussing what can be characterized as the parent
group, that is, those citizens whose children are enrolled in the school
or district concerned.

Clearly, this interpretation of community relations includes all
activities that fall under public relations as previously defined and
much more. Gordon McCloskey, whose careful study has long been
the standard work for educators interested in community and/or

public relations, seems to agree with the approach we have taken toward the meanings of *community relations* and *public relations*. In a discussion of what name to give to a committee, McCloskey states:

"Community Relations Committee" connotes civic unity and cooperative enterprise. Unfortunately, "Public Relations Committee" may connote a high-pressure effort to "sell" an unwanted service. The term "Publicity Committee" over-emphasizes one aspect of a sound communication program and may cause some people to believe that educators' purposes are similar to those of irresponsible press agents. (1967, p. 298)

McCloskey is alluding to the negative connotation of public relations, a connotation that has become fairly widespread owing to frequent misuse of the term. *Public relations* was used by one of the principals in the Watergate incident to denote a hostile propaganda barrage: "Mr. Colson referred to the networks as 'the other side' and told Mr. Haldeman, 'I think it is time for us to generate a PR (public relations) campaign against the Democrats and CBS' " ("Memos," 1973).

The lack of respect for public relations is captured in a piece by columnist Charles McCabe. McCabe suggests that public relations has such a bad reputaton that it needs a "public relations program for public relations itself" (1982). Although he is speaking of business and industry, his comments are applicable to public relations in any enterprise.

Despite such unfortunate associations with public relations, we intend to use the term as previously defined. It is but one phase, and a perfectly acceptable phase, of community relations. Perhaps someday the term will need to be redefined if the misuse continues. Something similar occurred with the word *propaganda* and we had finally to abandon the value-free use of that word for we knew readers would assume that the intent of propaganda is to distort or mislead.

A problem with our definition of community relations is its all-inclusiveness. That is, if the curriculum, as communicated to citizens by pupils, is a matter of concern, that concern becomes community relations. If the cost and the supplier of gym suits or band uniforms become matters that gain the attention of citizens, we are dealing with community relations as well as with the other obvious tasks of finance and pupil personnel. Almost anything that may cross the invisible boundary between school and community (in either direction) is potentially a community relations phenomenon. When interpreted in this fashion, it is extremely difficult to point to anything that may not, under some circumstances, be considered as having to do with community relations. That is exactly what we wish to suggest by the meaning given to *community relations*. Almost nothing happens in a school that is not or cannot become the community's business. Little happens in the community that cannot become the school's business.

If this seems a radical approach to take, it is probably because so many of us (educators) accept the protective wall of anonymity, shored up by apathy and inability to participate, that we associate with parents in giant urban school districts. If we were teaching or administering in small towns or villages, we would not be amazed at the magnitude of the task of community relations as we have defined the term. In small towns we would acknowledge that that is the way it *is.* Whether or not we would acknowledge that that is the way it is *supposed to be,* is an issue that is better postponed until Chapter 3, where we can give extended attention to the attitudes of educators—professionals—about community—lay—relations.

Students of community relations recently seem, by implication at least, to give additional support to the broad view of community relations adopted here. For example, Johansen, in his systems approach (1973), shows the essential overlap of the school district and potential subsystems. His flow chart of communication further supports our position that events in one system (the community) *can* become important data for the other system (the school).

Richard Gorton indirectly supports a broad interpretation of community relations in his discussion of a graphic illustration of "Individuals and Groups Which May Hold Expectations for the School's Role." Gorton identifies nineteen generic groups (e.g., taxpayers' associations) that "may possess expectations for the role of the school in regard to any specific or problem" (1972, p. 23).

PROPRIETY OF PROMOTING COMMUNITY RELATIONS

Regardless of how it is defined, there is even an element of controversy about whether it is proper for educators to become involved in attempts to do something about community relations. Obviously, if our preferred meaning of community relations has been accepted, there can be no argument about whether educators choose to participate in attempts to influence community relations. They *are* influencing community relations whenever they do anything in their roles as teachers and administrators. For those favoring other interpretations of the term—especially interpretations that take on more the nature of public relations—there is a valid concern for the propriety of participating in activities deliberately designed to influence community relations.

A recent publication expressed perfectly the ambiguity about deliberate efforts of educators to influence community relations: "School administrators act as though it is not only possible but right to influence public opinion and behavior in the interest of a school's purposes, but they often *talk* and write as though such actions were wrong" (Committee for Informed Detroit Schools, n.d.).

The real danger of ambitious efforts to influence public attitudes, aside from a possible waste of resources, is that the process might be confused with the substance, that is, to mount an extensive public information campaign as though the campaign itself could make a difference—regardless of what was actually happening in the schools! It is patently absurd to expect the public relations campaign to improve the schools. Other actions that become the substance of the public relations communications thrust can make the schools better, not public relations. A lawyer addressing a seminar on school-community relations put it this way: "What needs to be changed is not communications, public *appreciation* of what happens on campus, or image, or rapport with the community. What needs to be changed is *what takes place on campus!*" (Weltmer, 1973, p. 6).

In view of the particular focus of community relations identified—citizens' participation in school matters—there is ready justification for the propriety of studying and working on community relations. At one time all citizens had a say in the determination of school policy and practice by means of a gathering such as the revered New England town meeting. Even when the growth of towns and cities made this impossible, large boards and large operating committees of boards were devised to attempt to keep the public in close touch with its schools. It was not until after 1800 that the governance of education ceased to be lumped with all other municipal governmental functions. (Campbell, 1977, p. 95, puts the date of school government's differentiation from general government at 1827.)

Even after professional superintendents and trained staffs were employed, the public seemed still to need other sources of reliable information about their schools. One example of this can be seen in the rise and proliferation of school surveys. (See, e.g., American Association of School Administrators, 1964; Sears, 1925; Caswell, 1929.) Such surveys continue.

Current evidence of the public's need to know, and possibly their lack of complete trust in professionals, can be seen in the accountability emphasis. Sunshine laws, student- (Jaeger and Tittle, 1980) and teacher- ("Add-On's," 1982) mandated competency testing, and increased legislative curriculum requirements (Wise, 1979) all attest to this ambiguity of securing professional educators and at the same time a reluctance really to trust these professionals to do their jobs and report honestly on the progress they are making. Vouchers (see Coons and Sugarman, 1978) and tax credits (Moriarity, 1981) are other obvious devices to return an important measure of the control of education to the individual citizen. These and other such developments are in the American tradition to inform citizens about their schools and to participate in some way in the determination of educational policy.

If further justification of the need for citizens' participation in school matters is needed, it can be found in Cremin's *The Genius of American Education* (1965). After describing the strained relationship between educators and citizens, Cremin points out that "the profession is obligated, both in its own interest and in the interest of the service it performs, to assist the public in developing an ever more sophisticated body of opinion about education" (p. 110).

THE WISDOM OF PROMOTION

Even if it is agreed that it is quite proper for administrators to study and engage in community relations, it still may not necessarily be wise to do so. For, as we shall soon see, community relations is literally a two-way street. To implement a program of community relations as conceived in these pages will mean to open the schools in new ways to the participation and influence of citizens—who are not educators.

We intend to examine the traditional attitudes of educators in detail and to provide evidence to support our conclusions. However, to anticipate that argument, it can be asserted here that educators almost instinctively "know" that opening up the school system leads inevitably to criticism; in short, opening up leads to trouble. For most, the ideal climate heretofore would have been one characterized by an apathy tempered by feelings of mild support for the schools. Why then is it prudent to seek a change that must certainly add to demands on the time and talent of educators?

The most compelling argument in support of changing school-community relations is political. It is now necessary to earn the support and approval of the public. In 1975 we argued that it was necessary to protect the schools from attack. The situation has deteriorated since then to the point that there is a real need to reestablish the legitimacy of public schools. Gooler, in a persuasive plea for more sharing of evaluation data with the public, supports the political rationale for increased community involvement. He goes beyond that in a logical progression:

One of the principles underlying widespread involvement has to do with our understanding of the systems that govern us. If we understand, we are in a better position to make wise decisions, or to respond more adequately to decisions that are made for us. It is difficult to control what is not understood. And it is important from the viewpoint of a quest for quality of life that we are able to feel we are a part of the process of control. (1973, p. 307)

For these reasons Gooler assumes that it is possible and desirable for the public to understand what happens in schools; that the public should have access to the policy-making process; that increased citizen involvement is desirable even if it is less efficient; and that some people desire to be more involved than others with their schools. We think Gooler is correct, but changing old ways to act in accordance with these assumptions will be a most difficult assignment for all of us—the public as well as professional educators.

Hopefully, it is clear that there is a modern imperative to involve more citizens in school affairs. For reasons known to all of us, there is a crisis in the legitimacy and authority of all of our national institutions: government, school, church, even family. Young people are not alone in questioning the legitimacy of educational programs and even of their duty to support the public schools by their tax monies. Free schools, alternative schools, defeated bond issues and levies are all symptoms of discontent. This lack of confidence in institutions is complicated by the pervasive social problem of mass society: a feeling of powerlessness, of anomie.

Reasoning this way, one feels that institutions, including and especially the schools, need to regain the trust and support once so freely, almost unquestioningly, given. This kind of trust can only be renewed if schools can become more responsive and if people are involved in important ways with matters that concern them. In this way the overall community may support the schools again as new, mutually advantageous relationships are established. A new sharing and responsiveness can be initiated by opening up school-community relations.

SUMMARY

In this discussion we have noted that problems of meaning confound efforts to discuss community relations. The term *public relations* will be used to refer to that phase of community relations that consists of deliberate efforts by the schools to influence community opinion. *Community relations* refers to all interactions between any element of the school and any element of the community. A particular focus for our purposes will be placed upon the participation of citizens in school affairs.

Elements peculiar to American history and democratic ideology support efforts of educators to affect community relations. It seems both wise and proper to promote good school-community relations. Powerful social and economic forces have mandated a new attention to, and a more open approach to, community relations if schools are to continue as viable educational institutions.

Exercise 1.1

SOME ARE MORE EQUAL THAN OTHERS

1. Using our definition of school-community relations, identify one common school activity that is a highly visible example of school-community relations.

2. Now try to identify another common school activity that is most unlikely to become an example of school-community relations.

Share your answers with others. What can you say about the class of activities identified under 1?

Look at the activities noted under 2. See if you can visualize a situation where the examples *may* become important influences on school-community relations.

SUGGESTED ACTIVITIES

1. Find out who are the persons given primary responsibility for public relations and community relations in a school district.
2. Ask a superintendent and a principal to rank the tasks of administration (curriculum and instruction, finance and business management, pupil personnel, physical facilities, school-community relations, staff personnel) in order of importance. Predict in advance which one will rank school-community relations higher. Ask then which task the administrator feels most competent to deal with, and which least competent to deal with.
3. From your experience describe briefly an episode or action that you would classify as predominantly a community relations activity. Do the same for public relations.
4. Poll the members of a school faculty or your colleagues in a graduate class and find out what preparation they received for parent-community relations either in their academic program or in-service. Obtain also an indication of how helpful they perceived the preparation to be. Analyze the results of your poll and derive appropriate implications.
5. Interview or invite a veteran administrator to talk to your class about educational administration "then and now."

SUGGESTED READINGS

Davies, Don, ed. *Communities and Their Schools.* New York: McGraw-Hill, 1981.

Hilldrup, Robert P. *Improving School Public Relations.* Boston: Allyn & Bacon, 1982.

Kindred, Leslie W.; Bagin, Don; and Gallagher, Donald R. *The School and Community Relations.* 3rd ed. Englewood Cliffs, N.J.: Prentice-Hall, 1984.

McCloskey, Gordon. *Education and Public Understanding.* New York: Harper & Row, 1967.

Rioux, William et al. *You Can Improve Your Child's School.* New York: Simon & Schuster, 1980.

REFERENCES

"Add-On's to Teacher Competency Testing—New Shape for Teacher Training Programs." *Legislative Review* 12(6) (March 15, 1982):1.

American Association of School Administrators. *Management Surveys for Schools: Their Uses and Abuses.* Washington, D.C., 1964.

Blumenfeld, Samuel L. *Is Public Education Necessary?* Old Greenwich, Conn.: Devin-Adair, 1981.

"Building Public Confidence Wins Award." *NASSP Newsleader* 29(1) (September 1981).

Buskin, Martin. *Parent Power: A Candid Handbook for Dealing with Your Child's School.* New York: Walker and Co., 1975.

Campbell, Roald F.; Bridges, Edwin M.; and Nystrand, Raphael O. *Introduction to Educational Administration.* 5th ed. Boston: Allyn & Bacon, 1977.

Caswell, Hollis. *City School Surveys.* New York: Teachers College, Columbia University, 1929.

Committee for Informed Detroit Schools. "Keep Informed Detroit Schools." Detroit, n.d.

Coons, John E., and Sugarman, Stephen D. *Education by Choice: The Case for Family Control.* Berkeley and Los Angeles: University of California Press, 1978.

Cremin, Lawrence A. *The Genius of American Education.* New York: Vintage, 1965.

Crim, Alonzo. "Crim Says Schools Need Community of Believers." *Communicator* 5 (April 1982):7.

Everhart, Robert B., ed. *The Public School Monopoly.* Cambridge, Mass.: Ballinger, 1982.

Gallup, George. "The 14th Annual Gallup Poll of the Public's Attitudes Toward the Public Schools." *Phi Delta Kappan* 64(1) (September 1982):37-50.

Gooler, Dennis D. "Evaluation and the Public." In *School Evaluation: The Politics and Process.* Ed. Ernest R. House. Berkeley: McCutchan Publishing Corp., 1973, pp. 306-18.

Gorton, Richard A. *Conflict, Controversy, and Crisis in School Administration and Supervision: Issues, Cases, and Concepts for the '70's.* Dubuque, Iowa: William C. Brown, 1972.

Hubbell, Ned. "What Is School Community Relations?" *Seminar on School-Community Relations.* ERIC No. ED 044 820. Muncie: Indiana Public School Study Council, 1970.

Illich, Ivan. *Deschooling Society.* New York: Harper & Row, 1972.

Jaeger, Richard N., and Tittle, Carol Kehr, eds. *Minimum Competency Achievement Testing: Motives, Models, Measures, and Consequences.* Berkeley: McCutchan Publishing Corp., 1980.

Johansen, John. "Serving the Client System." In *A Systems Approach to Educational Administration.* Ed. Robert C. Maxson and Walter E. Sistrunk. Dubuque, Iowa: William C. Brown, 1973, pp. 238-55.

Kindred, Leslie W. *School Public Relations.* Englewood Cliffs, N.J.: Prentice-Hall, 1957.

Kohl, Herbert. *36 Children.* New York: Signet, 1967.

McCabe, Charles. "Doing Public Relations: Honesty Shunned." *Toledo Blade,* April 28, 1982.

McCloskey, Gordon. *Education and Public Understanding.* New York: Harper & Row, 1967.

McGuire, Willard, president, NEA. Letter to life members, May 7, 1982.

"Memos Reveal White House Plotted Attack on Networks." *Toledo Blade,* November 2, 1973.

Moriarity, Ann. "Tuition Tax Credits." *Ohio School Boards Journal* 25(5) (May 1981):2.

National Urban Coalition. "Restoring Confidence in Public Education: An Agenda for the 1980s" Conference Proceedings. Washington, D.C., 1979.

Raywid, Mary Anne. "The Novel Character of Today's School Criticism." *Educational Leadership* 37(3) (December 1979):200-03.

Scribner, Harvey, and Stevens, Leonard. *Make Your Schools Work.* New York: Simon & Schuster, 1975.

Sears, Jesse B. *The School Survey.* Boston: Houghton Mifflin, 1925.

Seeley, David S. *Education Through Partnership: Mediating Structures and Education.* Cambridge, Mass.: Ballinger, 1981.

Wasserman, Miriam. *The School Fix, NYC, USA.* New York: Outerbridge & Dienstfrey, 1970.

Weinberg, Richard L., and Weinberg, Lynn G. *Parent Prerogatives: How to Handle Teacher Misbehaviors and Other School Disorders.* Chicago: Nelson-Hall, 1979.

Weltmer, Charles L. "A Citizen's Viewpoint on School-Community Relations." In *Citizens, Businessmen, and Educators: The Elements to Better School-Community Relations.* Conference report by W. Arthur Darling. Dayton, Ohio: Institute for the Development of Educational Activities, 1973, p. 6.

Wise, Arthur E. *Legislated Learning.* Berkeley and Los Angeles: University of California Press, 1979.

2

SCHOOL DISTRICT ORGANIZATION, BUREAUCRACY, AND SCHOOLS

For forms of government let fools contest;
Whate'er is best administer'd is best.
(Alexander Pope, *Essay on Man*)

In this chapter we shall maintain that schools as presently constituted take on some aspects of bureaucracy. Contrary to the trend apparent in much writing about education, we do not perceive bureaucracy to be at the root of all current problems. The bureaucratic organization at its best or worst cannot be held responsible for some of the incredibly myopic actions of a few members of the educational hierarchy. Despite this perhaps unexpected kind word for what has become a traditional whipping boy, we shall imply that bureaucracy *at its best* is no longer able to respond to current needs in school-community relations. In its typical form it has proved a barrier to effective school-community relations.

BACKGROUND

At first, mothers or relatives or no one taught our children; then there was the dame school. We are told that in colonial days education in New England was characterized by the broad participation of citizens in policy formation. The notion of the town meeting, which dealt with education as with other governmental functions, comes to mind. As towns became more populous and schooling more complex, certain persons accepted particular responsibility for the governance of education. This development, accompanied by the appearance of professional school administrators, eventually grew into the familiar model of the school district. This is usually represented schematically as shown in Figure 2.1. The hierarchical arrangement, with its several layers and implicit chain of command, is a harbinger of problems associated with bureaucracy. Concurrently with the growth of cities and the beginning of specialization by educators there was an industrial revolution. And there was Max Weber, who is generally given the dubious distinction of founding the concept of the ideal bureaucracy. Bureaucracy is a way of organizing the administration of an enterprise to coordinate the various specialized activities needed to accomplish the goal of the enterprise. Bureaucracies are characterized by:

A high degree of specialization.
Hierarchical authority structure with limited command and responsibility.
Impersonality of relationships among organizational members.
Recruitment of officials on the basis of ability and technical knowledge.
Differentiation of private and official income.
Files and official jurisdictional areas, regularly ordered by rules, policies, regulations, bylaws.
Administration based on written documents.
Administration by stable and comprehensive general policies.[1]

Because of the problems of growth and the existence in society of ways of dealing with bigness and specialization, the schools followed along and adapted bureaucratic organizational practices. Callahan (1962) and Cremin (1972) describe this relationship of schools to society (the larger community). F. W. Taylor, the founder of the scientific management movement, is acknowledged as having almost as important an influence on education—through society—as Weber. A philosopher and reformer, Mary Parker Follett (see Metcalf and Urwick, 1940), aided by the empirical research of Elton Mayo (1933), launched a counterforce to the mechanistic and inhuman approach to education that was growing out of forces fed by Weber (bureaucracy) and Taylor (efficient management). The resulting wave of democratic

---

[1]For detailed discussions of bureaucracy, see Mouzelis, 1967, p. 39; Weber, 1958, Ch. 8, esp. p. 214; Lane et al., 1966, Ch. 7.

Figure 2.1

The Typical Model of a School District (simplified)

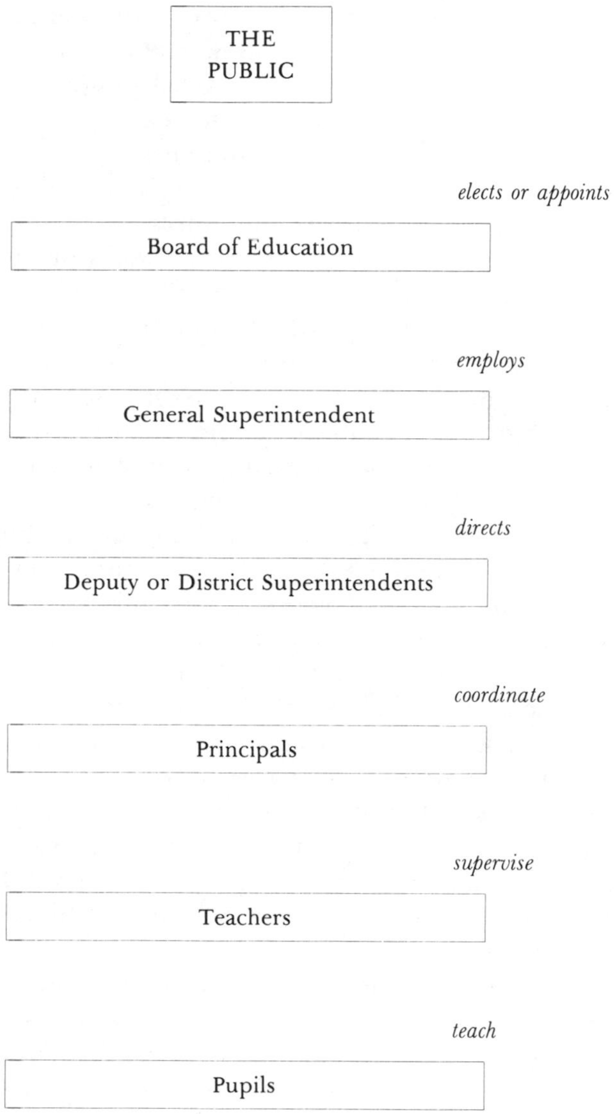

```
          ┌─────────────────┐
          │      THE        │
          │     PUBLIC      │
          └─────────────────┘
```

elects or appoints

```
┌────────────────────────────────────────┐
│            Board of Education            │
└────────────────────────────────────────┘
```

employs

```
┌────────────────────────────────────────┐
│          General Superintendent          │
└────────────────────────────────────────┘
```

directs

```
┌────────────────────────────────────────┐
│     Deputy or District Superintendents   │
└────────────────────────────────────────┘
```

coordinate

```
┌────────────────────────────────────────┐
│                Principals                │
└────────────────────────────────────────┘
```

supervise

```
┌────────────────────────────────────────┐
│                 Teachers                 │
└────────────────────────────────────────┘
```

teach

```
┌────────────────────────────────────────┐
│                  Pupils                  │
└────────────────────────────────────────┘
```

human relations in education seems to have restrained the Taylor influence but not to have had much impact on the movement toward a better bureaucracy in schools. (For the thrust of the democratic human relations reaction to scientific management, see Koopman et al., 1943.) About 1900, bureaucracy seems to have become a corrective for school reform groups wanting to abolish the corruption and abuse of patronage associated with ward politics in the sprawling cities. Bureaucracy became the educator's attempt to raise the quality of education and to be fair to all students.

It seems then that bureaucracy in schools came about with the best of intentions. It has become so commonplace that some find it almost impossible to conceive of alternatives. Professor Steven Miller of Loyola University in Chicago put it this way: "The paradox is that we cannot function in today's world without burocracy [sic]. The educational establishment has to be administered by someone whether we like it or not" ("Bureaucracy," 1971). It is interesting to see how people will organize groups of people to accomplish any task (e.g., the annual charity collection). Almost invariably they break the task down into groups and establish some kind of hierarchy.

Despite our acknowledging Weber as the father of bureaucracy, it is possible to see elements of bureaucracy in antiquity. One such ancient illustration is found in the Toledo Art Museum. There, together with a sarcophagus, are the items found enclosed in the Egyptian burial tombs. Among these are small clay figures called "ushebtis." These are to be the servants of the dead in the next world. The intriguing aspect to students of administration is that for every ten ushebtis there is a supervisor or steward in charge.

Evidence of a hierarchy and supervisor can even be found in the Bible where we find the suggestion that third level supervision should have two subordinates; second level, five; and first level, ten. "Thou shalt provide . . . rulers of hundreds, rulers of fifties, and rulers of tens" (Exod. 18:22).

So, bureaucracy is endemic and international. And, almost invariably, it seems associated with stupidity and frustration. We read of Ram Chundar, an Indian in New Delhi denied a passport to attend the funeral of his wife in New Orleans (she died while visiting there with their three children) because: "Now she is dead, what useful purpose will be served by you going there and wasting foreign exchange?" (Hawkins, 1970).

In a chapter titled "Red Tape and Registers," a British writer, Gerald Haigh, comments on the sanctity of the attendance register kept in red ink:

No mistakes were permitted. If you marked present some child who was absent, the only way of putting the matter right was to go out and fetch the absentee in from his sick bed or hospital ward. The risk of epidemics or complications was less to be feared than the wrath of the Head who saw scratching out and alterations in the register. (1972, p. 59)

As we can see from the last quotation there is also a tendency, almost a need, to poke fun at bureaucracy and bureaucrats. All administrators must have read one or another of the books about Parkinson's Laws (Parkinson, 1957). Teachers have taken special delight in the administrators in Bel Kaufman's staircases (1964) or Peter's various levels of incompetence (Peter and Hull, 1969). This writer has also lampooned the absurdities of bureaucracy as misconceived by American educators (Saxe, 1970). Not a month goes by without an addition to the growing body of works critical of bureaucracy—and now see Martin (1973). Yet it proliferates.

Some of the antipathy toward bureaucracy is a misplaced hostility directed at administrators rather than at the concept of bureaucracy. One of the first thoughts of a citizen bent on economy is to cut out all that waste downtown. "Think of what it would do for the pupil-teacher ratio if all the non-teaching personnel were set to work teaching." When bureaucracy was blamed for the high cost of education in Chicago, Hope Justus, a reporter for the *Chicago Tribune*, gathered the financial information necessary to determine the accuracy of the charge. It was believed that there was no money for teachers because the system was "overburdened with highly paid administrators." Justus found that the 222 members of headquarters staff together accounted for only 0.6 percent of the school budget. And so it went with other accusations of the ill effects of bureaucracy ("Bureaucracy Costs," 1973).

Although the charge of "too many chiefs and not enough Indians" can sometimes be refuted, other attributes of bureaucracy do seem ill suited to education. To the degree that these attributes exist, it is possible to hypothesize that they may be especially harmful to school-community relations. Bureaucracies are supposed to be impersonal; sometimes schools should not be impersonal. Depersonalization for schools is questionable. The standardization of products is a worthy goal provided one does not talk of pupils and teachers as products. Hierarchy of command is not compatible with professional autonomy. Conformity was once a goal of those who thought that schools should be melting pots. It continues to be part of the bureaucratic model. Some wonder to what extent the inculcation of conformity should be part of the mission of the school. Perhaps the important question we are raising is: To what extent are conformity, depersonalization, and other such functions necessary characteristics of bureaucracy?

PROBLEMS OF TYPICAL SCHOOL DISTRICT ORGANIZATION

Since our purpose here is not to consider modifications of the bureaucratic model but to point out ways in which bureaucratically organized schools are barriers to good school-community relations, considerations of other models must be put off until the final section of the book. It is necessary now to review the typical model of school organization presented in Figure 2.1.

In school systems functioning according to Figure 2.1, the citizen was to be represented by the elected or appointed board of education. In theory the individual participation of the town meeting model was replaced, in the typical model, by delegates or representatives. Of course the citizen, particularly the parent of a school pupil, also had direct relationships with administrators and teachers at the local school building level. These relationships were circumscribed by the concept of professionalism and the tenets of bureaucracy, which, accompanying the typical model, structure the roles of educators and citizens. The educator is the professional responsible to other professionals who are ultimately responsible to the representative board. The citizen does not meet the professional at the building level to discuss objectives. These are determined at the top of the organizational chart.

In effect, there is nothing in the model to guide or explain the role of citizens at the building level. There is a general dictum that school administrators should "have good public relations." Sometimes the term *community relations* may be used. In either case it may be interpreted to mean only that the building administrators should prevent anything that would lead to attention that might be unfavorable or even embarrassing to the superordinate school administrators. This is an extremely negative view of the matter, but I believe it is a fair statement of the case and indicates the absence of a working model or conceptual design to guide administrators and the public.

At any rate, there is this general notion that local administrators should cultivate cordial rather than hostile relationships with citizens. This condition is, however, effectively neutralized by elements of the bureaucratic professional model. Educators deal with parents from a position of superior knowledge and status and they are, as bureaucrats, supposed to be unemotional and detached. A superior bureaucrat is not ideally suited to establishing rapport.

Another negative aspect of the local school-community relations climate is caused by the administrator's need to protect pupils and to preserve a safe environment for learning. This is evidenced by placards such as those reproduced in Figures 2.2 and 2.3. Even though the wording in such signs could be improved upon, the intended message remains: Keep Out! Administrators in giant urban schools have even found it necessary to station uniformed guards to enforce the message of the signs. Mechanisms such as this help preserve a learning environment of sorts (an island, an oasis?). They also create a schism between school and community. They intimidate citizens and discourage visitors. Figure 2.4 shows one principal's attempt to soften the tone of the message, which he embellished with a drawing of a cartoon character as well.

Figure 2.2
Visitors Sign, Ohio

All Visitors
Must Report to The Principal's Office
VISITORS—STATE STATUTE 2917.21.1 OF THE OHIO CODE PROHIBITS THE TRESPASSING ON SCHOOL PROPERTY. THIS REGULATION PERTAINS TO THE BUILDING AND GROUNDS.

Figure 2.3

Visitors Sign, Chicago

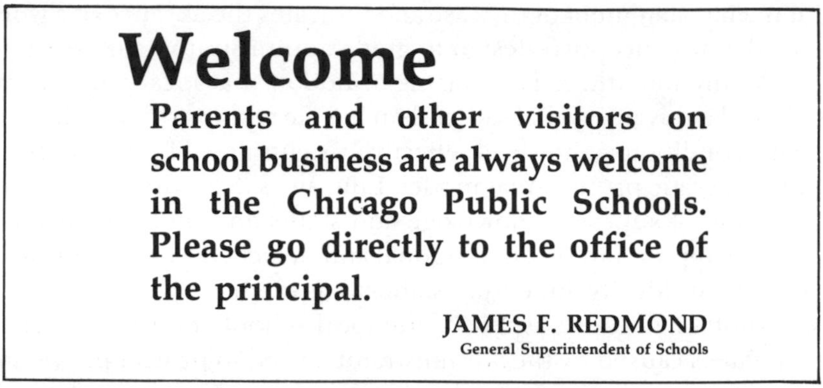

Welcome
Parents and other visitors on school business are always welcome in the Chicago Public Schools. Please go directly to the office of the principal.
JAMES F. REDMOND
General Superintendent of Schools

Note: "A person commits disorderly conduct when he knowingly: (1) Does any act in such unreasonable manner as to alarm or disturb another and to provoke a breach of the peace; . . . A person convicted of a violation . . . shall be fined not to exceed $500. . . . " (Criminal Code of Illinois Ch. 38, Par. 26-1, Ill. Rev. Stat. 1967)

Figure 2.4

Homemade Visitors Sign

Welcome—
We're glad you came, but please report to the office.

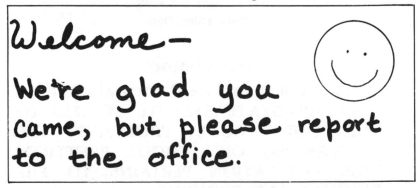

Note: The formal signs required by law were also displayed, but there were fewer of them and they were smaller.

If the attitude of the public schools toward parents is merely restrictive, it is well-nigh prohibitive to other citizens. Clearly they do not belong and the burden is theirs to show cause why they should pause on school premises. This is quite proper for, according to the typical model, there is no valid role for any adult other than a parent or an employee in the school environment. The *public* is shown once, and only once, at the top of the figure where it is placed to select a representative school board.

Adding to the difficulty of the administrator's task at the building level is the teachers' seldom-voiced but quite real fear of parents. This is related to elements of professionalism; that is, the professional cannot be questioned by the client in matters professional. But, because education is often viewed as a pseudoprofession, the professional is not really protected from his clients by the intricate mysteries of his calling. Anyone can understand and discuss education. So, the teacher, not having a secure professional armor, is vulnerable to the parents of his assigned clients (Saxe, 1969).

Teachers in this situation look to administrators to protect them from parents. And, because teaching is so far from being a science, the teacher expects precisely that the administrator will back him in all situations, whether he has acted wisely or unwisely, rightly or wrongly. The belief among teachers is that a united front must be presented to outsiders and that any criticism of the teacher that the administrator might have must be delayed until the confrontation is over and then given in strictest confidence. Such behavior by administrators will be perceived as loyal and good by teachers.

The attitude of teachers toward parents is illustrated by a headline: "New York Teachers to Walk Out If Parents Walk In" (*Educators Negotiating Service*, 1972). This refers to a new union policy that provides that "if a group attempts to enter a classroom, the teacher shall, first, notify the principal that, unless the intruders leave immediately, no teacher will be able to remain in the classroom." The policy could permit groups to observe teachers maintaining surveillance over pupils but not teaching them, the purpose being to prevent community boards or principals from allowing groups of parents to observe and evaluate.

Much more could be said about the built-in rigidity of the typical model, which, though it protects the school system from isolated attacks, fails to allow local school units to respond appropriately to changing situations. Concerns of individuals or groups that cannot be accommodated at the local level must be passed, like the ubiquitous bucks they are, up the hierarchy to the top. Or they may be shifted directly from the local school to the top. However, at the top they are quite properly perceived as local and perhaps peculiar to one or only a few individuals or schools. And the top must deal with the broad perspective.

Thus, we have a stalemate of sorts built into the typical model. Local problems are out of place at the top but the local level does not seem capable of taking the initiative to solve them. When such problems do reach the top (and there are countless ways in which they can be diverted on the tortuous route) they are usually routed back down through the levels of the organization chart for appropriate action. One cannot explain precisely how or even where it happens, but somewhere in this rerouting, there is invariably added an implication that each level is being censured (mildly or severely depending upon circumstances) for disturbing the equilibrium of the higher levels. Again this is dysfunctional in the typical model. The previously mentioned general policy to refrain from rocking the boat, to grease the squeaking wheel, or to oil the troubled waters implies that something must be done to remove the pressure (threat?) that has found its way to the top. However, the addition of explicit or implicit criticism of the levels intervening between the top and the point of pressure creates hostility toward the offending citizen who started the whole thing. This hostility, whether communicated overtly or covertly by the school administrator who deals with the citizen, creates tension and distrust that exacerbate the situation and nullify the intent of the general desire for "good" community relations.

There is a procedure that throws much light on this malfunction of the typical model. It is the procedure of "going over the head" of an individual at any level in the organizational chart. The model suggests (a better word might be *requires*) that communications proceed "through the channels." When levels are bypassed, the model has been circumvented and, quite naturally, this is somewhat embarrassing to all those who, by virtue of their positions in the organization, must preserve and use the model.

BUREAUCRACY MISPERCEIVED

We shall come back to the general problems of the citizens' access to schools when we examine decentralization, community control, and new models for citizen participation. For now, it should be noted that the prevailing model of district organization is similar to that suggested by Figure 2.1. (For a complete description of the typical model of organization, see Griffiths et al., 1962, p. 21.) The other ways in which bureaucratic procedures are harmful to community relations will be discussed throughout the book. However, since our discussion has been mainly theoretical to this point, it is necessary to introduce a few specific instances to put this chapter in its proper perspective.

The first incident can be titled: "Thirty days have September, April, June, and November, except bureaucrats have only twenty-eight." The essence of the incident is a rule that pupils cannot be absent more than a specified number of days and still receive credit for the term. The seventh-grade pupil in question underwent emergency surgery to repair an inguinal hernia and was out of school for three weeks. The school authorities were fully informed of all developments and his classmates picked up assignments that were completed and returned by the recuperating pupil. Upon the pupil's return to school, his parent was immediately and officially informed that the child would have to repeat the grade because his attendance record showed excessive absences.

We need not pause here to examine all of the ramifications of the incident. Readers merely need to know that there was no malice intended to the pupil or his parents. There was no previous pattern of problems to explain what seems to be a clear case of arbitrary action. The sole explanation lies in the existence of a rule and the unemotional, detached decision made when a bureaucrat applies the general rule to a particular case.

A second case involving absence from school adds a new dimension to one's understanding of the simplistic, dispassionate decision making of a bureaucrat. This incident may be captioned: "Insult and Injury." A freshman in high school suffered a serious fracture during wrestling practice while competing against a boy in a heavier weight class as a favor to the coach and to the other boy who needed an opponent. Upon his first day back at school (with his arm in a cast) after hospitalization and recuperation, the student was given a test by his algebra teacher. The ensuing low mark was duly recorded and weighed against him in the subsequent cumulative average grades he obtained throughout the year.

Without considering possible alternative procedures open to the algebra teacher, we need to understand the unemotional fearlessness of this teacher-bureaucrat who did not hesitate to place the administration and his colleague, the wrestling coach, in serious jeopardy. Coach and administration were vulnerable for several reasons, most important for suggesting that the student compete out of his weight class. Even with the good will of the injured student and his parents, coach and administration would be fortunate to weather the incident unscathed by legal action or official sanction. The algebra teacher knew all that, but he was giving a test that day and bureaucrats have to "call them as they see them." Again, it is necessary that readers believe that there is no reason to suppose that the algebra teacher harbored malice toward any of the parties potentially injured by his adherence to procedure.

Seemingly, bureaucracy as an organizing element for the educational institution has some utility, perhaps more as a buffer against an uncertain external environment than as a set of procedures to carry on internal activities. The formal bureaucratic structure was seen in the upheavals of the late sixties as a symbol of educational oppression and as a prime target of reformers. Wasserman saw schools at that time as preserving status differences and conjectured that student and community attacks might lead to the demise of school systems (1970). Arnstine likened schools to factories and also associated the problems of schools with bureaucracy: "If freedom is to flourish in schools, if teachers and pupils are to behave like self-directed, intelligent, and increasingly mature human beings, then the bureaucratic structure of school control must eventually disappear" (1971, p. 24). Arnstine continued his analysis to make a more telling argument against bureaucracy as he perceived it: "For all their current bureaucratic organization, nothing more inefficient could be imagined than American schools" (ibid.).

Those who attack bureaucracy often explain its longevity by what seems to us (the reader who expects a biased perception at this point will not be disappointed) a gratuitous attack on educational administrators. The reasoning of critics is that administrators see their role as maintenance rather than change.[2] Arnstine puts it this way: "Far from being 'impartial' officials, administrators in a school system are deeply committed to the maintenance of the system which maintains their own jobs. . . . It is not likely that school administrators, as presently trained and appointed, will ever constitute anything but an obstacle to the creation of freedom in education" (1971, p. 25).

There is little to be gained by rhetorical rejoinders to the philosophical attack (although the temptation is well-nigh irresistible). The challenge is rather for administrators and, of course, all educators to demonstrate their ability to circumvent bureaucracy when it is stupid and dysfunctional and to create alternative structural arrangements more appropriate for their task. Romantic critics to the contrary, this is not an easy assignment.

ALTERNATIVES TO BUREAUCRACY

In a well-reasoned, dispassionate paper, Firestone presents five alternative organizational patterns to bureaucracy. The characteristics of each are delineated and their utility to different school situations is suggested (1980). In *New Ways of Managing Conflict* Likert and Likert (1976) describe four systems of management. One of these, termed "System 4," seems well suited to avoid the pitfalls of bureaucracy, at least for internal participants. System 4 makes use of cooperative work throughout the organization and features a person-to-person pattern of relationships.

SUMMARY

In this chapter we have demonstrated that the typical organization of school districts does not provide adequate means for citizens to participate. The absence of these means leads to situations in

---

[2]Readers unfamiliar with the perennial argument on this issue will find it reviewed in Saxe, 1980, pp. 16, 17.

Our focus is not on the internal structure of schools but on the interaction between schools and communities. The critics of bureaucracy have made their point—bureaucracy is not conducive to free and open school-community relations. We do not need to accept the drastic cures advocated by some critics (Down with the system!), but neither can we ignore the blunders committed in the guise of following bureaucratic procedures.

which citizens are rebuffed by schools and frustrated in their legitimate concerns.

Elements of bureaucracy are a part of the school organization model. Although intended to increase the quality of education and ensure fair treatment for all, the ritualistic observance of bureaucratic rules and procedures can lead to incidents that may cause irreparable harm to school-community relations. There are ways of living within this system and there are alternatives to the system. We shall consider both of these palliatives to the dismal situation we have portrayed in these pages.

Exercise 2.1
TO ERR IS HUMAN,
BUT WHAT ABOUT BUREAUCRACIES?

After reading the horror stories in the "Bureaucracy Misperceived" section, describe one or more beautiful bureaucratic blunders that you have endured. Share these with your colleagues. Try to analyze the reasons for the mindless treatment. What suggestions can you make to prevent a reoccurrence of the same type? Finally, consider what the effect of the bureaucratic blunder was on those involved.

SUGGESTED ACTIVITIES

1. Draw a schematic model (similar to Figure 2.1) to represent the organization of a school or district with which you are familiar.
2. Visit a school or school district office building and see if you can find their version of a "Visitors Sign." Copy down the exact wording of the sign. Show it to some parents of school children and find out how they perceive it. Try to design a better wording for such a sign. Find out how parents perceive your version.
3. Visit any bureaucratically organized agency on a real, but simple, errand (the drivers license agency to obtain a booklet of rules of the road; a post office to inquire the price of one ounce of first class mail to Tanzania). Then visit the office of your local school or central office on a similar errand (to find out, for instance, what date kindergarten pupils may be enrolled; if Russian is offered as a foreign language in any high school). Compare the two visits, including the physical arrangements and your treatment by the person responding to your query. In what ways were the two experiences similar? How might you improve on the response of the educational institution? What are the reasons behind your suggestions?
4. Create the design of an alternative organizing concept to bureaucracy, and tell how it would be applied to a school or school district.

SUGGESTED READINGS

Firestone, William A. "Images of Schools and Patterns of Change." *American Journal of Education* 88(4) (August 1980):459-87.

Hoy, Wayne K., and Miskel, Cecil G. *Educational Administration.* 2nd ed. New York: Random House, 1982, Ch. 5.

Katz, Daniel, and Kahn, Robert L. *The Social Psychology of Organizations.* 2nd ed. New York: Wiley, 1978, Ch. 9.

Likert, Rensis, and Likert, Jane Gibson. *New Ways of Managing Conflict.* New York: McGraw-Hill, 1976.

Saxe, Richard W. *Educational Administration Today: An Introduction.* Berkeley: McCutchan Publishing Corp., 1980, Chs. 2, 3.

Tyack, David B. *The One Best System.* Cambridge, Mass.: Harvard University Press, 1974.

Weick, Karl E. "Educational Organizations as Loosely Coupled Systems." *Administrative Science Quarterly* 21 (1976):1-19.

_____. "Administering Education in Loosely Coupled Schools." *Phi Delta Kappan* 63(10) (June 1982):673-76.

REFERENCES

Arnstine, Donald. "Freedom and Bureaucracy in the Schools." In *Freedom, Bureaucracy, and Schooling.* Ed. Vernon F. Haubrich. Washington, D.C.: Association for Supervision and Curriculum Development, 1971, pp. 3-28.

"Bureaucracy and Chicago Schools." *Chicago Tribune,* October 29, 1971, sec. 1, p. 20.

"Bureaucracy Costs of City's Schools." *Chicago Tribune,* January 19, 1973.

Callahan, Raymond E. *Education and the Cult of Efficiency.* Chicago: University of Chicago Press, 1962.

Cremin, Lawrence A. *Transformation of the School.* New York: Knopf, 1961.

Educators Negotiating Service, July 1, 1972, p. 193.

Firestone, William A. "Images of Schools and Patterns of Change." *American Journal of Education* 88(4) (August 1980):459-87.

Griffiths, Daniel; Clark, David; Wynn, Richard; and Iannaccone, Laurence. *Organizing Schools for Effective Education.* Danville, Ill.: Interstate, 1962.

Haigh, Gerald. *Beginning Teaching.* London: Pitman Education Library, 1972.

Hawkins, Frank N., Jr. "Bureaucracy Impeding Progress in India." *Pittsburgh Post-Gazette,* November 18, 1970.

Kaufman, Bel. *Up the Down Staircase.* Englewood Cliffs, N.J.: Prentice-Hall, 1964.

Koopman, G. Robert; Misner, Paul; and Miel, Alice. *Democracy in School Administration.* New York: Appleton-Century-Crofts, 1943.

Lane, Willard R.; Corwin, Ronald G.; and Monahan, William G. *Foundations of Educational Administration.* New York: Macmillan, 1966.

Likert, Rensis, and Likert, Jane Gibson. *New Ways of Managing Conflict.* New York: McGraw-Hill, 1976.

Martin, Thomas L., Jr. *Malice in Blunderland.* New York: McGraw-Hill, 1973.

Mayo, Elton. *The Human Problems of an Industrial Civilization.* Boston: Harvard Business School, 1933.

Metcalf, H., and Urwick, L., eds. *Dynamic Administration: The Collected Papers of Mary Parker Follett.* New York: Harper, 1940.

Mouzelis, Nicos P. *Organization and Bureaucracy: An Analysis of Modern Theories.* Chicago: Aldine, 1967.

Parkinson, C. Northcote. *Parkinson's Law.* Boston: Houghton Mifflin, 1957.

Peter, Laurence J., and Hull, Raymond. *The Peter Principle.* New York: William Morrow, 1969.

Saxe, Richard W. "An Unstudied Problem: Parent Visiting." *Educational Forum* 33(2) (January 1969):241-45.

_____. "Toward a Feary of Administration." *National Elementary Principal* 49 (April 1970):26-30.

_____. *Educational Administration Today: An Introduction.* Berkeley: McCutchan Publishing Corp., 1980.

Wasserman, Miriam. *The School Fix, NYC, USA.* New York: Outerbridge & Dienstfrey, 1970.

Weber, Max. *Essays in Sociology.* Trans. H. H. Gerth and C. Wright Mills. New York: Oxford University Press, 1958.

3

PROFESSIONAL BARRIERS TO SCHOOL–COMMUNITY INTERACTION

Community relations are usually in the teacher's zone of indifference

Some myths survive despite an abundance of evidence that they no longer serve the purposes that led to their creation. For example, only recently have educators openly abandoned the once serviceable myth that education must be outside politics—that education and politics do not mix. This concept supported an educational reform movement and made it possible for educators and boards of education to use the concept as a barrier to keep out unscrupulous ward politicians. But time passed, and the apolitical concept became a self-serving strategy for professional educators. In a way, the most political position a professional educator could assume was that of the righteous protector of schools from all external pressures; that is to say, "Leave the schools to the professionals."

The problem with myths is that they endure beyond their time and sometimes prevent necessary reforms and adaptations. There are still professional educators who attempt to use the apolitical-political shield to insulate themselves. The trouble is, of course, that the myth is no longer credible to citizens and groups who clearly perceive elements of the educational system as political resources worthy of political action. For them, the myth is no longer an effective shield. The demonstration of political action for the resources of education follows in the next two chapters on interest groups and power structures. We mention the issue now to introduce the chapter on professional barriers to school-community relations to anticipate our assault on another venerable myth in education—the partnership of parents and teachers.

41

Figure 3.1

Promotional Sticker on Parent-Teacher Relationship (National Educational Association, 1981)

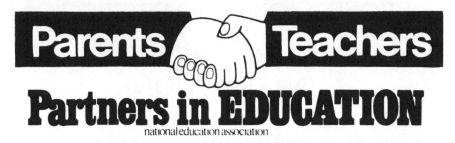

The symbolic representation of the relationship between parents and teachers is demonstrated in Figure 3.1 distributed by the National Education Association. The handshake between parents and teachers is intended to suggest that (1) there is a natural partnership between parents and teachers; (2) the partnership exists; and (3) the partnership "should" exist. We have no quarrel with the third element in the list above ("should" exist) but will present data to question the other elements.

One of the no-longer-hidden problems of school-community relations is the attitude of educators toward the "lay" community. We shall maintain that educators in general view the participation of citizens with a mixture of resentment and apprehension, educational rhetoric to the contrary. The public, for its part, returns both of these attitudes in kind. It fears the professional and the persons who presume to assess the worthiness of its progeny. Moreover, there is deep in the American tradition a distrust of the academic, an anti-intellectualism.

SYMPTOMS OF PUBLIC DISTRUST
OF PROFESSIONALISM

As we noted in the Introduction, there are symptoms of a nation-wide lack of trust in educators—all types of educators, not merely or even especially administrators. The first piece of evidence supporting the lack-of-confidence argument is Table 3.1, which shows the increase in the percentage of Gallup poll respondents favoring standardized examinations as requirements for earning a high school

Table 3.1

**Public Attitude on Nationwide Examination
for High School Graduation (percentages)**

"Should all high school students in the United States be required to pass a standard
nationwide examination in order to get a high school diploma?"

	1958	1976	1981
Favor	50	65	69
Oppose	39	31	26
No opinion	11	4	5

Source: Gallup, "Taking Education's Pulse," 1981, p. 12.

diploma. These data are reinforced by a related finding reported in
State Education Leader[1] that almost forty states have some form of
minimum competency testing requirement. There are many
unsolved problems associated with minimum competency tests, but
they are, for now at least, part of the educational process in most of the
nation (Pipho, 1982). The requirement of these two kinds of testing is
evidence of a public desire for external validation of teaching effectiveness, for there should be no need for such requirements if the educational system were functioning properly.

A similar need for external validation of teacher competence is
demonstrated in Table 3.2 concerning the percentage of Gallup
respondents favoring the requirement of a state board examination
for teachers. Since this would be a requirement in addition to the
college or university requirement and the school district's own selection procedures, it shows lack of trust in the educational institutions.
Competency testing for teachers before the award of state certificates
is now required in fourteen states (*School Administrator,* 1982).

Another exhibit that reflects the reservations of the public about
teacher competence, as sampled by Gallup, is Table 3.3 on tenure. In
1981, 63 percent of the sample disapproved of the tenure policy. In a
further probe of this issue, Gallup pollsters asked: "If teachers must be
laid off to save money in a school system, do you believe that those
who are to be kept should be chosen on the basis of performance or on
the basis of seniority?" Only 17 percent favored seniority rights

---

[1]This is a journal that began in Winter 1982; it replaced *The Interstate Compact for Education.*

Table 3.2

Public Attitude on Examinations for Teachers (percentages)

"In addition to meeting college requirements for a teacher's certificate, should those who want to become teachers also be required to pass a state board examination to prove their knowledge in the subject(s) they will teach before they are hired?"

	National Totals	No Children in School	Public School Parents	Nonpublic School Parents
Yes	84	84	84	86
No	11	10	12	8
Don't know/No answer	5	6	4	6

Source: Gallup, "Taking Education's Pulse," 1981, p. 9.

Table 3.3

Tenure for Teachers (percentages)

"Most public school teachers have tenure; that is, after a two-or-three-year period, they receive what amounts to a lifetime contract. Do you approve or disapprove of this policy?"

	Approve	Disapprove	No Opinion
1972	28	61	11
1974	31	56	13
1981	28	63	9

Source: Gallup, "Taking Education's Pulse," 1981, p. 9.

compared with 78 percent who believed that teachers should be kept on the basis of performance (Gallup, "The 13th Annual," 1981, p. 43). Both tenure and seniority are not only important professional perquisites to teachers; they are symbols of alleged competence. The public disagrees: they seem unwilling to allow teachers the status of professional experts.

One final indicator from the Gallup poll shows an increase in the percentage of respondents opposed to teacher strikes. The interview question was: "Should public school teachers be permitted to strike or not?" The percentage answering "No, they should not" increased from 48 to 52 to 56 over the years 1975, 1980, and 1981 (Gallup, "Taking Education's Pulse," 1981, p. 10). On a related issue the same poll noted only 18 percent reporting that unionization has helped the quality of education compared with 37 percent who perceived that unionization has hurt the quality of education (p. 11). It can be inferred that these data support our rejection of the happy partnership myth and, moreover, suggest that the public's trust in teachers is deteriorating. We shall examine the preferences of parents and other citizens in greater detail in other chapters. Now, we consider the attitudes of educators about citizen participation in education.

PROFESSIONALISM AND THE VESTED INTERESTS OF TEACHERS

Teachers have good reason to be sensitive to citizens' intrusions into educational affairs. Only recently have teachers attained a position of relative power in educational decision making. They have a long history as menials. The collective memory of teachers goes back past Pete Dixon, Mr. Peepers, Miss Brooks, Miss Dove, and Ichabod Crane to a time when teacher-bondservants were offered at a lower price than craftsmen—often without buyers. At long last, teachers abandoned their passive, reacting stance and assumed a more acting, initiating posture. When they did this, they discovered what they should have known all along, that their adversaries were not the administrators but the citizens—parents of school children and others.

Even at this "sophisticated" age we find pervasive—although not completely successful—attempts to create a new rhetoric that proclaims a coalition of parents and teachers against their adversary the administrator. Arnstine, writing for the Association of Supervision and Curriculum Development, argues that "if any significant change is due to appear in education, it is not to be sought from boards of education or from school administrators. If it comes at all, it can come only from those who are most directly involved in the processes of education and most directly affected by those processes; the teachers, the students and the local parents" (1971, p. 25).

Much of the radical rhetoric, after denigrating everything that happens in schools, attempted to salvage something for the new free schools advocated by assuming that there was an alliance between parents and teachers. The events at Ocean Hill-Brownsville destroyed this rhetoric with harsh empirical data. (See, e.g., Carter, 1971.)

If liberal reformers and would-be revolutionaries have not grasped the realities of the controversy about power distribution in educational governance, the organized teachers' leaders have. They know that community control would cost them hard-won privileges. (Several of Albert Shanker's weekly columns in the *New York Times* present the position of the American Federation of Teachers on community control and the participation of citizens; see, e.g., his "Continuing Conflict in Brownsville," 1973.)

TEACHER WELFARE ISSUES AS BARRIERS

Two incidents reported by *Educators' Negotiating Service* demonstrate the stance of organized teachers versus citizens in regard to issues of teacher welfare. In Denver the PTA president asked that the PTA be a third party in contract talks between Denver teachers and administrators, even if only as observers. The contract talks were secret and dealt with new salaries and work rules for teachers. The PTA president based her request on the position that "these are our children and our tax dollars." The reply of the Denver Classroom Teachers Association is revealing:

We don't want them here. We don't think it helps to have outside special interests there. . . . We're going to negotiate the teachers' contract, not the parents' contract. It's not their livelihood. It's not their life. It's our life. ("Parent Group," 1982, p. 102)

This incident is not reported to suggest an unnecessary hostility between parent and teacher groups but rather to establish a (probably) necessary difference in perspective.

The second incident reports the impending loss of jobs by about 4,000 teachers in Minnesota because of reduction in state aid to schools. The head of the Minnesota Education Association (MEA), commenting on the cutbacks, had a major concern about the probable use of volunteers to replace the teachers:

It's very definitely going to happen that volunteers will try to teach. I imagine we'll see every crazy cockamamie kind of volunteer program next year. . . . The state cannot replace teachers with volunteers. ("Volunteers," 1982, p. 122)

The association head warned that he might resort to litigation "if teachers perceive that union work is being done by unpaid mothers and fathers." A principal of the "lighthouse" program in regard to use of volunteers disagreed with the position taken by the MEA head. "What people don't seem to understand is that a successful volunteer program depends on management and the willingness of people on the inside—teachers and staff—to give more of themselves to help the volunteer. Volunteers create more work, not less" (p. 123). This incident reveals the very real concern of the teachers association that unpaid parents might perform some "union work." Such concerns might not be demonstrated in the same way in better economic times, but they would still be part of the teachers' attitudes about this particular form of parent-citizen participation—volunteer work.

PROFESSIONALISM AS A BARRIER

When we leave the issue of power and self-interest, we find another obstacle in the concept of professionalism. Whether or not teaching is a profession can be argued elsewhere. The point here is that to the extent that teaching is a profession, the professional and his professional reference groups determine good practice—not the clients. In view of their long history as poor but (probably) worthy public servants, teachers, not surprisingly, may wish to take advantage of whatever perquisites accompany professional status. Among these perquisites is being allowed the status of experts.

This tenuous professional/expert status can be viewed as a probable determiner of teacher attitudes on different forms of parent-citizen participation. It can also be viewed as a screen that admits certain kinds of parent participation as good and appropriate and rejects other forms of participation as bad and inappropriate. A study by Stallworth demonstrates this notion based on a survey using a sample of 1,983 elementary school teachers from six states.

Data for the study were gathered by a Parent Involvement Questionnaire of eight parts. The parts of the questionnaire were:

1. Opinions—Parent involvement and school personnel
2. Opinions—Parent involvement and parents
3. Decisions—School decisions and parent participation
4. Experiences—Training experience about working with parents
5. Roles—Specific roles parents can play in schools
6. Activities—Parent involvement activities in current use
7. Goals—Specific goals for parent involvement activities
8. Demographic information

TEACHER OPINIONS ABOUT PARENT INVOLVEMENT

We cannot review all eight areas of the study but will note the results in areas of most concern to our focus on teacher attitudes about participation. In part 1, opinions about parent involvement, teachers were asked to respond on a four-point scale (1 = strongly disagree to 4 = strongly agree). The results were:

Teachers agreed most strongly with opinions stating that teachers are having to take on responsibilities parents used to assume, that teachers need to be involved in school policy decisions, that teachers need to provide parents with ideas about helping their child with homework, and that principals need to provide teachers with guidelines about parent involvement. They disagreed most with statements that teachers should avoid conferring with parents about the child's home life, that parents should evaluate school staff, or that teachers do not need training to prepare them for working with parents. (Stallworth, "Parent Involvement," 1982, pp. 6-7)

TEACHER OPINIONS ON PARENT INPUT
IN SCHOOL DECISIONS

The responses of teachers to items in part 3, parent input in school decisions, are good examples of the way teachers' concepts of their roles as professionals affect their attitudes on parent participation. For this reason, Table 3.4 shows responses to the entire list of twenty items. As you can see by inspection of the table, items seen as most useful were those least threatening to the role of the teacher as expert and most supportive of the parent role as primary in matters of related areas specific to their own children (e. g., deciding if family problems are affecting school performance, placing children in special education). The evidence on the negative side is even more supportive of our prediction. Decisions where parent input was deemed least useful were those which intruded on professional and welfare issues: making

Table 3.4

Teachers' Ratings of Usefulness of Involving
Parents in School Decisions[a]
(N = 873)

Decisions	Weighted Means
1. Grouping children for instruction	2.325
2. Amount of homework assigned	2.648
3. Choosing classroom discipline methods	2.810
4. Evaluating pupil performance	2.337
5. Selecting teaching methods	1.980
6. Selecting textbooks and other learning materials	2.349
7. Emphasizing affective skills rather than cognitive skills	2.430
8. Placing children in Special Education	3.199
9. Curriculum emphasis on the arts rather than basic skills	2.038
10. Hiring/firing of school staff	1.508
11. Evaluating teacher performance	1.947
12. Deciding priorities for the school budget	2.262
13. Emphasizing multicultural/bilingual education	2.368
14. Setting promotion and retention standards of students	2.183
15. Formulating desegregation/integration plans	2.744
16. Making assignments of teachers within a school	1.486
17. Deciding if family problems are affecting school performance	3.884
18. Setting school discipline guidelines	2.760
19. Providing sex role instruction and sex education	2.986
20. Setting guidelines for grading students	2.075

[a]Using a five-point rating scale from 1 (Not Useful) to 5 (Very Useful).
Source: Stallworth, "Parent Involvement," 1982, p. 10.

assignments of teachers, hiring/firing, evaluating teachers, selecting teaching methods, and the budget.

ROLES FOR PARENTS

The pattern of responses predicted continued throughout other areas of the survey. Concerning seven identified parent involvement

Table 3.5

Rank Order of Teachers' Ratings of the
Most Important Parent Involvement Roles

Rank	Roles	Weighted Means
1	Audience for school activities (e.g., attending special performances, etc.)	4.242
2	School program supporter (e.g., volunteers for activities, field trip chaperones, etc.)	4.212
3	Home tutor for children (i.e., helping children at home to master school work)	3.858
4	Co-learner (i.e., parents participate in activities where they learn about education with teachers, students, and principals)	3.651
5	Paid school staff (e.g., aides, parent educators, assistant teachers, etc.)	3.202
6	Advocate (i.e., activist role regarding school policies and community issues)	3.104
7	Decision maker (i.e., partners in school planning, curriculum, or administrative decisions)	2.407

Source: Stallworth, "Parent Involvement," 1982, p. 12.

roles, teachers preferred parents in the roles of audience for school activities and school program supporter. Teachers perceived it least important for parents to take the roles of either decision-makers or advocates. These data are found in Table 3.5.

Types of Involvement Preferred by Teachers

Stallworth's study gave teachers an opportunity to react to four major types of parent involvement. Each type of involvement would seem to require different skills of parents and different behavior from teachers. The four types of involvement identified for the study were:

1. Parent involvement in support of school activities
2. Parent involvement in home learning
3. Parent involvement in curriculum and instruction
4. Parent involvement in school governance.

Once again readers can accurately predict the rank order of teacher preference using the teacher professional-expert role as a guide. Stallworth's conclusion was that

... elementary school teachers in this survey support the types of parent involvement where parents contribute their time for social or fund raising events and the type where parents assist their children in learning at home. In contrast, these teachers do not support the idea of having parents involved in either curriculum and instruction decisions or in decisions related to school governance. (p. 19)

In another analysis, part of the same continuing study, Stallworth compared the attitudes of teachers and principals concerning parent participation. The results of this comparison finds them in general agreement with a most interesting difference. The difference gives yet another guideline to ways of predicting the attitudes of educators. In this survey Stallworth found that "the responses of principals and teachers revealed that teachers tended to see parent input as more useful in decisions which were usually made by principals, and that principals also gave parent input higher ratings for decisions usually made by teachers" (Stallworth, "Identifying Barriers," p. 14). The nuance added by this comparison suggests that educators will be more supportive of parent participation in areas that do not affect them directly than they will in areas of direct, personal importance to themselves.

Before we turn to a focus on administrator attitudes, readers should review the findings presented on teacher attitudes. In broad terms, they should be able to set down the agenda of teachers concerning parent participation. It will be necessary and helpful to recall this agenda later for comparison with those of other groups.

A good way to introduce our consideration of the attitudes of administrators on parent-community participation is to begin with the implications of the teachers' agenda for administrators' behavior. We know the general set of teacher preferences, and, thanks to Waller (1932), Becker (1953), and Lortie (1975), we know that teachers are willing to defer to administrators to deal with relations with the community and even with parents. This same phenomenon is apparent in Gold and Miles (1981), which is highly recommended as a case study of the divergent interests of parents and teachers. In this report the authors found that "the majority of teachers ignored the external environment; the main device for maintaining organizational boundaries was the delegation of authority to the principal to buffer, negotiate with, and possibly co-opt community groups" (p. 346).

ADMINISTRATORS IN THE MIDDLE

The preceding quotation serves as a good introduction to a consideration of administrators' attitudes. The administrator is truly "the man in the middle." We are always wary of dealing in clichés because, at least in this chapter, one of our goals is to raise serious questions about some clichés in education, e.g., that parents and teachers are natural partners; that there is a unity of purpose of parents and teachers; that all are concerned only with good of the child. Nevertheless, we describe the administrator as the "man in the middle" because he finds himself between a pair of legitimate demands: teachers demand professional authority to determine the methods of teaching, pupil relations, assessment, etc., and parents and the community demand the democratic right to affect the processes and participate in the governance of "their" schools. In this role he serves as an arbiter and sometimes as a negotiator. If the administrator is not successful in his negotiations, he can be accused either of abusing professional privileges (of teachers) or denying legitimate educational concerns (of parents and community). Often in this apparent dilemma the administrator can, if he is trusted and has acquired a substantial bank of "idiosyncrasy credits," persuade one of the parties to the disagreement to make appropriate concessions. Idiosyncrasy credits are, according to Hollander (1964, p. 12), credits accumulated by a leader by his performing as a member of a group. These credits the leader may "spend" to innovate in attempting to meet the goals of the institution.

For example, faced with the likelihood of the parents' refusing to pay for additional work materials required by teachers and the likelihood that the teachers will insist (and threaten sanctions for noncompliance) that the materials (i.e., the parents' money) are essential, the administrator is in an unenviable position. His decision of what action to take will be an analysis of best practice and feasibility, "ideal" solutions seldom being tenable. Administrators must negotiate the best possible solution, the solution that, given present limitations, is the closest approximation of the ideal. Simon (1965, pp. xxv, xvi) coined a set of terms that nicely describe the nuances of finding the best feasible solution. A *maximizing* decision is one in which the best alternative is selected from among all the possibilities available. A *satisficing* decision is one that is satisfactory, one that, given all the ambiguities of the real world, will do. Needless to say, administrators, according to Simon, must usually "satisfice" rather than "maximize."

In order to secure the best possible solution, the administrator, using Hollander's idiosyncrasy credit notion, cashes in some of the credits he has earned by his previous behavior. In effect, if he asks the parents to honor the request to purchase additional materials, they may be persuaded to do so because of the administrator's credits. In effect, they are saying "OK, you have done several very good things for our children, so we will go along with you on this request for extra money." Conversely, if the administrator asks that the teachers withdraw their request for additional funds, they acquiesce because, they might reason: "OK, you have really helped us accomplish a lot of our objectives, so we owe you this one."

Analyzing the hypothetical issue in this way, we have the advantage of emphasizing the central role of the administrator. Neither side (teachers or parents) needs to have acknowledged the superiority of the other's position. The decision, if arrived at in this fashion, belongs to the administrator as well as to the other parties. Despite the fact that he has "earned" the right to influence the decision, he now has future credit vested in how the solution works out for all concerned. Finally, administrators with no credits in their bank may have to "borrow" influence with implicit or explicit good deeds in the future.

In order to make our point, we have deliberately ignored other ways of dealing with the issue. For one thing, the administrator could attempt to stay clear of the controversy. Or he might seek to avoid such disputes by convening a group to formulate a policy governing conditions and amounts of future assessments for additional funds. He might also rule according to his evaluation of the soundness of the plan regardless of whether it, in effect, alienated one party or another to the argument and so let the chips fall where they may. "Be sure you are right and then full steam ahead." Or he might determine which group is the more powerful and accede to its demands.

It is to be hoped, even as the administrator is spending idio-syncrasy credits to influence a solution, that he would go beyond "satisficing" and work toward a solution that would take on the characteristics of a Mary Parker Follett "integrating" decision—one that includes the desires of both parties and is, in fact, a gain for each. Bertram Gross (1964) provides a succinct analysis of Mary Parker Follett's concepts. Integrating decisions are contrasted with domina-tion and compromise. In the example about the extra money, we have already alluded to a decision by domination. A compromise would be to reduce the amount of funds required by half. An integrating decision might find parents contributing services or material resources better than those to be purchased but at no additional cost.

Since our focus at the moment is on the attitudes of administrators toward community relations, this is not the place to deal with the strategy and tactics of creating and implementing new relationships. We have developed the theme of administrator as man in the middle—between teachers and the community. We consider now the administrator as being in the middle between teachers and students.

The administrator, whenever he is brought into a dispute by either a teacher or a student, is again in the position of an arbiter who becomes a participant in the decision, once it is made. Unless it is really a routine decision where the administrator's participation is more cere-monial than anything else, his actions will, in effect, make new policy, strengthen existing policies or change policies that affect community relations.

Suppose, for example, that a teacher decides to withhold the grade of a student who has completed all course requirements except for a homework assignment. A decision for the teacher is to confirm the professional autonomy of the teacher, but at the cost of seeming unconcerned with student interests. Supporting the student would indicate an appreciation for individual differences but might well alienate many teachers who would perceive it as an appalling lack of support for them. Perhaps the administrator could engineer another Follett integrating solution and use the dispute as a vehicle to work with the faculty to design alternative programs that provide for individual differences. Realistically ("satisficing"?) we cannot expect happy endings to all such controversies. (What would Solomon have done if both mothers had been prepared to relinquish the child rather than settle for half?) The administrator is, once again, in the middle.

Should additional examples of the student-teacher issue be needed, they are easily found. What about the girl who cannot receive a grade in physical education until she "makes up" twenty showers? Then there is the nasty problem of denying an educational experience (a pleasant field trip) to a boy because his conduct suggests that he is a bad risk.

The role of the superintendent as the person in the middle is represented in Figure 3.2. It shows the superintendent as a link between other groups for some purposes. Of course, many of the groups and others that we could place on the circle can and do communicate directly with one another. However, when there is a dispute, it is the superintendent who is called upon to arrange a solution. The superintendent is generally placed in the central position for systemwide issues. However, he may be brought into the same role on appeal from a local situation.

In the local (school building) situation it is the principal who is in the middle as shown in Figure 3.3. The relationships at the local level are, in many ways, analogous to the systemwide relationships. In some ways, the principal deals with the same groups as the superintendent, only on the local level. If the community shown in Figure 3.3

Figure 3.2

The Superintendent as Person in the Middle

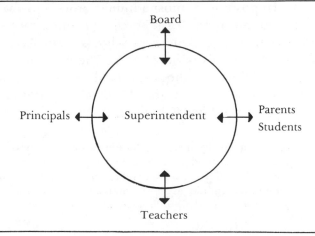

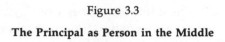

Figure 3.3

The Principal as Person in the Middle

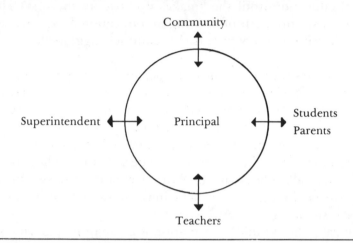

should be formalized and represented by a regularly constituted board of control, there would be a parallel to the systemwide board of education. There is, however, nothing analogous to the line relationship of principal as subordinate to superintendent to be found in the systemwide scheme.

ADMINISTRATORS' ATTITUDES

The official position of most administrators is probably similar to the position taken by the Task Force on Community Education for Building Confidence in America's Schools of the American Association of School Administrators (AASA). The mission statement of the task force proclaims that the AASA (and the National School Public Relations Association and the National Community Education Association) are committed to building public confidence in education.

The ideals of citizen involvement in educational decision making, public use of school facilities, neighborhood self-help and interagency and private sector cooperation are central to that effort. . . . All members of these organizations are urged to support maximum community involvement, not only to enhance the education of people but also to improve the public's attitude toward its schools. ("Community Education," 1982, p. 31)

There is little at this general level with which administrators can quarrel.

As with teachers, however, we find administrators much more enthusiastic about some types of community involvement than others. In a companion study to those of teachers reported by Stallworth ("Parent Involvement," 1982) Williams analyzed elementary principals' opinions on the same issues (1982). In general, the opinions of the principals were the same as those of the teachers. In summing up, Williams wrote:

Finally, principals are clearly in favor of parent involvement goals or purposes which enhance children's development and parent participation in that development. However, they *do not* give importance to those aims which promote direct parent participation in matters considered to be the province of school staff. As a result, these findings lead to the conclusion that principals *value most* the broad, general concepts of parent involvement, but *value least* parent involvement, which trespasses on their perceived domains of governance in schools. (1982, p. 20)

A training program for administrators that seems designed to prepare them for the role implied in the preceding quotation from Williams was prepared for Teacher Corps (Barr et al., 1980). The objectives of the module "School/Community Involvement" were:

1. School administrators will be able to utilize community resources in the teaching/learning process in their schools.
2. School administrators will be able to solicit and gain the involvement of community members in the improvement of the teaching/learning process in their schools. (p. 143)

The activities described in the module are valuable and would give administrators insight into other types of community involvement as well as the school support and home learning functions addressed by the objectives. Our purposes in noting these objectives are to reinforce the finding that administrators favor home learning and school support functions and to challenge readers to formulate objectives for a module that would be more suited to parent involvement in curriculum and instruction and governance of the school.

SUMMARY

We have presented evidence to challenge the myth of the "natural" partnership between parents and educators. Both teacher welfare concerns and concepts of professionalism can be seen as barriers to community involvement in schools. Educators subscribe to community involvement in the abstract. In particular, however, they tend to favor involvement in the domains of school support and home learning. They do not really desire community involvement in the domains of curriculum and instruction or educational governance.

The implications of these findings will become more apparent after we complete a similar review of parent and community attitudes about participation. For now, it can be inferred that there will be few attitudinal or procedure barriers, aside from the lack of training and resources, to the types of involvement favored by educators. Involvement in governance or curriculum and instruction, on the other hand, will meet with formal and informal resistance from educators.

Administrators, whom we have placed in the middle, between teachers and parents, will need to develop strategies and skills to accommodate the types of involvement feared and resented by educators (teachers did not say they feared or resented such involvement; this is our inference) in order to avoid the loss of support *from both groups,* parents and teachers.

The studies reviewed in this chapter should enable us to understand the apparent schizophrenia or hypocrisy of educators who go on record in favor of community involvement while in practice they seem to want no part of it. Obviously, involvement is not a single, monolithic concept. One can favor involvement in general as well as specific types of involvement and, at the same time, resist other types of involvement for good reason. Identifying these barriers is an essential first step to surmounting some of them and, perhaps, accepting and strengthening others.

Exercise 3.1
SOME OF MY BEST FRIENDS ARE IN THE COMMUNITY

Below is a list of school activities. Next to each describe briefly the present practice in your school or district. Then in the "Ideal" column enter an alternative practice that seems more appropriate for educators who literally and sincerely favor parent-community participation in school activities. Compare the two columns, and see what inferences seem justified about the degree of commitment to parent-community participation.

Activity	Way It Is	Ideal for Parent Participation
Open house		
Parent conferences regularly scheduled		
Parent conferences other than usual parent conference day		
PTA/PTO meetings		
Preschool children		
Class visits by parents/others		
Selection of personnel		
Selection of materials		
Policies on extracurricular treats, parties		
Others		

SUGGESTED ACTIVITIES

1. Interview five or ten parents of school-age children. Find out the date of their most recent visit to the school attended by their children. Find out also the general purpose (i.e., open house, sports event, parent interview, etc.). Finally, ask whether the visit was initiated by the parents or by the school. Present your data in tabular form and draw inferences. To what extent do you think your findings are typical or atypical?

2. To experience vicariously the dilemma of the administrator in a situation where a teacher has clearly acted unwisely, try to place yourself in this situation:

   A second grade boy has spent the entire day behind the piano in the classroom because he persisted in disturbing other pupils by talking and distracting their attention in various ways. The parent has questioned the teacher about this procedure and now they seek to have you, as principal, resolve their differences. The parent "doesn't want her boy sitting behind the piano because he won't learn anything there." The teacher maintains that "he can sit with his class anytime so long as he observes the rights of other boys and girls to learn."

   Try to design a solution that will preserve the "face" of both parent and teacher. Consider whether you can:

   1. As an educational leader, support the "behind-the-piano" tactic.
   2. Seemingly remove from the teacher the means of controlling the learning situation in the classroom.

   After you have solved this relatively simple incident, prepare others based on your own experience, for example, the failing grade given apparently arbitrarily without supporting evidence or warning. Are there administrators who invariably support the parent's side of such controversies? The teacher's side? If so, would one have good public relations and the other good staff relations?

3. Interview five or ten parents of school-age children to describe briefly one incident which caused them to feel good about the school or any of the personnel associated with the school. Then ask them to do the same for any issue that caused them to be unhappy about the school or any of the personnel associated with the school. Analyze the responses and compare your results with others in your class. What inference can you draw about the most likely source of support or hostility toward schools?

4. Prepare ten or twenty examples of each kind of parent involvement described. Samples of each follow:

   School support—Hold bake sale to raise money for school needs.
                   Attend open house.
   Family benefit—Tutor children at home.
                   Assist children with homework.
   Curriculum and instruction—
                   Set classroom goals for children with teachers.
                   Help evaluate a school program.
   Governance—Participate in decision to hire a new principal or teachers.
                   Participate in teacher evaluation.

After you have your pool of items, arrange them in alphabetical order, and ask a group of educators to indicate their agreement about each as a useful kind of parent involvement. Use a 4-point scale with:

1 = Strongly disagree
2 = Disagree
3 = Agree
4 = Strongly agree

Compute mean scores for each item, and then arrange your items in rank order. Analyze the results, comparing the results of your survey with those reported in the chapter. Then compare your pattern of results with others in your class.

SUGGESTED READINGS

Duea, Jerry. "School Officials and the Public Hold Disparate Views on Education." *Phi Delta Kappan* 63(7) (March 1982):477-79.

Gold, Barry, and Miles, Matthew. *Whose School Is It Anyway?* New York: Praeger, 1981.

Holcomb, John H. "Don't Let Advisers Run Your Schools." *American School Board Journal* 169 (April 1982):39-40.

Saxe, Richard. "Teachers in Administration." In his *Educational Administration Today: An Introduction.* Berkeley: McCutchan Publishing Corp., 1980, Ch. 6.

Tucker, Harvey J., and Zeigler, L. Harmon. *Professionals Versus the Public: Attitudes, Communication, and Response in School Districts.* New York: Longman, 1980.

REFERENCES

"Across the Nation." *School Administrator* 39(6) (June 1982):3.

Arnstine, Donald. "Freedom and Bureaucracy in the Schools." In *Freedom, Bureaucracy, and Schooling.* Ed. Vernon F. Haubrich. Washington, D.C.: Association for Supervision and Curriculum Development, 1971, pp. 3-28.

Barr, Donald; Elmes, Robert; and Walker, Bruce. *Educational Leadership for In-School Administrators: Participants Manual for an Experiential Training Program.* Omaha, Nebr.: Center for Urban Education, 1980.

Becker, Howard. "The Teacher in the Authority Structure of the Public School." *Journal of Educational Sociology* 27 (November 1953):128-41.

Carter, Barbara. *Pickets, Parents, and Power.* New York: Citation Press, 1971.

"Community Education and Public Confidence." *School Administrator* 39(6) (June 1982):31.

Gallup, George. "Taking Education's Pulse: The 13th Annual Gallup Poll of the Public's Attitudes Toward the Public Schools." Special Publication of the National Association of Secondary Principals, 1904 Association Drive, Reston, Va., 1981.

_____ . "The 13th Annual Gallup Poll of the Public's Attitudes Toward the Public Schools." *Phi Delta Kappan* 64(1) (September 1981):33-47.

Gold, Barry, and Miles, Matthew. *Whose School Is It Anyway?* New York: Praeger, 1981.

Gross, Bertram. "The Scientific Approach to Administration." In *Behavioral Science and Educational Administration*. Ed. Daniel E. Griffiths. Chicago: National Society for the Study of Education, 1964, pp. 33-72.

Hollander, E. P. *Leaders, Groups, and Influence*. New York: Oxford University Press, 1964.

Lortie, Dan C. *School Teacher: A Sociological Study*. Chicago: University of Chicago Press, 1975.

"Parent Group Seeks Access to Teacher Talks." *Educators' Negotiating Service*, April 5, 1982, p. 102.

Pipho, Chris. "A Survey of State Legislative Activity." *State Education Leader* 1(1) (Winter 1982):1, 8-11.

Shanker, Albert. "Continuing Conflict in Brownsville." *New York Times*, November 18, 1973, sec. E, p. 11.

Simon, Herbert A. *Administrative Behavior*. 2nd ed. New York: Free Press, 1965.

Stallworth, John T. "Identifying Barriers to Parent Involvement in the School: A Survey of Educators." Paper presented at American Educational Research Association Meeting, New York, 1982.

———. "Parent Involvement at the Elementary School Level: A Survey of Teachers, Executive Summary of a Report." Austin, Tex.: Southwest Educational Development Laboratory, 1982.

"Volunteers May Replace Teachers, Union Head Says." *Educators Negotiating Service*, May 20, 1982, pp. 122-23.

Waller, Willard. *Sociology of Teaching*. New York: Wiley, 1932 (Science Edition Printing, 1965).

Williams, David L., Jr. "Parent Involvement at the Elementary School Level: A Survey of Principals, Executive Summary." Austin, Tex.: Southwest Educational Development Laboratory, 1982.

4

INTEREST GROUPS

Power abdicates only under stress of counterpower.
(Martin Buber)

In this chapter we shall consider the relationship of special interest or pressure groups to school-community relations. Such groups include informally organized groups of citizens seeking to change something about a school as well as formally organized, powerful, national pressure groups. Some, perhaps most, will owe their existence to dissatisfaction with some aspect of education. Others will invariably support educators on certain issues. Many will only enter into educational disputes when their particular interest is involved; when their ox is being gored. All are potentially important to school administrators, who should be aware of their interests, tactics, and influence. They are a part of the local community as well as the city, state, regional, and national communities. They are neither completely benevolent nor malevolent.

Our previous discussion has anticipated some aspects of the role of interest groups. We noted in Chapter 2 that a parent or a citizen with a concern might be rebuffed at the local school level. One of the things that the concerned parent might do would be to seek a hearing at another level in the school district hierarchy. Another possible reaction would be to seek the support of existing or temporary ad hoc groups to aid or represent the parent in dealing with the bureaucratic organizational structure. This latter strategy is an example of the use of an interest group to augment the influence of individual parents or a small group of parents with a common concern.

In our discussion of interest groups we shall adopt a very general meaning of interest groups that includes many different types of individuals and organizations. We shall use the terms *interest groups* and *pressure groups* interchangeably. An interest group, then, is any collection of individuals or any organization that presents demands or attempts to affect policy formation or implementation. Because this usage is so all-inclusive, it is necessary to present some ways of classifying interest groups.

Davies and Zerchykov (1981) classify interest groups by structure and function. Under *structure* they provide four divisions:

A. Multiissue
B. Noninterest group forms which take on interest group function
C. Delegate groups
D. Trustee groups (p. 180)

There are also four divisions under function:

I.   Episodic
II. Moral: Values
III. Material: Grievance
IV. Material: Benefit

When the dimensions of structure and function are combined, they generate a sixteen-cell, 4 x 4 matrix (see Figure 4.1). According to Davies and Zerchykov, although four of the cells will be empty or virtually so, the other twelve cells provide examples of the variety of interest groups. Cell 14, for example, would represent Davies's own organization, the Institute for Responsive Education, a trustee group functioning on behalf of values. Cell 1 would represent "a neighborhood association or interest group mobilized to prevent the closing of a local school" (p. 181). Rather than provide representative occupants of the other cells here, we shall refer back to Figure 4.1 from time to time as we consider other interest groups.

Figure 4.1

A Matrix of Interest Group Forms

FUNCTION

Structure	I	II	III	IV
A	1	2	3	4
B	5	6	7	8
C	9	10	11	12
D	13	14	15	16

Source: Reprinted from Ron Davies and Ross Zerchykov, "Parents as an Interest Group," *Education and Urban Society,* Vol. 13, No. 2 (February), p. 181. Copyright © 1981 by Education and Urban Society. Reprinted by permission of Sage Publications, Inc.

Steele and his colleagues (1981) provide a "Three-Descriptor Model of Interest Groups." Each descriptor has two divisions. The descriptors and their divisions are:

1. Relative Permanence
   Ad Hoc
   Standing
2. Origin
   Appointed
   Emerged
3. Organizational Structure
   Formally organized
   Informally organized

Using these descriptors, Steele et al. are able to "configure expectations for each of the eight differently characterized groups" (p. 204).

Using the same two groups that we classified according to Davies and Zerchykov will show how the two schemes compare. The Institute for Responsive Education (IRE), which was located in cell 14 for Davies and Zerchykov, would be classified as standing, emerged, and formally organized by Steele et al. The neighborhood association mobilized to prevent a school closing would be ad hoc, emerged, and informally organized. Readers should review both systems. Neither is perfect, but a careful analysis of both may suggest the most appropriate system for various purposes. Kirst and Somers (1981) discuss types of interest groups and cite other sources (p. 238).

There is a directory of national organizations that maintain their headquarters or have an office in Washington, D.C. (Hawley, 1969). It lists entries according to these headings:

Associations of Professionals.
Associations of Institutions.
Organizations Concerned with Curriculum.
Councils, Commissions, and Conference Boards.
Accrediting Agencies and Spokesmen for Professional Standards.
Media and Materials Groups.

There are ninety-seven entries in the directory, ranging from the Adult Education Association of the USA to the World Confederation of Organizations of Teaching Professions. These are all pressure groups.

The late Stephen Bailey compiled a summary of education interest groups in Washington, D.C. (1975). Bailey placed the 250-300 organizations into these categories:

Umbrella Organizations
Institutional Associations
Teachers Unions
Professions, Fields, and Discipline
Librarians, Suppliers, and Technologists
Religion, Race, and Sex
"Lib-Lab" Lobby
Institutions and Institutional System
Administrators and Boards
Miscellaneous[1] (p. 9)

Bailey warned that the categories were certain to overlap.

Those who wish to study a more thorough treatment and more careful classification of pressure groups should see the work of Campbell and his colleagues: *The Organization and Control of American Schools* (1980, Chs. 13-14). Campbell first discusses school-oriented groups, such as the PTA, the National School Boards Association, the

---

[1]Examples of this category are the Council for Basic Education and the National Committee for Citizens in Education.

National Committee for Support of Public Schools, and the Council for Basic Education. Campbell also describes types of locally based groups.

Finally, Kimmelman (1981) provides a novel taxonomy that may strike a responsive chord among veteran school administrators. Kimmelman's classifications are:

> Exploiters
> Righteously Indignant
> Uninformed and Overwhelmed
> Enlightened Critics (p. 35)

One problem with this system is that the categories are not discrete, and one group may fall into three of the four categories at any one time, changing from one to another as the school administrator interprets their tactics.

School Superintendent Steele and his colleagues (1981) lend support to Kimmelman's guarded approach to interest groups when they report that, if the truth were known, administrators view interest groups as "negative, disruptive, time-consuming, uninformed, unreasonable, myopic, emotional, and otherwise generally antagonistic to the purposes and procedures of the school district" (p. 259). These are harsh, but probably accurate, words. Creative readers are challenged to discover for themselves how administrators feel about interest groups. Since there is a well-known "correct" answer to the research question (How do educational administrators perceive interest groups?), it would be necessary to arrive at the answer by inference as well as by anonymous interview or questionnaire approaches.

SCHOOL-ORIENTED GROUPS

Undoubtedly, the best-known school-oriented pressure group is the PTA. For years the PTA or an equivalent mothers' club (really a more descriptive term for most PTA's of the past) was the best supporter of school policies. The PTA was the best vehicle available for parents at the local level according to the organization of the typical model represented in Figure 2.1. For most, participation through the PTA room mother, executive board, and monthly meeting was more ceremonial than real.

However, even the harmless, actively school-supporting PTA was feared, resented, and resisted by teachers. Attendance at PTA meetings by teachers was in my case a great concession paid to me as principal for past and possible future good deeds. This attitude shows rather nicely the difficult position of administrators in the typical model. Teachers recognized that it was part of the *administrator's respon-sibility* to "have good community relations" and were willing to cooperate with an administrator whom they believed could protect them from the risks involved in relating to the community. Moreover, it was a tradeoff of the administrator's idiosyncrasy credits (see our discussion of Hollander's concept of idiosyncrasy credits in Chapter 3). The teachers were willing to do something that they would other-wise be reluctant to do in return for some action of the principal that they had seen as being supportive of their best interests. Further indication that attendance was a quid pro quo was the absence of those teachers with whom the administrator was temporarily persona non grata.

At many PTA elections, I observed teachers voting as a bloc for candidates for office perceived as less threatening to the school sanctuary. Often, because in slum neighborhoods parents cannot or will not participate, the teachers' bloc vote was enough to carry the election. It seems that the implications of this are clear. The partner-ship between home and school is at best an uneasy alliance. Neither partner has complete trust in the other. Perhaps the situation is analogous, to some extent, to the place of administrators in the teachers' association. For a time administrators were accused of dominating proceedings. They were finally forced out on the grounds that they did not have common cause with the teachers who were members and might even be adversaries. Are the *P* and the *T* of the PTA partners or, as they seem to imply in so many ways, psychological adversaries?

In July 1972, a politician analyzing lobbies at the state level (in California) assessed the influence of the PTA in these words: "The PTA has all the muscle of a piece of wet spaghetti. It has always been a fourth rate tool of the school system" (Greene, 1972). Despite this uncomplimentary evaluation, there are signs that the PTA, along with the rest of society, is changing. With the loss of the traditional wide-spread acceptance of school practices, the PTA could not long survive with a policy of supporting schools and minding its own business (i.e., staying out of school business).

In September 1972, Elizabeth Mallory, national PTA president, described the new philosophy: "If it affects the life of the child, it's PTA business" (Lawrence, 1972). Mallory clearly rejected the old role of the PTA: "I think PTA members are beginning to see that what they need to be is a force working for the children rather than a fund-raising auxiliary." If anything, the move to a more aggressive role is a bit tardy for the PTA, which has lost 3 million members since 1963. Membership in 1972 was 8½ million members in 40,000 local units (ibid.).

An action that most clearly signaled the new, more active role of the PTA was also taken in 1972. The National PTA dropped a section of their bylaws that required local PTA units to "cooperate with the schools to support the improvement of education in ways that *will not interfere with the administration of the schools,* and shall not seek to control their policies." The new inserted statement read: "PTA shall work with the schools to provide quality education for all children and youth, and shall *seek to participate in the decision-making process establishing school policy,* recognizing that the legal authority to make decisions has been delegated by the people to Boards of Education" (Sparling, 1980, p. 25).

Lillie Herndon, 1973 national president, accepted the new version of the PTA. In her first remarks as presiding officer she urged members:

As we begin another year of work, I would like to ask each of you as a PTA member to determine the needs of children in your community. Set new goals based on these needs and then plan an action program designed to achieve, in greater measure than ever before, that which is desirable for every child. And as all of us—parents, teachers, and students—focus on every child in our work, PTA will surely grow in power and credibility. (1973)

The PTA used to take the word of the school authorities about the needs of children. Moreover, it would not have been considered proper for the old PTA to "plan" a program. Planning was a task for professionals.

In September 1977 the PTA opened an Office of Governmental Relations in Washington, D.C., "to secure adequate laws for the care and protection of children and youth" ("National PTA Legislative Activity," 1981, p. 5). It is the responsibility of the national vice-president for legislative activity and the staff of the Office of Govern-

mental Operations to implement and interpret the National PTA
Legislative Program. The program "is a compilation of policy statements and legislative directives that originated with local PTA's or
their representatives" (ibid.). It has been approved by all of the state
PTA congresses or their representatives on the National Board of
Directors. In 1981 the Office of Governmental Relations began
publishing (eight issues annually) *What's Happening in Washington.* In
the first issue the vice-president for legislative activity set the tone:
"Through the National PTA we have a power and clout in influencing
legislation that cannot even be realized by unaffiliated parents'
organizations" (Ungar, 1981, p. 1). In addition to presenting the
essential information concerning issues, the publication gives the PTA
position and suggests appropriate action for local as well as state and
national levels.

The interests of the National PTA identified in the first issue of
What's Happening in Washington were "relate[d] to the very preservation
of public schools; opposition to tuition tax credits; juvenile justice;
school lunch and child nutrition; adequate funding of educational
programs; banning of drug paraphernalia; truth in testing; and
children with special needs" ("National PTA Legislative Activity,"
1981, p. 5). The PTA has formed coalitions with other interest groups
to advance their common agenda. The National Coalition for Public
Education, chaired by Grace Baisinger of the PTA, claims a
constituency of over 70 million persons in its member organizations.
This organization joined the PTA in its fight against tuition tax credits
(Fege, 1982). The PTA joined with other education groups to oppose
the Reagan fiscal 1983 budget. This was the first time that the PTA
(eighty-five years old in 1982) had opposed the policies of an
incumbent president (White, 1982)!

Coalitions at all levels abound. In Ohio the PTA started the Ohio
Coalition to Oppose Tuition Tax Credits ("No Longer Just Mothers'
Clubs," 1981). In Illinois, the PTA pulled together nine statewide
organizations "that support public education for a concerted effort to
change public attitudes and to defeat legislative proposals that could
hurt the public schools" (O'Connor, 1980; see also "New Jersey
Groups Unite," 1982). The Illinois coalition agreed to take a stand
only on issues upon which all of the member associations agreed.

The new stance of the PTA has not detracted from its role as the best-
known education interest group and the most reliable ally of adminis-

trators. Politically, this may not be taken as high praise by PTA's at a time when it is the fashion to deplore the lack of wisdom and to question the motivation of administrators in education. In support of the PTA, the president of the American Association of School Administrators (AASA) wrote a strong endorsement of the new category of sustaining membership. His closing comment was:

The American Association of School Administrators and the National PTA have a history of working together, as partners, to assure high quality education for students. It is a relationship we value very much. If we are to be successful in our schools, parents must be our partners. (Miller, 1981, p. 1)

The AASA platform and resolutions statement has this continuing resolution:

Support of National Congress of Parents and Teachers
    AASA supports the National Congress of Parents and Teachers and the local and state affiliates in their continuing efforts to improve education.
    AASA urges members of boards of education, administrators, staff and community to support and become active participants in PTA groups.

The endorsement was echoed by state-level administrators' organizations. In Ohio the Buckeye Association of School Administrators urged their members to welcome PTA's, and the president noted: "I can personally testify that when it comes to passing levies and garnering local support for school efforts, there is no organization that can match the PTA" (Boyd, 1982, p. 1). "The Principal and the PTA, Partners in Education," a four-page brochure published by the PTA, was bound into the September 1982 issue of *The Principal*, the publication of the National Association of Elementary Principals. Clearly, at least at the national and state levels, the rapprochement between administrators' organizations and PTA's is still secure.

The PTA will not easily shed its old image. Erma Bombeck's column of September 24, 1972, is not yet nostalgia. Her final paragraph captures the friendly-comic image of the PTA:

I know that someday when I go to that big PTA in the sky, someone will remember that brave little mother who single-handedly gave birth to 80 cupcakes, who drove 15 kids with bubble-gum breath to a turkey farm, and who got knocked in the face with a Frisbee and who carries a black eye with her today.

Doubtless, the forces that are questioning the role of women in society are working with other pressures to support the new direction of the PTA. Some of us will regret the passing of the old version even though we must endorse the need to change.

Whatever its contributions, and they were many, the PTA of the 1950s and 1960s certainly was not a vehicle for parents to communicate freely with their schools. The PTA had no authority. It could not in any real sense make legitimate the operation of a school in a community. As an organization it seemed to be better suited to the needs and life style of middle-class school patrons than to working-class patrons. It was supportive of the schools, harmless, respectful, and yet it was feared by teachers.

A problem with the typical model (see Figure 2.1) and the associated PTA is that provision is made only for very general participation. This is fine in theory because, at the general level, deliberations are not clouded by personal concerns. However, the parent of a school pupil is almost invariably motivated by a most particular, restricted interest in his own child.

Whether the PTA remains the staunch supporter of educators depends on many things. There is a real possibility that the PTA may need to consider a role as a possible third force[2] to represent parents and children in negotiations between teachers' organizations and boards. (For a case study of this phenomenon, see "Are Citizens Really Wanted?" 1979.) This much is clear, administrators must not take the PTA for granted. The PTA must be accorded respect and given timely information. Certainly, at the very least, the chief administrator or the best possible alternate should attend PTA board meetings and cover all events. The best antidote for misinformation is prompt and accurate information. The presence of a fully informed representative of the school can squelch rumors and alleviate needless concern.

Before leaving the PTA, we must, as promised, classify it according to the categories previously described. We place the local school PTA

---

[2]*Third force* has been given a new meaning in some discussions of community relations. This is not the sense of our use above where we envisage the PTA becoming *more* partisan, *less* objective advocates of their particular constituency and children. For a good overview of the new concept of third force, see L. Cunningham, 1981.

unit in cell 14 in the Davies-Zerchykov (1981) matrix—a trustee group with a moral values function. Apparently Davies would not agree since in one of his examples he lists the PTA as a noninterest group in cell 6. The problem here is not so much the questionable reliability of the classification scheme—although that is certainly open to question— so much as the possibility of an organization usually assigned to one classification operating in a different, atypical manner. It should also be noted that Davies has a more restricted definition of interest groups than we do.

Using Steele's (1981) classification, we would place the typical local PTA unit in the standing, emerged, formally organized category. And, in Kimmelman's (1981) system, the PTA could be placed in any of the four broad categories depending on the dynamics of the local situation. May you all be blessed with "Enlightened Critics"!

NATIONAL COMMITTEE FOR CITIZENS IN EDUCATION (NCCE)

NCCE is the successor to the National Committee for Support of the Public Schools (NCSPS). NCSPS emphasized increased federal support of education. This organization was founded in 1962 by Agnes Meyer, the philanthropist. For several years the committee operated mainly through annual conferences and nationally known consultants. Good publications were produced, but the impact of the committee's activities was limited. (See, e.g., National Committee for Support of Public Schools, 1970.) After the death of Meyer, NCSPS became inactive due to diminished funding. In 1973 the committee reorganized, changed its name, and broadened its focus. The purpose now was to increase citizen involvement in the affairs of the nation's public schools (National Committee for Citizens in Education, n.d.). Among the accomplishments of the NCCE are the following:

Published a major report, *Children, Parents, and School Records*, which received national attention in *Parade* Magazine, *Time* Magazine, *The New York Times*, and on ABC television.
Supplied necessary information upon request to Senator James Buckley, who sponsored the Family Educational Rights and Privacy Act of 1974, which became law in November 1974.
Conducted hearings across the United States on who controls America's public schools, taking testimony from hundreds of individuals and organizations.

Went to court to challenge the authority of the federal government to restrict nonprofit, tax-exempt organizations from attempting to influence legislation (lost) and to assert the due process rights of students (won in the U.S. Supreme Court).

Joined with other national organizations to convene a.National Conference of Title I parents.

Convened the first national meeting of active local parent groups held since 1910.

Established the first public-interest, toll-free telephone hotline, 800-NET-WORK, to help parents get rapid information and help.

Established *The Parents' Network*, to mobilize citizens for action to improve our nation's public schools, and to support existing local parent-citizen groups.

Established *Network,* a newspaper for parents about schools. (p. 1)

Educators are probably most aware of the pocket-sized parents' rights card published by NCCE in both English and Spanish. This card informs parents of their precise legal rights involving student discipline, instruction, records, and other common areas of concern. The card has been NCCE's most popular publication. A newly revised version is available for 10 cents per card (National Committee for Citizens in Education, 1982). Parents holding this card will know, for example, that they can visit their child's classroom at any time during the day, providing they give notice to the school office, in twenty-six states and Washington, D.C.—or twenty-seven states when Michigan, which requires a prior request to be granted by the principal, is included. The 800-Network phone was widely advertised on stickers. A call to Network brings informational material about services available from NCCE. The minimal expectation for administrators concerning the information disseminated by NCCE is that the administrator should be at least as well aware of the legal prerogatives and prohibitions as the parent or citizen who receives the information from NCCE. We predict that this is seldom the case and invite readers to test this prediction for themselves by diplomatically ascertaining if administrators in their area are aware of "parents' rights" as explained on the NCCE card. (NCCE is located at Suite 410, Wilde Lake Village Green, Columbia, Md. 21044.)

NCCE is attempting to form a nationwide network of groups and individuals to influence education. The progress in networking so far has not been impressive, but the organization still seems to be struggling to define itself more clearly. Meanwhile, the thrust on publications is most evident. Here NCCE has endeavored to oppose censorship by making censored books available. However, this thrust is blunted by the simultaneous effort to make good reading of any kind available and by the major emphasis on advice to parents on how to cope with schools. A casual reader of the Holiday 1982 catalogue might well perceive it as just another holiday promotion if it were not enclosed in the September 1982 issue of *Network,* the NCCE paper for parents.

We would place NCCE in cell 14 of the schema by Davies-Zerchykov (1981). Cell 14 is a trustee group concerned with moral value issues. Steele (1981) would classify it as standing, emerged, formally organized. Kimmelman (1981) would consider NCCE to be enlightened critics.

THE INSTITUTE FOR RESPONSIVE EDUCATION (IRE)

IRE was founded by Don Davies, its president and a former U.S. commissioner of education. It seeks to bring about improvement in education by encouraging better collaboration between educators and citizens. IRE is "a private, nonprofit organization which studies and assists citizen participation in education" (Institute for Responsive Education, n.d.). IRE, like NCCE, works mainly through publications. It makes available a journal, *Citizen Action in Education,* and serves as a clearing house for publications. "Major IRE concerns include school-community councils, citizens' roles in educational collective bargaining, federal and state policies affecting citizen participation, the role of citizen-initiated organizations, declining enrollment, and citizen action research for school improvement" (ibid.). Because of its emphasis on citizen participation, we shall give further consideration to IRE in Chapter 12.

IRE is located at 704 Commonwealth Avenue, Boston, Mass. 02215. Like NCCE, we would place it in cell 14 in the Davies-Zerchykov (1981) matrix and in standing, emerged, and formally organized in Steele's (1981).

COUNCIL FOR BASIC EDUCATION (CBE)

"The Council for Basic Education (CBE) was incorporated in the District of Columbia on July 3, 1956, as a nonprofit educational organization pledged to the encouragement and maintenance of high academic standards in American public schools" (Council for Basic Education, 1960, p. 4). Most educators quickly perceived CBE as a

critic of education with a program of emphasis on fundamental intellectual disciplines and social adjustment. It is my impression that time
and events have tempered this judgment so that CBE is no longer seen
as a hostile adversary but as a responsible critic of public education.

CBE operates mainly through publications, the monthly *Bulletin,*
books, and occasional papers. There is no network of state or local
units. Membership is now set at 20 dollars. A list of publications
currently in stock and available at a nominal cost will give an idea of
the orientation of CBE.

"Phonics in Beginning Reading: A Guide for Teachers and Parents."
"Inner-City Children Can Be Taught to Read: Four Successful Schools," by
   George Weber.
"Uses and Abuses of Standardized Testing in the Schools," by George Weber.
"A Sound Curriculum in English Grammar: Guidelines for Teachers and
   Parents," by Kenneth Oliver.
"Choosing a Science Program for the Elementary School," by Howard J.
   Hausman.
"Art in Basic Education," two papers by Jacques Barzun and Robert J. Saunders.
"What Are YOU Doing Here? Or, Schooldays for the Teacher," by Ellen
   Glanz.
"The Education of Gifted and Talented Students: A History and Prospectus," by
   James J. Gallagher and Patricia Weiss.
"Education's Stepchild, In-Service Training," by Peter Greer.
"Minimum Competency Testing: Guidelines for Policymakers and Citizens," by
   Dennis Gray.
"Improving Curriculum Management in the Schools," by Fenwick English.
"Teaching Mathematics: What Is Basic?" by Stephen Willoughby.
"Morality and the Schools," by Robert S. Wicks. (*Basic Education,* 1982, pp. 17-18)

   In addition to these occasional papers there are three citizen guides,
four books, and two other publications available from CBE. One of
the books is *The Literacy Hoax* by Copperman (1978).
   A letter from CBE (1982) to potential new members began this way:

Recent data on academic achievement demonstrate the low state of learning in the
basic subjects. *At least 15%* of students who are graduated from high school are func-
tionally illiterate, students' work habits are slothful, and textbooks are a scandal. The
Council for Basic Education is an association of individuals and institutions working
together to establish *sound* teaching and learning of the basic skills necessary for *all*
children to function effectively in today's society.

Educators *could* go through an entire career and never encounter evidence of the influence of CBE. On the other hand, two or three members in a district who receive the publications could raise difficult questions for the unprepared teacher or administrator. Readers who have not read *The Literacy Hoax* are fortunate that they were not challenged. Obviously, we think it best to keep informed and to make your own analysis of important books or events before you are asked to react to the perceptions of others better informed than you are on the particular issue in question. You need not even have one CBE member to receive the probing question. It could come from the local press, which has received a news release. A word to the wise: the October 1982 issue of *Basic Education* featured a review of *The Paideia Proposal: An Educational Manifesto* (Adler, 1982).

The Council for Basic Education is at 725 Fifteenth St., N.W., Washington, D.C. 20005. We place it in cell 14 on the Davies-Zerchykov (1981) matrix.

TEACHERS', ADMINISTRATORS', AND SCHOOL BOARDS' ORGANIZATIONS

The changed and changing relationships of the several professional organizations at the state level were well described by Campbell and Mazzoni (1976). With others, Campbell described the role of teacher organizations (1980; see also Wirt and Kirst 1982, Ch. 4; and Saxe, 1980, Ch. 6). Although the activities of these professional organizations affect education at all levels, they are not the focus of this volume. We turn our attention now to other interest groups.

OTHER INTEREST GROUPS

In Chapter 14 of the fourth edition of *The Organization and Control of American Schools* (1980) Campbell considers other interest groups. These groups may support, oppose, or seek to influence the schools whenever an issue on their agenda becomes active: textbooks, finances, religion, goals, etc. Among the groups are extremists of the left and right, black organizations, moral majority groups, scientific creationists, women's groups, tax-savers' organizations, and the like.

Extremist Groups

It is tempting to assume that groups such as the Ku Klux Klan can no longer find sufficient support to function in modern society. Unfortunately, hatred and bigotry are always with us, and they thrive in difficult times—and these are difficult times. In 1981 Klan activities were so numerous that the NEA prepared materials for use in teaching students the truth about the Klan. According to Albert Shanker, president of the American Federation of Teachers, the NEA materials were not suitable because they portrayed the United States as inherently racist and presented only one side of the issue of racial quotas (Shanker, 1981). A description of an incident of Klan involvement together with suggested resources and procedures may be found in the *American School Board Journal* for May 1982 (Cramer).

The Klan probably belongs in cell 3, multiissue, grievance (Davies and Zerchykov, 1981), and is standing, emerged, and apparently formally organized (Steele, 1981). Kimmelman (1981) would have trouble choosing between the righteously indignant and the exploiters categories.

In 1975 we noted that the John Birch Society was adopting a low profile and attempting to change its image (Saxe, p. 65). They have succeeded in maintaining the low profile but apparently have not been successful in changing their image. The society has educational goals associated with its mission of preventing the international communist conspiracy from enslaving the entire world.

Robert Welch personally headed the John Birch Society until his death in 1983. The society's agenda, although less strident, remains the same according to their public relations spokesman, who claims Birchers helped bring about the nationwide conservative trend, stopped the American Indian movement, helped defeat the Equal Rights Amendment, stopped the civilian police review board in New York, and "lots of little victories all over the country where we have been a factor" (Overend, 1982).

Society members receive *American Opinion, Review of the News,* and bulletins by Welch, and view tapes and films. They send out about twelve postcards a month to legislators or newspapers. We place the society in cell 3, multiissue, grievance (Davies and Zerchykov, 1981). In the Steele (1981) classification the Birchers are standing, emerged, and formally organized. Kimmelman (1981) would find them to be righteously indignant.

The scientific creationists have capitalized on political and social forces with surprising effectiveness. Chris Pipho has a definitive, objective treatment of these groups and their tactics (1981). Gordon Hoffman, superintendent of a school district receiving the attention of scientific creationists, prepared an analysis: "The New Right: Its Agenda for Education" (1981; see also three other case studies in the same issue of *The Generator*). Most scientific creationists at the local level will probably be trustee groups seeking a benefit (Davies and Zerchykov, 1981, cell 16).

For perhaps the first time there are prominent and well-organized groups with an openly hostile position on public schools. These groups may make common cause with the traditional private and religious school interest groups, but they differ in their emphasis on pointing out flaws in the public schools in order to demonstrate the superiority of their alternative proposals. *Inform,* published originally by the Center for Independent Education sponsored by the Cato Institute, "is a bimonthly newsletter that provides information on the independent education movement, on alternatives to government schools, and on legislation that affects those alternatives" (*Inform,* 1980). *Inform* is now published by the Education Voucher Institute (*Inform,* 1982).

The September 1980 issue of *Inform* contained a centerfold that reflects the new, more openly hostile stance toward public education. Headed "Official Proclamation, State Department of Education, Rights of Parents," the proclamation listed seven "rights of parents" to sacrifice and do loving things for their children such as:

> Parents may give of their own lives, their resources, and their patience to raise children.
> Parents may love and cherish children and hold their needs ever above their own.

The proclamation ends with this sentence in large bold-face type: **But . . . Under No Circumstances Shall Parents Themselves Formally Educate Their Children At Home!** (*Inform,* 1980, pp. 4-5). Concerning the proclamation, *Inform* reported:

> This issue of *Inform* also contains our first centerfold, which we hope many education bureaucrats will find obscene. We also hope that many of you involved with the independent school movement will be as delighted with this poster as we are. We have the "centerfold" available in large poster format for those who wish to use it either as

an appropriate office decoration or as a fund-raising aid. For example, some organizations have bought the poster in quantities at a discount and then given them away to their membership for prompt payment of dues and/or tuition. (p. 1)

We leave the analysis of the merits of the approach and the relevance of the proclamation as a criticism of public schools to readers. The point to be underscored is that *Inform* has an audience and the editors write with the apparent assumption that there are sympathetic and supportive readers to these assaults on "the public school monopoly." Although a degree or two more toward the center of the ideological continuum, *Education Update,* the publication of the Heritage Foundation, is hardly cordial in its treatment of public education and educators. (The editor is Onalee McGraw, and the Heritage Foundation is at 513 C Street, N.E., Washington, D.C. 20021; see *Education Update,* 1982.)

Racial and Ethnic Groups

When Campbell's second edition of *The Organization and Control of American Public Schools* was published in 1970, blacks were dominating the media and causing Campbell to give special emphasis to black organizations such as NAACP, CORE, SCLC, and SNCC. These groups lost center-stage to Spanish-speaking and Native American groups, who in turn gave the media spotlight to Asiatic immigrants, then back to Castro's refugees and Mexican children. All of these groups seemed to stir up other existing groups who felt a need to protect their territories. Most of the crucial issues of the 1970s have found their way to the courts. The grief of balancing competing demands from different groups has been taken from educational administrators, but so too has a large measure of autonomy, flexibility, and local control. A colleague will analyze the new role of the courts in Chapter 7. Women's organizations are regrouping after the defeat of ERA, but much of their agenda has also been taken up by the courts.

Taxpayers' Organizations

Powerful basic forces—inflation, recession, unemployment, and energy shortages—are having predictable effects on taxpayer groups. This is especially evident in regard to financing education. In most instances there is no direct way that a taxpayer can say no to an expenditure. Taxpayers cannot veto carriers or bombers or raises in utility fees, but they can vote against new funds for schools and even against renewing current levels of support. It is not surprising that taxpayers' organizations advocate the only direct cost-saving within their control. They need not be opposed to any aspect of public education to advocate cost-cutting. Good public relations and the obvious relationship of good education to competent future workers and citizens and a sound economy can lessen this pressure, but hardly when unemployment is endemic.

The finance issue in California was taken to the state level with Proposition 13. Kirst and Somers describe the way educational interest groups became involved at the state level in response to the deteriorating financial situation (1981). They see the contest for resources for schools transferred to the state level and suggest that education interests must reunite and declare a truce in regard to fiscal policies. The implications of this development for educators are, by now, familiar. Building and even district level administrators have lost another bit of autonomy. Their associations must now carry on the political battle in another arena. And, as with the issues now decided by the courts, local control of schools has deteriorated again.

Business-Fraternal Groups

Administrators seem well aware that some groups not primarily interested in education are nonetheless of major importance in regard to policy formation. For example, it is routine for schoolmen to belong to Lions, Kiwanis, and similar business-professional groups. The exclusion of women from such groups presents a special problem for administrators and has not yet been fully dealt with by the courts. Nevertheless, many administrators still assiduously cultivate the good will of the business elite and the Chamber of Commerce. One such, when queried about the effect of his frequent absence from his administrative post on goodwill meetings, commented that this phase of his job was more important than curriculum development or the other in-service tasks he might be needed for (W. Cunningham, 1972). In some situations he may well be quite right. However, the times are such that acceptance by the business elite is no longer sufficient political legitimation for the administrator. In fact, one wonders whether the obvious affiliation with one interest group—together with the absence of affiliation with those of different persuasions—is even good practice.

Our attention to noneducation groups is supported by a growing body of research. A researcher in Chicago found that

the organizations which dominated school politics were not concerned primarily with education issues. They were small businessmen's leagues, property and homeowner's associations, and civic improvement groups that were generally unconcerned with drop-out rates, low achievement test scores, or the selection, training, assignment, and promotion of teachers and administrators. Instead, they were concerned with the effect of school policies on the ecology of the community—the migration of population and the aesthetic appearance of school buildings. (Weeres, 1971, p. 2)

ATTITUDES ABOUT PRESSURE GROUPS

There is much ambiguity surrounding the role of pressure groups in education. It seems obvious that such groups play an important role in a democracy by providing another way for the individual to secure access to governing bodies and to make possible the communication of his needs to authorities. This is part of the same network of communication as are letters to newspapers or elected representatives. The difference is that the pressure group is readily available and has been created to represent the special interest concerned.

The ambiguity about pressure groups and education may be related in some ways to the now thoroughly debunked myth of the separation of education and politics.[3] The notion that education as a kind of public religion should be above partisan attempts at influence might have slowed the development of permanent organizations designed to lobby and engage in other pressure group tactics.

In support of this quaint notion that such groups are not seen as exactly proper in education, we note the denial of their influence on decision making as reported to us by Ohio legislators. In a survey completed in May 1969, we asked members of the Ohio legislature to indicate the sources of influence of importance to them in arriving at their positions on three different bills on education. The bills dealt

---

[3]According to most of the recent professional literature on the topic of politics and education, education is, and ought to be, political. Our own research supports this; see Saxe (1969). An especially cogent discussion of the relationship between education and politics is found in Bailey (1967). A comparison of perceptions of interest group legitimacy is found in Saxe (1981).

with districting, finance, and curriculum. The results showed clearly that legislators wished to be perceived as being influenced by constituents, themselves (i.e., their own values and judgment), and—in a very low third place—the position of their political party (Saxe and Rosenberger, 1970, p. 15).

The role of pressure groups, according to our legislator respondents, was negligible. One respondent was so offended at our even suggesting that he could be affected by other groups that he told us he would oppose increased support for a university where professors wasted their time on such nonsense. This particular respondent had never been a strong supporter of universities, so his threat was meaningless. Nevertheless, it is symptomatic of an important attitude that may be characteristic of many legislators.

In interpreting the survey it seemed to us that legislators were, in effect, telling us: "Look here now, we are our own men, not to be swayed by anyone, but *if we were* to listen to outside influences, the following might be among them." In the cluster mentioned were: the Ohio Education Association, the State Department of Education, the Republican Speaker of the House, the Buckeye Association of School Administrators, and the Ohio School Boards Association (p. 15). Note, first, that two of these, the Speaker and the State Department, cannot be considered, in themselves, pressure groups nor spokesmen for such groups.

With the exception of the Speaker of the House, the group of organizations of some importance consists of members of Conant's educational establishment (1963, pp. 15-16). The group did not vary from bill to bill. We make no conclusions from this survey other than the clear finding that legislators possess an idealized image of themselves as independent decision makers, influenced only by their values and the needs of their constituents, and sometimes perhaps by the position of their parties.

It does not matter whether the image is accurate or not. What is significant, for those of us who may deal with legislators on educational matters, is knowing that the legislator needs to perceive himself in this way. Among organizations receiving minimal attention as sources of influence on the bills surveyed were: Retail Merchants Association, PTA, newspapers, Farm Bureau, and various individuals such as the governor and some committee chairmen.

To this point we have suggested that pressure groups are part of the process of educational governance and should be so considered by administrators. We also noted that state legislators, at least, acted as though it were not in keeping with their idealized concept of their role to be influenced by pressure groups. Nevertheless, we know that pressure groups are active at the state level as well as all other levels. There is ample documentation of the success of special interest groups at the state level in the enactment of laws requiring the attention to one interest or another in the required school curriculum. Attention to the evils of tobacco and alcohol comes to mind most readily. (See, e.g., Marconnit, 1966.)

STRATEGIES AND TACTICS OF INTEREST GROUPS

A happy aspect of permanent or semipermanent interest groups is that the administrator knows their goals. True, this does not always make it possible to find a way of relating to such groups, particularly when there may be two or more with diametrically opposed platforms (sex education versus no sex education; integration versus segregation).

There are existing groups with a plan of action and resources to support widely held general goals that will advance the interest concerned. From time to time they may intervene in local affairs in response to special organizational programs or in response to a local appeal for assistance. In these cases there is often as great a problem between the representatives of the broadly based pressure group and their local supporters as there is between the educational institution and the pressure group. This often leads to some tragic and absurd effects on the local level.

This is an area of concern for administrators as well as for local members of nationally affiliated pressure groups. There is assumed an interest in a broadly conceived goal that may not always represent the particular concern of a given local unit. I was urged by one interest group of principals of which I am a member not to buy a certain brand of trousers (communication from the Chicago Principals' Association on behalf of William A. Lee, President, CFL, IUC). I know nothing of the merits of the controversy concerned, but it has little to do with my present concerns about the principalship. Some years ago the National Association of Secondary School Principals wished to ban *Life* magazine because it was seemingly dealing unfairly with American schools in a series of articles entitled "Crisis in Education." Here was a case of being invited to join in an ill-advised sanction determined unilaterally at some distant national headquarters. The point is that administrators may find themselves under attack tomorrow for some issue that, today, is of no local concern whatever. However, if the organization of the pressure group is in good order, local spokesmen may loyally report the new grievance. When this happens it is difficult not to liken the national pressure group's tactic to a physician who advocates a given surgical procedure, at which he excels, regardless of the actual ailment of his patient.

Tactics

The tactics of pressure groups will vary greatly from violent demonstration to subtle influence. The nature of the organization has much to do with the activities considered appropriate. The PTA, for example, is constrained by its objectives as well as its tradition. The Students for a Democratic Society have a different, more active style of operation. Patriotic organizations may use all the communication media to ban a book that they perceive as subversive but they may not forcibly remove and destroy the volumes. It is part of their orientation to see that their cause is just under law. To secure their objective through secret or illegal means would make no sense at all. They must be open and extremely moral in their tactics.

Probably militant confrontation tactics have been most disturbing to administrators and board members. The rise and fall of one such group is revealing of the tactics and their effects. In 1971, two community organizers trained in Saul Alinsky's methods—a Jesuit priest and a Jesuit seminarian—started the Central Toledo Action Committee. CTAC was funded by the Toledo Diocese. Neighborhood groups were formed and encouraged to seek solutions to their problems through confrontations with city officials and landlords. Members of the CTAC groups picketed the homes of officials, disrupted meetings, and were accused of making disturbing phone calls. A judge announced that he was resigning from the housing court because he and his family were being harassed by the Jesuit organizers.

At the end of the first year of the program, the majority report of the Central City Ministry Department supported CTAC, saying of their tactics: "While others find them distasteful, they are no more pressure tactics, for all their visibility, than a phone call from a rich contributor to a politician." The minority report noted that "some tactics of them-selves are offensive to many people. To this extent, the tactics tend to cloud the issues and cause adverse reactions among the general public" ("Abrasive Tactics," 1972). Such tactics were termed totally unacceptable by the minority, who were outvoted by ten votes to two.

Early in the second year of operations, the city manager issued new rules "for city officials to follow in dealing with any citizen groups that specialize in the harangue and harass school of social concern." An editorial wondered whether, "having now got the attention of public officials, there is a need to indulge in the kind of boorish behavior ascribed to CTAC—including use of obscene language and signs, personal threats, harassing members of families of city officials in their own homes and distributing objectionable literature" ("Dealing with Disrupters," 1973, p. 20).

Near the end of the second year of operation, CTAC claimed credit for repairs to over 300 rental units and the destruction of 144 firetraps. With the support of organized labor, the city manager's ruling against picketing at the homes of officials was defeated by city council. The Reverend Redding, Director of Community Relations for the diocese, said he would not have done things in the same way as the Jesuit organizers but would not have accomplished one-tenth as much: "I wonder if my nice little hat-in-hand approach would have gotten us that far?" Father Redding acknowledged that an alleged stabbing by a "marginal" CTAC member was a serious setback ("CTAC Report," 1973).

At about the same time, it was reported that CTAC was seeking funding from other sources. Father Redding hoped that the organizers would continue and noted "that the fact that the diocesan funding will cease does not mean they leave" ("Diocese Funding," 1973). A city commissioner of inspection (buildings) reported that he had been ready to resign because CTAC's "sixteen weekend marches on his home had disrupted his family life to the point of making his wife extremely nervous and having traumatic effects on his eight-year-old son . . . the worst thing was the fear tactic" (Lindeman, 1973).

Finally, an editorial noted that CTAC, being disbanded, blamed its demise on inner-city residents who did not want its help. "Is it any wonder, then, that inner-city residents may well have come to feel that CTAC really had little to offer them in resolving their crucial concerns because it seemed so much more fascinated with its own continuous confrontations?" ("CTAC's Self-Martyrdom, 1973, p. 16).

Whatever the truth is about CTAC, the episode has implications for educators. Abrasive tactics are likely to be used if they prove effective. Most educators will find them personally repugnant. Board members are not prepared for personal abuse. The process is intended to be intimidating. The organizers of CTAC never abandoned the confrontation tactic despite growing concern by their supporters as well as protests by their targets. These tactics were widely disseminated in connection with federally funded Community Action Programs.

Organizations without so sacred a goal as the survival of democracy, or morality, or religion, or getting rats out of bedrooms cannot be so direct and forceful. In our own research (Saxe, 1965) we found that the giant Ford Foundation quickly learned this lesson—actually, the Fund for the Advancement of Education, created by Ford, was studied. After an unsuccessful direct attempt to reform teacher education in an entire state, the Foundation became more circumspect, realizing that it was important in the change strategy first to secure the cooperation of a prominent insider in the institution concerned. The institutions (universities) to be changed were selected because of their prestige and their geography. They were seen as centers of excellence in their several regions of the country. It was hoped that changes demonstrated in these "lighthouse" institutions would be quickly copied by others. The Foundation was to assist the influential insider, by its money and prestige, in implementing an innovation that included the Foundation's essential intentions. This relationship is different from the usual approach of a pressure group that is obviously wooing or forcing an educational institution. The Foundation at that time did indeed seek out certain institutions, but it appeared that the university had sought the Foundation's assistance for its—the university's—program.

The National Association of Manufacturers (NAM) for a time had an open, direct liaison with the American Association of School Administrators. This is further evidence of the long-standing notion that it is quite proper for the school administrator to be allied with business leadership. Now the NAM will supply free materials presenting its viewpoints. Because of the wealth of material available, many districts have established screening committees to examine and approve free and inexpensive material. This tactic is clearly very indirect pressure, but it is an important one for established, well-financed special interest groups (see Harty, 1979).

Not all groups are "supposed" to function as pressure groups, and tactics appropriate for one group may be improper for other groups. For example, a "Children's March for Survival" in Washington, D.C., drew severe criticism because materials critical of the president were being distributed in local schools and because ten thousand pupils were recruited to participate in the march. "The upshot was 1,000 children got lost and were found crying in a mess of chicken bones, garbage, and discarded bagfuls of bread; fierce denunciation in the press and in Congress for exploitation of children, and no apparent points scored at the congressional power center" (Thimmesch, 1972). Apparently this cause seemed so noble that the board and administrators departed from the tradition of avoiding any appearance of using pupils to secure an objective. This same lack of restraint and objectivity is sometimes evidenced in financial campaigns for bond issues.

The discussion by Campbell et al. on policy formation (1971, Ch. 16) provides an excellent perspective on the role of pressure groups. Such groups align themselves with movements to change education that are generated by basic social forces. The pressure groups get on the bandwagon and attempt to direct the process of change in a direction that will advance their own goals. They use press, TV, political action, money, and influence to bring about their goals. They will direct their efforts at the most accessible targets.

FUTURE PROSPECTS

If the past is a reliable guide for the future, we will see current efforts to reform education increase and culminate in many bills and some laws. Science and math are again needed to keep up with or surpass the Soviets. We shall have laws and rules to accelerate the rapid training and employment of a sufficient cadre of math and science teachers. Accountability in its many forms continues to be in vogue. We expect to see pressures to become more accountable continue to result in minimal competency testing for students and tests for future teachers as well as teachers seeking initial certification. It is too soon to predict with any certainty yet, but a good bet is that the attention to computers will result in computer literacy requirements for teachers as well as students. At this time, the counterpressure of more classical, traditional groups has not even begun. The new conservatism will probably result in more debates and a few rules about teaching some improved moral values curriculum.

It is intriguing to attempt to predict the future course of events that are only in their formative stages at this time. (In Saxe, 1980, Ch. 10, we explain the more reasoned approach of educational futurists to developing alternative futures.) The perceptive administrator can read the signs of coming events just as accurately as meteorologists forecast the weather.

Many of the actions of interest groups can be predicted precisely because of their announced special interest. For instance, we should expect patriotic organizations to reward patriotic virtues and to view with alarm actions perceived as unpatriotic. And the organizations will not disappoint us. We expect ethnic interest groups to favor the presentation of material complimentary to their groups and to oppose the teaching of anything that presents them in an unfavorable light. The downtown coaches' club will favor a new athletic facility and more night football games. They will oppose any curtailing of the number of games played and policies that prevent postseason bowl championships.

Sports interest groups are among the most predictable of all. It is a sign of their strength that varsity teams are among the last to be hit by financial or fuel cutbacks. During the 1982 extended teacher strike in Detroit the only activity of any observable kind was the regular practice of the high school football teams! As we all know there is much more involved in varsity sports than the contest between a handful of young athletes. Area superintendents testify that when the team has a winning season, vandalism goes down, morale goes up, and it is the optimum time to pass an operating levy (Saxe, 1970).

Some topical pressures seem well-nigh irresistible, but time can change that. It was once tradition for all male students to be absent at the beginning of each hunting season. One superintendent notes that now "hunting is a dying tradition. Fewer students are requesting permission to get out of school opening day. We have misgivings about letting any go, but we'll follow the policy" (Wolfe, 1972). Another superintendent required a hunting license and a note from parents. Yet another reports that the percentage of boys absent on opening day of the season is down from over 50 percent to less than 15 percent.

The demise of hunting fever is mentioned to underscore the relationship of issues affecting education to attitudes and conditions in the larger society. At one time educators would have been reluctant to confront this issue. The high school prom and the senior trip are not precisely examples of the effect of pressure groups but an administrator must be aware of their significance to others. There is a time for action, a time for discretion.

It is difficult to move to another issue in community relations without offering educators some hope of being able to deal with the pressures we have described in these pages. However, since the problems and issues in school-community relations are intertwined, we will attempt to discuss solutions at one time to reduce repetition. To anticipate that argument, it should be clear that educators will wish to keep issues in the open and be sure that all interested in schools have access to the processes of policy formation.

SUMMARY

Pressure groups are a part of the process of policy formation and decision making in a democracy. There is some ambiguity about them that may be associated with the long-held misconception that politics and education must be kept apart. The tactics of pressure groups vary depending upon many things but particularly upon the "sacredness" of their cause. They operate in concert with other groups using widespread concern as their legitimating force for particular concerns that, they purport, will relate to the remedy of the basic social discontent. There are numerous pressure groups. Some rise and fall; others will always be with us.

SUGGESTED ACTIVITIES

1. Interview a superintendent and ask him to identify pressure groups. Try to find out which groups are active on which issues. Ask the superintendent whether the pressure groups affect policy formation.
2. Interview a board member, asking the same questions.
3. Interview a principal, asking the same questions.
4. Interview the leader (or educational chairman) of a pressure group. Ask how the group identifies issues in which it will become active. Find out what tactics the group uses. Remember that the PTA and veterans' groups are pressure groups, as are business and professional associations.
5. Ask each member of your graduate class or each member of your school faculty to make a list of all the pressure groups to which he or she belongs. Have someone prepare a master list and make a frequency distribution of the memberships. Are

the ones to which most of us belong generally the most powerful? If not, what explains the power of some groups?
6. Select an educational issue of current national or local importance. Identify groups that will support the issue and those that will probably oppose the issue. Possible issues: accountability, work or career education, new procedures to finance schools, federal involvement. On what basis were you able to predict the pressure groups and the stands they would take?

SUGGESTED READINGS

Campbell, Roald F.; Cunningham, Luvern L.; Usdan, Michael D.; and Nystrand, Raphael O. *The Organization and Control of American Schools.* 4th ed. Columbus, Ohio: Charles E. Merrill, 1980, Chs. 13, 14.

Cigler, Allan J., and Loomis, Burdett A., eds. *Interest Group Politics.* Washington, D.C.: C Q Press, 1983.

Education and Urban Society 13(2) (February 1981). This entire issue is devoted to interest groups in education.

Gross, Neal. *Who Runs Our Schools?* New York: Wiley, 1958.

Parker, Barbara. "How the Radical Right Would Alter Schools." *American School Board Journal* 169(3) (March 1982):8,45.

Phi Delta Kappan 64(2) (October 1982). Theme articles for this issue were on "The New Right: Watchdogs Unchained?"

REFERENCES

"Abrasive Tactics Noted: Priests, Laymen in Six Parishes Back Political-Power Drive in Inner City." *Toledo Blade*, November 1, 1972.

Adler, Mortimer J. *The Paideia Proposal: An Educational Manifesto.* New York: Macmillan, 1982.

American Association of School Administrators. *1982 AASA Handbook*, Washington, D.C., 1982.

"Are Citizens Really Wanted?" *Successful School Administration* 6(9) (January 22, 1979):191.

Bailey, Stephen K. "Comment." *Leadership for Education.* Washington, D.C.: National Committee for Support of the Public Schools, 1967.

_____ . *Education Interest Groups in the Nation's Capital.* Washington, D.C.: American Council on Education, 1975.

Basic Education 27(2) (October 1982).

Boyd, Dick. "President's Message." *BASA Adminiscope*, February 18, 1982.

Campbell, Roald F.; Bridges, Edwin M.; Corbally, John E.; Nystrand, Raphael O.; and Ramseyer, John. *Introduction to Educational Administration.* 4th ed. Boston: Allyn & Bacon, 1971.

Campbell, Roald F., Cunningham, Luvern L.; McPhee, Roderick F.; and Nystrand, Raphael O. *The Organization and Control of American Schools.* 2nd ed. Columbus, Ohio: Charles E. Merrill, 1970.

Campbell, Roald F.; Cunningham, Luvern L.; Nystrand, Raphael O.; and Usdan, Michael D. *The Organization and Control of American Schools*. 4th ed. Columbus, Ohio: Charles E. Merrill, 1980.

Campbell, Roald F., and Mazzoni, Tim L., Jr. *State Policy Making for the Public Schools*. Berkeley: McCutchan Publishing Corp., 1976.

Conant, James B. *The Education of American Teachers*. New York: McGraw-Hill, 1963.

Copperman, Paul. *The Literacy Hoax*. New York: William Morrow, 1978.

Council for Basic Education. "CBE: What It Is and What It Is Not." *CBE Bulletin*, no. 4, April 1960, p. 8.

_____ . Letter to Concerned Citizens. September 7, 1982.

Cramer, Jerome. "Your Kids Are the Target When the Klan Comes Calling." *American School Board Journal* 169(5) (May 1982):23-27.

"CTAC Report Cites Progress in Housing Problems Battle." *Toledo Blade*, October 27, 1973.

"CTAC's Self-Martydom." *Toledo Blade*, November 15, 1973.

Cunningham, Luvern L. "Third Parties as Problem Solvers." In *Communities and Their Schools*. Ed. Don Davies. New York: McGraw-Hill, 1981, pp. 83-120.

Cunningham, William L. "Some Specific Techniques for Building a Positive Image." Speech made to the National Academy for School Executives. San Francisco, August 1, 1972.

Davies, Don, and Zerchykov, Ross. "Parents as an Interest Group." *Education and Urban Society* 13(2) (February 1981):173-92.

"Dealing with Disrupters." *Toledo Blade*, March 6, 1973.

"Diocese Funding to End August 31 for Action Unit." *Toledo Blade*, August 20, 1973.

Education Update, 6(3) (July 1982).

Fege, Arnold, Director, Governmental Relations, National PTA. Personal letter, May 28, 1982.

Greene, Leroy F. "The Image of Education Today: A Politician's Viewpoint." Speech made to the National Academy for School Executives. San Francisco, July 31, 1972.

Harty, Sheila. *Hucksters in the Classroom: A Review of Industry Propaganda in Schools*. Washington, D.C.: Center for the Study of Responsive Law, 1979.

Hawley, Anne. *Contact Washington: An Educator's Directory*. Washington, D.C.: Washington Internships in Education, 1969.

Herndon, Lillie E. "I Strongly Believe in the Power of the Local P.T.A. Unit." *P.T.A. Magazine* 68(2) (October 1973):i.

Hoffman, Gordon. "The New Right: Its Agenda for Education." *Generator* 12(1) (Fall 1981):2-13.

Hollander, E. P. *Leaders, Groups, and Influence*. New York: Oxford University Press, 1964.

Inform, 2(5) (September 1980).

Inform, 4(1) (April 1982).

Institute for Responsive Education. "Help for Citizens and Educators Working to Improve Schools." Brochure. Boston, n.d.

Kimmelman, Paul. *Education and Public Relations: Croft Leadership Action Folio 155*. Waterford, Conn.: Croft-NEI, 1981.

Kirst, Michael W., and Somers, Stephen A. "California Educational Interest Groups: Collective Action as a Logical Response to Proposition 13." *Education and Urban Society* 13(2) (February 1981):235-56.

Lawrence, Clive. "National P.T.A. Changes Image." *Toledo Blade*, September 10, 1972.

Lindeman, Tom. "Inspection Chief Planned to Quit, Glad He Didn't." *Toledo Blade*, August 20, 1973.

Marconnit, George D. "A Study of the Current Curriculum Requirements by the Legislature in Each of the Fifty States." *Research Digest Number 21*, pp. 1-32. Iowa City: University of Iowa, 1966.

Miller, Richard. "Parents Must Be Partners." *School Administrator* 38(2) (February 1981):1.

National Committee for Citizens in Education. *NCCE Report* 1(1) (January 1974).

———. *Fund Raising by Parent/Citizen Groups*. Columbia, Md., n.d.

———. "NCCE Publications and Films" Advertisement: Holiday 1982. Columbia, Md., 1982.

National Committee for Support of Public Schools. *How to Change the System*. Eighth Annual Conference. Washington, D.C., 1970.

National P.T.A. "The Principal and the P.T.A., Partners in Education." Brochure. Chicago, 1982.

"National PTA Legislative Activity and the Role of Local PTA's." *What's Happening in Washington* 1(1) (Fall 1981):5.

"New Jersey Groups Unite to Restore State Education Aid." *Education Week*, September 22, 1982.

Network. Paper published by NCCE, Columbia, Md., September 1982.

"No Longer Just Mothers' Clubs: Back to School Means P.T.A.'s Are Back in the Thick of Things." *Toledo Blade*, September 8, 1981.

O'Connor, Meg. "PTA Chief Forges Lobbying Coalition." *Chicago Tribune*, November 23, 1980.

Overend, William. "Whatever Happened to the John Birch Society?" *Toledo Blade*, October 10, 1982.

Pipho, Chris. "Scientific Creationism: A Case Study." *Education and Urban Society* 13(2) (February 1981):219-33.

"P.T.A. Opposing Ohio Tax Repeal." *Toledo Blade*, October 9, 1972.

Saxe, Richard W. "The Foundation Fund as Venture Capital." *American Behavioral Scientist* 8(6) (February 1965):23-29.

———. "Mayors and Schools." *Urban Education* 4(3) (October 1969):243-51.

———. "Manifest and Latent Functions in Educational Activities." *Bulletin of the National Association of Secondary School Principals* 54 (January 1970):41-50.

———. *School-Community Interaction*. Berkeley: McCutchan Publishing Corp., 1975.

———. *Educational Administration Today: An Introduction to the Field*. Berkeley: McCutchan Publishing Corp., 1980.

———. "Interest Groups in Education." *Education and Urban Society* 13(2) (February 1981):141-48.

Saxe, Richard W., and Rosenberger, David S. "A Survey of Sources of Influence on

Ohio Legislators Concerning Three Bills." *Ohio School Boards Journal* 14 (April 1970):14-16.

Shanker, Albert. "How Not to Teach About the KKK." *New York Times*, November 1981.

Sparling, Virginia. "P.T.A. Involvement in the '80s: New Concepts, New Directions." *NASSP Bulletin* 64(432) (January 1980):23-28.

Steele, Donald J., Jr.; Working, Russell J.; and Biernacki, Gerald J. "Care and Feeding of Interest Groups." *Education and Urban Society* 13(2) (February 1981):257-70.

"Tea-and-Cookies PTA Starts Twisting Arms." *Toledo Blade*, March 3, 1974.

Thimmesch, Nick. "Children's Survival March Scores No Apparent Points." *Toledo Blade*, April 2, 1972.

Ungar, Manya S. "Message from Vice-President for Legislative Activity." *What's Happening in Washington*, no. 1, Fall 1981, p. 1.

Weeres, Joseph B. "School-Community Conflict in a Large Urban School System." *Administrators Notebook* 19(9) (May 1971):2.

White, Eileen. "National P.T.A. Joins Campaign to Fight Cuts." *Education Week* 1(24) (March 10, 1982):1, 10.

Wirt, Frederick M., and Kirst, Michael W. *Schools in Conflict*. Berkeley: McCutchan Publishing Corp., 1982.

Wolfe, Don. "Young Hunters Aim at Better Grades." *Toledo Blade*, November 12, 1972.

5

EDUCATION AND COMMUNITY POWER STRUCTURES

All animals are equal, but some animals are more equal than others.
(George Orwell, *Animal Farm*)

This chapter is the logical successor to the consideration of pressure groups. Pressure groups were seen to be proponents of the particular interests of their members. They were, in general, visible and open advocates of their special interests. Not so the power structure, although the power structure will have its agenda and will favor it above the general interest.

We shall present brief descriptions of the two major approaches to the study of the power structure. We note, in advance, that both are in a primitive stage of development especially in relation to the few studies of the educational structure and educational issues. Implications for educators will be presented. Finally, we shall maintain that the strategies of policy formation of both pressure groups and the power structure are inadequate to represent the majority of citizens and their concerns with the governance of education.

BACKGROUND

Educators, especially superintendents of schools, have long been interested in determining who is influential in decision making about educational issues. It would be strange if they did not have this interest. It stems not merely from idle curiosity or a need for the administrator to retain his employment. Since it is a duty of the administrator to secure and use what resources he can to carry on the educational program of his district, he is almost required to possess some knowledge of the power structure.

It is almost certain that school administrators who have served in a district for more than a few months will have arrived at some conclusions about the influential. They will know "who is in charge," or "who calls the shots." When asked how they know these things about the power structure, administrators will have difficulty in explaining precisely how they arrive at their conclusions. For many, the question appears silly because "everyone around here knows that." Such a reply, far from being seen as avoiding the question, would be seen as highly significant, approximating a proof of the existence and correct identification of the power structure by one school of thought about community power and decision making. It would not at all satisfy another group.

The disagreement touched off by a comment such as that quoted alerts us to a major problem for students of decision making in education—and in other areas as well. There is as yet no generally accepted, all-inclusive way to study the various influences on the control of education. Tyler (1961) acknowledges this condition and notes that each of the social sciences has developed a conceptual scheme and tools to analyze the situation. "Hence, although we cannot obtain a single picture of forces influencing the schools which is comprehensive and accurate we can obtain several pictures, each of which provides a meaningful, accurate, and helpful interpretation of a major aspect of the current situation" (p. 4). This limitation should be kept in mind. It underlies everything discussed in this chapter.

Another caveat is also in order. Much, really most, of what we know about community power structure has been derived from studies of matters other than educational decision making. Cunningham (1971) faced this problem and his conclusion is not reassuring.

The preparation of this chapter was undertaken on the assumption that the research of an empirical nature on community power, community decision-making, and community change plus certain theoretical models (tested and untested) and the reflections of knowledgeable people in the behavioral sciences would indeed have implications for education. One of the unanticipated outcomes may be the discovery that this assumption is false. (p. 109)

For some there is no need to borrow insights from other disciplines to understand educational decision making. James Koerner, of the Council for Basic Education, devotes an entire volume to the question: *Who Controls American Education?* (1968). Koerner's answer is clearly that the professional educators control education. He describes the (deplorable) situation in the final chapter of his book.

We have seen that the important decisions in education emerge from a labyrinth structure of forces and countervailing forces, but that the interests of professional educators tend to be dominant. We have seen that other interests can have a strong and even controlling influence—as demonstrated, for instance, in the power that public opinion exerted after Sputnik on behalf of educational reform—but only on rare occasions. And we have seen that at least the beginnings of change are now evident in the militancy of teachers, the demands of Negroes in the inner cities, and in the work of the curriculum reform groups. We have, that is, described the complicated political pattern by which American education is presently governed. (p. 155)

Neal Gross, of Harvard University, had previously asked almost exactly the same question, *Who Runs Our Schools?* (1958), ten years before Koerner and received a different answer. Much of the problem, according to Gross, was inadequate financial support for schools. His study showed that the PTA, community officials, businessmen, housewives, and service clubs supported public schools, while community officials, businessmen, taxpayers' groups, older residents of the community, individuals with grudges, religious groups, newspapermen, and the "private school crowd" blocked public schools. The appearance of the same groups on the lists of blockers and supporters is testimony of the way communities vary.

A severe anticommunist critic of professional educators also finds the answer in an interplay of pressure groups—in this case a collusion of three in a kind of conspiracy

. . . at the very high levels of learning, tax receipts and tax-deductible donations have combined to establish a three-way line of coded communication between our educational system, the big charitable foundations, and the Federal bureaucracy. For their effective direction of our national policy, it is no longer necessary to let "outsiders" listen in on this esoteric conversation because the audition would serve merely to confuse them. (Manion, 1967, p. 2)

Koerner, Gross, and Manion were all dealing with the issue of control of education in terms of the activities of pressure groups as we described them in a previous chapter. They examined the complex but open rivalries of groups with different objectives in competition to influence the schools to accomplish their set of objectives. The common sense and the folk wisdom of school administrators suggests that the process of decision making is more complex. Those who endeavor to follow the bureaucratic model rigidly soon find ample evidence that outside influences are constantly at work to interfere with the proper functioning of bureaucratic processes. Speculation about which sinister forces are affecting the bureaucracy sometimes leads to the discovery of an informal organization within the school district or school. Often, however, it seems to signal the influence of important persons working unobtrusively.

Many contemporary observers of education assume that there is no longer a need to question the existence of an unofficial community power structure. Consider this comment made in a seminar of citizens, businessmen, and educators:

A public enterprise of such magnitude as the school is bound to be of concern at some time or place to the community power structure. Every community has a power structure which is the relative distribution of decision making among the groups of people in a school district. Decisions which are vital to the school are quite frequently of considerable concern to the power structure. (Darling, 1972, p. 9)

Subsequent comments make it clear that the power structure referred to is not that of the regular organizational-governmental structure.

In the past educators have turned their backs on the power structure in the mistaken belief they were separated from politics by a non-partisan, elected school board and an appointed superintendent. In many instances, they have been brutally manipulated as a result. A major characteristic of the power structure is its lack of social responsibility. Its power is wielded largely in attempts to influence the community to make decisions that coincide with its own ends. (ibid.)

If the preceding arguments about the probable existence of a power structure are not persuasive, consider the logic of Nunnery and Kimbrough in their book, *Politics, Power, Polls, and School Elections* (1971). They maintain that:

there must be a structure or system for making decisions concerning community living, for executing policies, and for maintaining the system. . . . The power structure of the community is the systematic, relative distribution of social power among the citizens in determining the kind of community they want and the kind of institutional arrangements that will best serve them. The exercise of power by citizens is not equal; there is an unequal distribution of influence in the system. (p. 8)

Early studies by sociologists, although not directed at educational decision making, provided evidence of the existence and the nature of a community power structure. Robert Lynd and Helen Lynd published two important studies of "Middletown" (Muncie, Indiana) in 1929 and 1937. The Lynds investigated community behavior and how the decision makers arrived at decisions. In 1929 they found the Ball family (of the mason jars) ruled Muncie like a "manorial system." In 1937 they found that the business elites were still in power and that there had been little change in power centers. The Lynds did not suggest that Middletown-Muncie was a prototype of all small cities. They did reveal how economic power was used to affect decision making. A third study of Middletown from 1976-1981 found important changes in the power structure. "The local dominance of a handful of rich families that looked so threatening in 1935 quietly faded away during the decades of prosperity that followed World War II" (Caplow et al., 1982, p. 12).

Another sociologist, Lloyd Warner, and his colleague Paul Lunt studied Yankee City (Newburyport, Massachusetts) (1941) because it seemed to represent a stable, integrated community. Actually, Yankee City was in transition, for the local ownership and management of industries (mostly shoemaking) was becoming absentee-ownership and absentee-management. Out of this study came the famous classification system for social class. Despite the interesting effect of this shift, Warner and Lunt's findings supported the Lynds who had questioned the popular notion that communities were governed by democratic pluralism.

Other early case studies of communities in regions other than the east and midwest are available: see Dollard, 1937; Davis et al., 1941; and West, 1945—all of whom also studied the power structures and identified the groups included in and excluded from the elite. The next study that should be reported is Hunter's study of Regional City (Atlanta, Georgia), made in 1953. However, since Hunter precipitated a major controversy between sociologists and political scientists and heightened interest in the study of community power structure, we should take time to define a few of the terms used in the resulting debate.

STUDYING POWER STRUCTURES

Power is variously defined, usually in a manner suitable to the research purposes and orientation of the person using the term. For our purposes—of discussing community power structure—*power* means the ability or authority to cause others to do what we want them to do. *Power* as we use it suggests that one has whatever resources are necessary to get his way.

Influence as we define it is difficult to distinguish from power. *Influence* means the ability to persuade others to act, think, or feel as we want them to. The main difference is that power may be considered coercive and influence persuasive. Many writers, especially political scientists, seem to use influence interchangeably with power. In Banfield's study of *Political Influence* (1961), many of his examples of influence would fall within our definition of power. He offers this example of different kinds of influence: "A mayor, for example, is likely to employ in a single act of influence the authority of his office, the respect he commands as a man, rational persuasion, 'selling,' and perhaps both rewards and punishment as well" (p. 5). Clearly, the authority of his office would be a use of power by our definition, as would the application of punishment. Of course, the behavior described would be influence, not power, if the mayor were dealing with persons who were not obliged to respect his authority. For instance, employees in the mayor's office will turn their thermostats down to save fuel because of his power; citizens, because of his influence.

Something like the idea of idiosyncrasy credits is involved in influence. It is also helpful when thinking of a school administrator and a faculty to think of power as "ascribed" status due to anyone in the prescribed administrative position and influence as "achieved" status earned by actions perceived as effective and sensible.

Authority is an element of power. It means the rights and privileges that belong to a certain position. It is seen as being the legitimate basis for power, as contrasted to strength, force, and violence, when employed without authority. Authority is usually formal, based on

status in an organization. Authority is sanctioned by law, by delegation, or by election.

Community almost defies definition. So many systems interact that it
is difficult to construct specific boundaries. To pursue all of the
myriad nuances suggested by the term *community* is neither necessary
nor feasible in these pages. We will mean by *community* the relatively
autonomous political and social systems that together make up a
single system. In other chapters we shall need to mean something else
by *school community.* Now, *community* is used to refer to the complex of
institutions of all kinds that make up a single system. We will need to
clarify this usage by modifiers from time to time. Woodlawn can be
considered a community within the community of Chicago, which is
within the community complex of greater Chicago.

Power structure refers to the relationships among those holding
power in a given community. Some students of power structure will be
able to show the relationships in a diagram.

Hunter and the Elitists

In 1953 Floyd Hunter, a sociologist, published his discovery that, in
effect, a small ruling elite of only a few persons was making the
decisions for the entire city of Atlanta. This group, the power elite, was
isolated from the mass of people in the community. The leaders were
persons of high status and the group of leaders "in specific instances
tends to act on policy matters without regard for various community
groups" (p. 256). The elite was able to enforce its decisions by
persuasion, coercion, intimidation, and even force, if necessary.
There was an old guard of elder statesmen whose approval was usually
necessary for the projects of a group of younger, new leaders.

The distribution of power suggested by Hunter's findings is
illustrated in Figure 5.1. At the apex of the pyramid in Figure 5.1
would be found the small homogenous group of influentials who
direct the affairs of everyone else in the community. Moreover, "there
appears to be a tenuous line of communication between the governors
of our society and the governed. This situation does not square with
the concepts of democracy we have been taught to revere" (p. 1).

Hunter's data were gathered by a procedure that may be described
as the reputational technique. First he identified persons who were at
the center of community activities (e.g., members of the Chamber of

Figure 5.1

Monolithic Power Structure

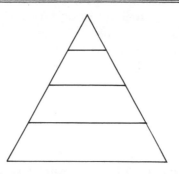

Commerce, League of Women Voters, community council, and newspaper editors and civic leaders). These persons provided lists of others prominent in economics, government, education, and religion, and citizens of wealth and social prominence. In Atlanta this activity generated a total of 175 names (p. 61).

The second step was to present the lists to a panel of fourteen judges composed of representatives of three religions, both sexes, various age and racial groupings, business executives, and professionals. The task of the panel was to narrow the list of 175 down to forty—ten each in economics, politics, community affairs, and society.

The third step required interviews of the chosen forty. The interviews took from two to six or more hours. Hunter asked each of the forty to name the five most powerful persons on the list and to add the names of other prominent persons if this seemed appropriate. The forty provided information about issues and decisions in the community, their participation, the participation of other leaders, friendship with other leaders, business ties, estimates of the relative influence of other leaders, kinship patterns, and related information.

Finally, Hunter and his associates organized and interpreted this mass of data to arrive at the findings with which we began the discussion of his work. These are the data that permit the use of the pyramid to describe the distribution of power in Regional City.

Hunter's study was followed by others using his approach. In general, they discovered monolithic power structures, often made of a group of influential businessmen, professionals, and politicians.

Political scientists were quick to respond to the intrusion of Hunter and his fellow sociologists into their territory. They responded with vigorous criticism, some of which provided ideas used later by political scientists in examining power structures. The first of many criticisms was made by Kaufman and Jones (1954) and the first political scientist to complete a study that met the criteria of political scientists was Robert Dahl.

Dahl and the Pluralists

Dahl is the person identified with the pluralist-political scientist approach to studies of power structure in the same way that Hunter represents the elitist-sociologist approach. Like Hunter, his study served as a model for subsequent studies by others.

Dahl organized his study (1961) of New Haven, Connecticut, to get the answers to questions about urban redevelopment, public education, and political nominations in the major parties. Unlike Hunter, Dahl found that decisions were not made by the same ruling elite. Influence was specialized, few individuals exercised important influence in more than one area, and there were different groups of decision makers for different issues.

Dahl found that the distribution of resources and the ways they are or are not used is a source of both political change and stability in a pluralistic political system. Interestingly, he found that the democratic creed to some extent placed limits on all concerned:

Citizens are very far indeed from exerting equal influence over the content, application, and development of the political consensus. Yet, widely held beliefs by Americans in a creed of democracy and political equality serve as a critical limit on the ways in which leaders can shape the consensus. (p. 325)

Dahl found that the social leaders and the wealthy were only influential in decisions directly concerned with business prosperity. He also found that, despite the many similarities in leadership in public education to leadership in urban redevelopment and political parties, there were significant differences. Most of the associations active in school affairs dealt only with public school concerns and played "a minor part in the political parties and in urban redevelopment" (p. 84).

Figure 5.2 is a schematic representation of the pluralistic power structure of New Haven. In each of the issue areas a different group is involved. The pyramids are truncated to suggest that the decision

Figure 5.2

A Pluralistic Power Structure

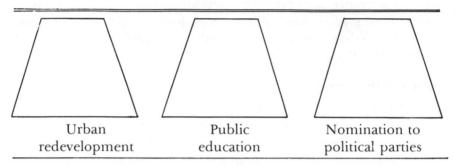

| Urban | Public | Nomination to |
| redevelopment | education | political parties |

makers at the top are not significantly more powerful than those at other levels as they would be in the monolithic mode used to represent Atlanta. Dahl emphasized the importance of the concept of "slack" in the system in that decisions are made by loose collections of persons, and citizens fail to use their full resources (p. 141).

Dahl and the pluralists are sometimes referred to as issue analysts or decision analysts, a reference to the method of data collection used in New Haven. The first step in their approach was to select the decision areas—nomination to political office, urban redevelopment, public education—and ask representative persons to identify the most important decisions made in the area during a specified time. The next step was to attempt to reconstruct each decision by documentary analysis, extensive interviews, and direct observation. Lengthy, sometimes multiple, interviews were held with persons who participated in the decisions. Dahl determined who initiated the process of decision making, how people exercised power, who controlled the outcome, how citizens participated, and who carried out the decision. (Dahl's procedure is summarized in his appendix B, pp. 330-34.)

Arguments continue between elitists and pluralists. The literature is too extensive to be reported here, but a colleague, John Spiess, has reviewed this controversy in *Community Power and Influence Studies: Two Positions* (1970). Dahl points out that the elitist position that someone behind the scenes ("they," old families, bankers, city hall, the party boss) runs things is virtually impossible to disprove. He maintains:

The ruling elite model can be interpreted in this way. If the overt leaders of a community do not appear to constitute a ruling elite, then the theory can be saved by arguing that behind the overt leaders there is a set of covert leaders who do. If subsequent evidence shows that this covert group does not make a ruling elite, then the theory can be saved by arguing that behind the first covert group there is another, and so on. (1971, p. 354)

Pluralists have been accused of confusing multiple ruling elites with the pluralistic model out of their dedication to the democratic ideology. The model for the type of power structure that consists of multiple ruling elites is shown in Figure 5.3. It would be termed a polylithic power structure (Clark, 1968, Ch. 2). There are plural issue areas but within each can be located an elitist monolithic decision-making structure. Even though a given person may be at the top of a pyramid for one issue, he may drop to the bottom for other issues. It is likely that the power structures of several large cities are of this type.

There is one important deficiency of issue analysis as a procedure. The absence of a decision, the refusal to permit an issue to surface may be an important function of power structure. Issue analysis cannot deal with such eventualities.

Combination Studies

As one would expect, there are now studies of community power that use a combination of reputational and issue analysis approaches. From the perspective of a school administrator, it seems most sensible

Figure 5.3

Polylithic Power Structure

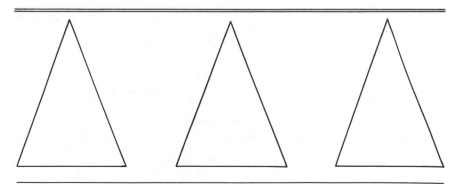

to consider reputational data about the community as well as data about actual participation in important issues. Separately these will not be adequate to analyze the process completely, but taken together the results will be superior to either approach taken alone. Kimbrough (1964, p. 88) and Spiess (1967), among others, support this position.

Apling's study (1970) of the influence of the mayor of a giant midwestern city on educational decision making is an example of the combination approach. It includes the identification and analysis of specific controversial issues as well as the identification of influentials.

A panel of persons knowledgeable about the school system, made up of the superintendent and the past and incumbent presidents of the board of education, nominated the most controversial issues facing the school system during a specified time. Four issues were selected for analysis: the Northwest Project, the Baldwin School, the ten mil levy campaign, and violence at Roosevelt High School.

Data were gathered from personal interviews, mailed questionnaires, news accounts, and minutes of board of education meetings. Each issue was reconstructed and analyzed to determine the relative influence of the mayor over educational decision making. A series of grids was used to represent the mayor's attributed influence for each and all issues. Coalitions of interest and/or action were noted.

The mayor was found to be significantly involved in decisions about the Northwest Project and violence at Roosevelt High School, deliberately less significantly involved in the ten mil levy campaign, and not involved with decisions about Baldwin School. Of the three issues in which the mayor was involved, he was judged to be influential in the two former and lacking in influence in the latter.

Apling concluded:

1. There is a relationship between politics and education; the relationship between municipal government and the schools is extensive.
2. The relationship of the mayor of this large city to educational decision making is extensive.
3. The mayor is an influential in controversial educational issues.
4. The mayor's involvement in controversial educational issues was largely the result of requests for assistance.
5. There are no coalitions between participants of one sector—municipal government, school government, and community—and participants of another sector.
6. For this particular study, a power elite did not exist to make the decisions about controversial educational issues.

Dunn (1980), in her study of influences on a school operating levy, also used a combination approach. Although not a major focus of her study, it is interesting to note that a sample of voters identified only visible officials and leaders of support groups as individuals who may have influenced their decision to support the school issue. Other data in the study show that members of an apparent power elite were at work, but the public, at least in a large city, is not aware of this.

THE STUDY OF COMMUNITY POWER STRUCTURES BY SCHOOL ADMINISTRATORS

The approaches to the study of community power structure discussed above are the best known. There are other approaches and school administrators will find the literature informative, although it should be obvious that they cannot employ the same methods. (See, e.g., Bell et al., 1961, pp. 5-23; Nunnery and Kimbrough, 1971, pp. 8-38.) Their relationship to boards and to communities would preclude the use of the usual methods of learning about the community power structure by school officials or their representatives. Nevertheless, it is well within the professional role of the school administrator to secure this kind of information. Actually, it is more than proper, it is necessary for administrators to have this kind of knowledge.

Sumption and Engstrom agree that the educator must identify the power structure. They point out that it will be most difficult to discover key figures in the power structure.

Discreet inquiries, casual conversations, study of past policy decisions, and above all, careful observation are essential. The delineation of a community power structure is somewhat like solving a crossword puzzle; each step toward the solution makes the subsequent step easier. (1966, p. 26)

They then go on to advocate tactics of elitists—asking well-informed persons to identify influentials—and pluralists—listing opponents and proponents of defeated and successful issues.

Nunnery and Kimbrough, in *Politics, Power, Polls, and School Elections* (1971), also agree that "studying the power structure is not an avocation of the superintendent of schools and his colleagues, but a serious part of the modern school leader's job" (p. 28). They offer detailed suggestions about how to discover the power structure. The first step is for the school leader to prepare himself by examining the professional literature (such as the works listed at the end of this chapter) and attending conferences, courses, or workshops. on the politics of education.

The second step is termed "Learning the problems, issues, and decisions." Educators initiate informal discussions with leaders in areas of importance to the school district. This step is clearly influenced by the reputational approach. The persons to be inter- viewed will vary according to the characteristics of the district, but might include the executive secretary or president of the chamber of commerce, politicians, bankers, leaders in women's clubs and social activities, union leaders, clergymen, political party chairmen, editors or publishers, farm agents or prominent farmers, and leaders of ethnic and racial groups. The conversations should arise naturally out of the normal activities of the administrator, not by special arrange- ment. In conversation the educator should encourage discussion about those who are influential in the community and remember the names of persons frequently mentioned in connection with issues and decisions—a pluralist tactic (p. 28).

The third step is called "Piecing together conversations and documents." The educator records the names of persons identified as prominent and notes the interrelationships among them. Documents of organizations and membership lists also confirm and supplement interview data. Newspapers will help to identify community leaders.

Step four is "Recording and compiling information." Because few can mentally organize and recall all of the information gathered, Nunnery and Kimbrough recommend a clipping and filing system. They also suggest that lists be made of persons interested in working for better schools and of persons "who express predispositions to oppose school proposals" (p. 29). When they were writing, the famous list of enemies of the Nixon administration had not been revealed ("Committee Disclosures," 1973, p. 10). In the light of recent events, it seems most unwise for school administrators to prepare "enemy lists." It needs to be mentioned that the purpose of the list of potential opponents of school issues was to enable the administrator to include such opponents in educational affairs and to provide them with information about educational needs in the hope that opponents would cease opposing once they understood the position advocated by proponents of educational proposals.

The final step is "Direct observation and participation in com- munity activities." As a guide to focus observation, it is suggested that educators formulate ideas (hypotheses?) about the type of power structure they believe exists. Obviously the educator-observer must be an active participant in community and civic functions in order to have ample opportunity for observing. Finally the authors recommend "thoughtful engagement in political activities by school leaders [to] provide a 'gut-level' conceptualization of the power structure" (Nunnery and Kimbrough, 1971, p. 30).

THE SIGNIFICANCE OF POWER STRUCTURE STUDIES

Although many studies of community power structure were not specifically concerned with educational issues, the conclusions are, nevertheless, of interest to educators. Cunningham wryly notes the "contemporary discovery of local school systems by political and social scientists" (1971, p. 114).

An early study of "Springdale" by Vidich and Bensman (1958) still offers a realistic description of school politics in one type of rural community. Springdale schools enrolled about six hundred students in grades one through twelve from all sections of a township. An informal agreement at the time of consolidation gave four out of five board of education seats to farmers and one to the village. The budget of a quarter of a million dollars made the school the major industry of the village. The school was also the community center for social, cultural, and athletic events.

Decisions of the school board had important consequences for the entire community. The board dealt with such problems as:

1. The budget; specifically [for] school buses, expanded curriculum, and expanded plant facilities, which together determine the school tax rate.
2. The proportioning of the agricultural curriculum as against college preparatory and industrial and business crafts curricula.
3. Appointments and reappointments of teachers and the granting of tenure.
4. The appointment of janitors, bus drivers, and motor repairmen.
5. School food and supply services. (p. 172)·

Because these are matters of great interest, the Springdale board went to great lengths to make its decisions in secret so as to give the outward appearance of unanimity.

The example of the selection of a new board member by the "invisible government" shows how the prosperous farmers retain their dominance (pp. 176-80). Village business interests can cooperate with the farm interests because both desire low taxes and a low level of spending. Businessmen speak through the business bureau in favor of law and order (namely, keeping adolescents orderly and off the streets) and local purchasing.

The school principal (in effect, the superintendent, owing to peculiarities of the districting in New York State) attempted to advance his own educational concerns through the PTA. In controversies, the board would often allow the administration "to absorb the resentment and [guarantee] the continuation of rural dominance on the board in exchange for a minor concession to business interests at the costs of the administration's program" (p. 186).

The principal, always called "The Professor," was perceived as "the personal embodiment of education," a condition that made him a central figure on the political scene. The way in which one school leader responded to his relationship to the particular power structure is shown in the extended quotation from the chapter "School Politics." In order to accomplish his ends "which are necessarily in the selfish interests of education," the principal must

recognize differences of power. He must recognize the interests of the farmers, professionals, industrial workers, party politics, the generalized desire for low taxes, and he must give each of these elements their due weight in his educational calculations. To the extent that he makes an accurate assessment of local power relations and acts on this assessment he has a chance, at least in the short run, to succeed with his program.

While giving due weight to these various interests he must at the same time try not to alienate any one of them. As a result he publicly tends to agree with everyone and his public statements are of sufficient generality as to be satisfactory to almost all groups. However, when pressed, he agrees most, in terms of his rhetoric, with the rural interests since this is the dominant group within and through whom he must work.

This he must do even though his underlying educational program is against a lopsided, farm-dominated school system. Vocational training, college preparation, a guidance program and modern methods are central to his educational philosophy. But in order to accomplish his program, he must constantly make concessions to the dominant interests behind school policy and attempt to implement his program through more indirect and subtle means. As a consequence of this, it frequently happens that he is forced to dissociate himself from his own ideas in the PTA and to take public positions which are inconsistent with his long range program. (pp. 195-96)

While surely not an admirable stance for the Professor to assume, his strategy seems well suited for survival and long-term change in Springdale schools. Before we condemn the Professor, it would be well to examine the wealth of data presented in *Small Town and Mass Society* and attempt to devise a more ethical strategy that can also be effective.

Alan Campbell would acknowledge the need for the Professor to provide day-to-day leadership in the school district. However, he adds this observation:

On the other hand, it is probably unrealistic to look to these people (school administrators) to introduce changes on their own initiative. In many ways they are captives of the community in which they operate. Further, their day-to-day responsibilities are so great that their primary role is to keep the system operating. They tend to make every effort to avoid controversy and, in general, to keep the boat from rocking. It is ridiculous to be critical of this behavior, for their positions make it inevitable. (1968, p. 50)

We already know, even if some of us will not admit it, that the answer to all our problems is not found in operating a good educational program for the boys and girls in the schools. Make no mistake, a good program is important and it must always be central to the arguments of educators. But, in fairness to the Professor in Springdale and to his counterparts, we must acknowledge that there can be no good program without a successful vote on the next operating levy, no outstanding open school if the bond issue is defeated.

The question of what difference knowing the power structure makes and how to deal with the power structure remains to be answered. The Springdale example showed how one particular school administrator responded to one particular power structure. There are any number of variations of power structures and there is some evidence to suggest that school boards and superintendents are both forced into different types in order to respond appropriately (see McCarty and Ramsey, 1967). For what it is worth, we can assume that life would be simpler for a superintendent working with an uncompetitive, monolithic power elite than it would be for his counterpart working with competing elites or competing pluralistic power structures. But, and this is an important, albeit obvious, analysis of the literature on power structures: knowing is not enough! Knowledge of the power structure will not, of itself, result in more effective administration. Teasing out the existing power structure will not yield a panacea. This seemingly gratuitous truism is a response to the positions of many colleagues who conclude their discussions of power structure with the observation that his possessing such helpful knowledge will undoubtedly make the administrator more effective. Maybe it will.

Nunnery and Kimbrough (1971) list seven ways in which educators may act on the basis of knowledge of the power structure. Simple inspection of the list will reveal that if administrators adopted *some* of these ways of acting, they would most probably be less effective! Here is their list of ways in which to approach the power structure:

1. Attempt . . . to organize latent centers of power (e.g., managers of absentee-owned corporations) and the public to defeat the existing power structure.
2. Bring . . . pressure from outside sources to bear to change the opinions of some of the influentials (e.g., the threat of losing the school's accreditation or eventual loss of economic growth, because of poor schools).
3. Organize . . . studies of school needs in which key influentials participate and grow in their understanding of school needs (e.g., cooperative school surveys, citizens committees).
4. Acquiesce . . . in the wishes of the influentials until school conditions get bad enough for public pressure to force a change in their opinions.
5. Forget . . . about the idea of pressing for school improvement.
6. Consider . . . changes in the school proposal that might make it acceptable to the leaders of the community. . . .
7. Attempt . . . to bargain with the influentials for their support by promising advantages to them for supporting the proposal. (p. 35)

The authors point out that these strategies will have different results with different power structures and that all have been used in practice.

Another pair of authors, although surely aware of the infinite variety of power arrangements possible, offer some specific general "guidelines for his personal conduct which will stand the administrator in good stead in meeting this problem." Sumption and Engstrom advise administrators to avoid entangling alliances by observing these rules.

First, he will maintain a complete independence and freedom of action. This means he will make no deals and accept no favors which are predicated on a return in kind. To do this he need not isolate himself. He can, and should, be active in community affairs. . . .

Second, he will judge each issue on its merits and act accordingly. Insofar as possible, he will avoid personalities and give battle only on the issues.

Third, he will never align himself with any group which is self-serving at the expense of the people he serves. . . .

Fourth, he will conduct himself in such a manner as to develop a reputation for fairness, consistency, and impartiality in his relations with all groups in the community. Even members of the power group respect a man who will not yield to influence from any quarter and as long as he treats all groups alike, are more or less content to leave him alone most of the time.

Finally, he will recognize that losing his job is not as bad as losing his integrity. (1966, p. 32)

Sumption and Engstrom take an ethical position based on the assumption that the power structure is hostile to the best interests of school programs. The advice will surely serve the administrator until he has been able to identify the power structure. Then, it would seem that a more pragmatic, less moralistic orientation might enable him to make good use of information about decision makers, hidden and visible. For example, it might be better in the long run for the school administrator to pull out of a hopeless struggle at least until his estimate of the situation gives him some hope of winning. Putting a $48 million bond issue before the voters when all the community spokesmen except for a school-supportive PTA oppose it is sometimes a good strategy, if the subsequent defeat will help arrange a compromise that can win. It is perhaps courageous, but probably harmful to education in the long run to stick to one's guns and go back time and again for the same, ideal $48 million.

One hears, sometimes from the ubiquitous "reliable sources," of administrators who invariably arrange an informal assessment of major proposals by the power structure before making the project public. In the $48 million issue mentioned above, such an administrator would first secure the approval of the identified influentials. This would need to be done covertly lest the administrator be perceived as a tool of the power structure. There would be a vigorous campaign, supported by the power structure, which could—in the present state of affairs—go down to a crushing defeat because of opposition coming from persons who were not under the influence of the elite. As the losing superintendent goes back to the drawing board to plan his next move, he needs to ask himself whether it makes any difference losing with the support of influentials or without it. The answer to this question will be easier after he has analyzed the sources and strength of opposition to his program.

Dealing with hypothetical issues is frustrating but so, too, is the political world of educators. Of course, there are issues so important that one must not withdraw even in the face of certain defeat. But is every issue such a matter of life or death? Compromise will sometimes result in an important gain but this must be evaluated against the possible long-term loss. Perhaps the voters will approve a $2 million levy now but this may make the $48 million project forever impossible.

Enough has been said, it is hoped, to support the position that school administrators need to be aware of the power structure and to consider the power structure in their planning. There is unlikely to be a handbook of how to deal with the power structure. However, it should be apparent that knowing the basis of possible opposition makes it possible to deal in advance with important obstacles without injuring an overall design. That is, if an administrator, by knowing his community, can put together a program that will be sure to bring enough support to succeed, he need not suffer remorse for modifying a plan that will engender enough opposition to ensure its failure.

Two important points remain to be made. The first is that neither pressure groups nor power structures, however defined, provide adequate means for a citizen to participate in education. A structure that would represent an adequate level of participation by citizens is represented by Figure 5.4.

Needless to say, there are few examples of organizations governed in accordance with Figure 5.4. The old New England town meetings would be something like this. When one reads A. S. Neill, it seems as though he were trying to make Summerhill become a mass participation model. There are small differences in status and leaders are easily

Figure 5.4

**Power Structure for Significant
Participation by Citizens in Decision Making**

replaced. People participate in any or all issues on an almost equal basis. Clearly, this model can never be achieved in a large, centralized system. We do not yet know if it is even feasible with decentralization to small, local school units.

The second point is a bit more optimistic. Power structures and pressure groups may well have denied certain citizens the chance to participate in decision making about education. New forces, including federal support and attendant controls, are providing a vehicle to involve new groups in decision making. What this new development will mean in the long run remains to be seen.

Finally, in opposition to the mass of data we have collected about pressure, influence, and power, there is always the potentially disproportionate influence of one persistent ordinary citizen. School administrators are always sensitive to the effect of valid, vigorous criticism, no matter what their relationship to pressure groups, or power structures, or ethical codes of conduct. It is still likely that the squeaky wheel will be greased if the squeak is persistent and loud enough.

SUMMARY

In this chapter we discussed the community power structure. Sociologists emphasized a reputational approach and were more likely to discover ruling elites. Political scientists stressed issue analysis and more often found different centers of influence, depending upon the area of the issue. School administrators are well advised to use a discreet approach in discovering the power structure. Knowledge of the power structure is one more source of important information to serve as a guide to planning and action. The power structure does not permit meaningful participation by ordinary citizens in decision making about education. The failure of pressure groups and the power structure to offer appropriate means for citizens to become involved and the barriers of bureaucracy and professional hostility contribute to the demand for alternative structures of educational governance.

Exercise 5.1

INFERNAL INTERNAL INFLUENCE

One of the assumed truths of education is that the school custodian or secretary is the most powerful individual in a given school building. Readers have an opportunity to test this assertion and to judge its appropriateness. Below are two lists of persons usually found in schools. The assignment is, first, to rank each individual in terms of his/her actual power and then to rank her/him according to how important the individuals ought to be.

Way It Is	Rank	Way It Should Be	Rank
Principal	_____	Principal	_____
Custodian	_____	Custodian	_____
Secretary	_____	Secretary	_____
A particular teacher	_____	A particular teacher	_____
Teachers in general	_____	Teachers in general	_____
Lunchroom attendant	_____	Lunchroom attendant	_____
Students	_____	Students	_____
Parents	_____	Parents	_____
PTA	_____	PTA	_____
Guidance counselor	_____	Guidance counselor	_____
Other ( )	_____	Other ( )	_____

After your individual rankings have been entered they should be collected and tabulated for the entire class. An average ranking may then be obtained for each position, and if time permits, a third statistic, "discrepancy," can be computed for each position. This would be the average rank for "Way It Should Be," less average rank for "Way It Is."

Your interpretation of this exercise must be tentative because, of course, raters are not from the same school and are not rating the same position-incumbents. However, it would be appropriate for purposes of discussion to approach an analysis by assuming that the ratings are all by persons in the same school of persons in that school.

Exercise 5.2
WHO'S IN CHARGE HERE?

Directions. Try a reputational survey in your class. Identify an educational area familiar to the entire class (e.g., a district, the university, the region, the state). Assume that all members of the class have been identified as knowledgeables in regard to leadership, both informal and formal, concerning education. Agree on the best wording of a question to elicit information about possible influentials. For example, "Who in (insert the area you have agreed on) has the most influence on educational issues such as (insert appropriate topics such as the ubiquitous operating levy or important reorganization)?" The wording of the question should be one that best describes important power in local usage. In Chicago we might have said: "Who in Chicago has the most clout on educational issues such as the threatened teacher strike?" Limit the responses to five per person in your class.

Make a frequency distribution of all responses for the entire class. Drop the names of persons cited fewer than three times from your list. If you and your colleagues were proper knowledgeables, the reduced list of names would represent the influentials concerning education for your chosen area. To verify your list you would go to some of the most cited individuals on your list and ask the same question. The answers should be close to those you prepared from your own panel of knowledgeables. However, it is also possible that you would add to your list the names of others identified by the most cited persons and not by your panel.

If your class feels knowledgeable about another issue area, you could repeat the process to determine if the influentials specialize in issue areas or if the same persons are seen as influential regardless of the issue area.

Exercise 5.3
ETERNAL EXTERNAL INFLUENCE

This exercise is a companion to Exercise 5.1 on internal influence. This time you are asked to rank the two lists of external participants according to how much power they have over what happens in your school and again according to how much power you think they should have over what happens in your school.

Way It Is	Rank	Way It Should Be	Rank
Superintendent	_____	Superintendent	_____
Board of education	_____	Board of education	_____
Central office personnel	_____	Central office personnel	_____
Teachers' professional association	_____	Teachers' professional association	_____
A college or university	_____	A college or university	_____
Lions, Kiwanis, Rotary, etc.	_____	Lions, Kiwanis, Rotary, etc.	_____
Booster clubs	_____	Booster clubs	_____
Real estate interest	_____	Real estate interest	_____
Chamber of Commerce	_____	Chamber of Commerce	_____
Court	_____	Court	_____
City council	_____	City council	_____
Law enforcement body	_____	Law enforcement body	_____
Social agency	_____	Social agency	_____
Other ( )	_____	Other ( )	_____
Other ( )	_____	Other ( )	_____

SUGGESTED ACTIVITIES

1. Using issue analysis, identify influential decision makers in the area of education for your community. Are these the same persons you would expect to find important in another area, such as housing or medical care?
2. Using the reputational approach, try to find the influentials in your community. Which power structure description is most appropriate to typify the relationships among influentials and others?
3. Make a list of the knowledgeable persons you might interview to discover who is important in educational decision making.
4. Interview some members of a board of education. Try to find out what individuals or groups influence their decision making.
5. Interview a school superintendent. Find out if he can distinguish the degrees of influence he has with different members of his board. What explanation does he give for these differences?
6. Read *Small Town in Mass Society* and try to devise a better approach to the power structure than the one taken by the Professor.
7. Describe and compare the power structures for two public service agencies in your community—make one the education agency.
8. Make a table of words or phrases associated with the two major approaches to studying community power structure. Head one column *Elitists,* the other *Pluralists.* Include names of proponents as well as words describing the approaches. Try to find corresponding but different terms for each side of your table whenever possible.

SUGGESTED READINGS

Bonjean, Charles M. "Community Leadership: A Case Study and Conceptual Refinement." *American Journal of Sociology* 68(6) (May 1963):672-81.

Clark, Terry N. *Community Structure and Decision-Making: Comparative Analyses.* San Francisco: Chandler, 1968, Chs. 2, 4, 5.

Dahl, Robert A. *Who Governs?* New Haven: Yale University Press, 1961.

Franklin, Herbert, and Kimbrough, Ralph B. "Leadership Practices Needed in Personalized PR Program." *NASSP Bulletin* 63(429) (October 1979):106-11.

Hawley, Willis D., and Svara, James. "The Study of Community Power: A Bibliographic Review." Santa Barbara: American Bibliographic Center/Clio Press, 1972.

Hawley, Willis D., and Wirt, Frederick M., eds. *The Search for Community Power.* 2nd ed. Englewood Cliffs, N.J.: Prentice-Hall, 1974.

Hunter, Floyd. *Community Power Structure.* Chapel Hill: University of North Carolina Press, 1953.

Kimbrough, Ralph B. *Political Power and Educational Decision Making.* Chicago: Rand-McNally, 1964.

Peshkin, Alan. *Growing Up American: Schooling and the Survival of Community.* Chicago: University of Chicago Press, 1978.

Peterson, Paul E. *School Politics Chicago Style.* Chicago: University of Chicago Press, 1976.

Polsby, Nelson W. *Community Power and Political Theory.* 2nd ed. New Haven: Yale University Press, 1980.

Sergiovanni, Thomas J., and Carver, Fred D. *The New School Executive: A Theory of Administration.* 2nd ed. New York: Harper & Row, 1980, Ch. 13.

Smith, Martha L., and Smith, Milton L. "Identifying Power Structures." Paper presented at annual meeting of American Educational Research Association, Boston, 1980. ED 185 645.

Spiess, John A. "Community Power Study: Applications to Educational Administration. Toledo, Ohio: University of Toledo, 1971.

Wirt, Frederick M., and Kirst, Michael W. *Schools in Conflict.* Berkeley: McCutchan Publishing Corp., 1982, Ch. 5.

Zeigler, L. Harmon, and Jennings, M. Kent, with Peak, G. Wayne. *Governing American Schools: Political Interaction in Local School Districts.* North Scituate, Mass.: Duxbury Press, 1974.

REFERENCES

Apling, Daniel L. "An Analysis of a Large City Mayor's Influence with Regard to Educational Decision-Making." Ph.D. diss., University of Toledo, 1970.

Banfield, Edward C. *Political Influence.* New York: Free Press, 1961.

Bell, Wendell, Hill, Richard J., and Wright, Charles R. *Public Leadership.* San Francisco: Chandler, 1961.

Campbell, Alan K. "Who Governs the Schools?" *Saturday Review,* December 21, 1968, p. 50.

Caplow, Theodore, et al. *Middletown Families: Fifty Years of Change and Continuity.* Minneapolis: University of Minnesota Press, 1982.

Clark, Terry N. *Community Structure and Decision-Making: Comparative Analyses.* San Francisco: Chandler, 1968.

"Committee Discloses 'Enemies List' Given to IRS by Former Nixon Aide." *Toledo Blade,* December 22, 1973, p. 10.

Cunningham, Luvern. *Governing Schools: New Approaches to Old Issues.* Columbus, Ohio: Charles E. Merrill, 1971.

Dahl, Robert A. *Who Governs?* New Haven: Yale University Press, 1961.

_____ . "A Critique of the Ruling Elite Model." In *Decisions, Organizations, and Society.* Ed. F. G. Castles, D. J. Murray, and D. C. Potter. Harmondsworth, England: Penguin Books, 1971, pp.354-63.

Darling, Arthur (conference reporter). *Better School-Community Relations.* Dayton, Ohio: Institute for Development of Educational Activities, 1972.

Davis, Allison; Gardner, Burleigh; and Gardner, Mary. *Deep South.* Chicago: University of Chicago Press, 1941.

Dollard, John. *Caste and Class in a Southern Town.* Garden City, N.Y.:Doubleday, 1937.

Dunn, Sally A. "Educational Policy Making in an Urban School System with Regard to an Operating Levy." Ed. D. diss., University of Toledo, 1980.

Gross, Neal. *Who Runs Our Schools?* New York: Wiley, 1958.

Hunter, Floyd. *Community Power Structure.* Chapel Hill: University of North Carolina Press, 1953.

Kaufman, Herbert, and Jones, Victor. "The Mystery of Power." *Public Administration Review* 14 (Summer 1954):205-12.

Kimbrough, Ralph B. *Political Power and Educational Decision-Making.* Chicago: Rand-McNally, 1964.

Koerner, James D. *Who Controls American Education?* Boston: Beacon Press, 1968.

Lynd, Robert S., and Lynd, Helen M. *Middletown.* New York: Harcourt, Brace and World, 1929.

_____ . *Middletown in Transition.* New York: Harcourt, Brace and World, 1937.

Manion, Dean Clarence L. "Professional Educators Play 'Musical Chairs.'" *Manion Forum,* February 5, 1967, p. 2.

McCarty, Donald J., and Ramsey, Charles I. *A Study of Community Factors Related to the Turnover of Students' Community Power, School Board Structure, and the Role of the Chief School Administrator.* Ithaca, N.Y.: Cornell University Press, 1967.

Nunnery, Michael Y., and Kimbrough, Ralph B. *Politics, Power, Polls, and School Elections.* Berkeley: McCutchan Publishing Corp., 1971.

Spiess, John A. "Community Power Structure and Influence: Relationships to Educational Administration." Ph.D. diss., University of Iowa, 1967.

_____ . *Community Power and Influence Studies: Two Positions.* Toledo, Ohio: University of Toledo, 1970.

Sumption, Merle R., and Engstrom, Yvonne. *School-Community Relations.* New York: McGraw-Hill, 1966.

Tyler, Ralph. "The Purpose and Plan of This Yearbook." In *Special Forces Influencing Education.* Sixtieth Yearbook of the National Society for the Study of Education, part 2. Chicago: University of Chicago Press, 1961.

Vidich, Arthur J., and Bensman, Joseph. *Small Town in Mass Society.* Princeton: Princeton University Press, 1958.

Warner, W. Lloyd, and Lunt, Paul S. *The Social Life of a Modern Community.* Vol. 1, "Yankee City Series." New Haven: Yale University Press, 1941.

West, James. *Plainville, U.S.A.* New York: Columbia University Press, 1945.

6

MULTIPLE AND CHANGING SCHOOL COMMUNITIES

by

Joseph C. Sommerville

Before the Lord; for he cometh to judge the earth: with righteousness shall he judge the world, and the people with equity.

(Psalm 98:9)

The effort to equalize educational opportunities for all students has created a need for diversity and cooperation among distinctive groups. Student populations in school communities throughout the United States are rapidly changing. Several major developments— the thrust for school desegregation, multicultural education, and a free public education for all handicapped children—have contributed to more diversified and dynamic school populations and communities.

One need not go far to find multiple and changing school communities. They exist in every sizable school district in the nation. For example, in the Toledo area, there are (1) school districts that provide special education programs in a single school building for students from several different attendance areas, (2) schools that were almost all white a few years ago and are now changing or have changed to a predominantly black school population, (3) schools that have a growing population of Latino and Asian students, (4) vocational and magnet schools that attract students from diverse neighborhoods because of the specialized curricula offered, (5) schools that have increased racial balance as a result of the board's policy which encourages students to transfer to another school if the transfer will enhance racial desegregation, and (6) schools that are attempting to meet the educational needs of an increasing number of academically and physically handicapped students. Similar developments and school-community population changes are evident in other areas of the country.

The changing school-community population presents a special school-community relations challenge for school personnel. The changed communities are special in that the usual approaches to school-community relations are often ineffective and counterproductive. Barriers to communication—mistrust, language problems, past negative experiences, and stereotypes—block effective school-community interaction. Frequently, past experiences have led to parents' (1) suspicion that the school will not address the unique needs of their children, (2) mistrust of school authorities, and (3) fear that their ideas would not be welcome. Thus, the routine newsletters, open houses, PTA's, and Parent Teacher Organizations (PTO's) are inadequate as strategies for improving school-community relations with multiple and changing communities.

Approaches and strategies for meeting the new school-community relations challenge are the focus of this chapter. They will be discussed within the context of three developments that directly affect school communities. These developments are (1) desegregation and sometimes resegregation of schools, (2) emphasis on bilingual and bicultural education, and (3) efforts to provide special programs to meet the needs of the exceptional students, especially programs for the handicapped as mandated by Section 504 of the Vocational Rehabilitation Act of 1973 and Public Law 94-142 of the All Handicapped Children Act of 1975.

SCHOOL DESEGREGATION AND
SCHOOL-COMMUNITY RELATIONS

Since the *Brown* v. *Board of Education* (1954) Supreme Court decision, the desegregation-integration struggle has been at the forefront of educational problems throughout the nation. The struggle has resulted in conflicts and strains in the relationships of students, parents, school personnel, and specifically between the school and community. This writer recalls 1966 when as a school administrator and a coordinator of an initial effort to desegregate the Inkster, Michigan, schools, he was the focus of a conflict between school and community that made national news. The scene of the writer under verbal attack by an angry citizen and the related story appeared on

NBC's evening news. Other administrators in other cities were "experiencing" similar attention. Such incidents left lasting effects in many communities. The desegregation of schools continues to affect school-community relationships.

Some school districts that have been desegregated by court order or by edict of the local boards have resegregated. "White flight" has been widely discussed as a reason for resegregating school communities. Coleman et al. (1975), Green and Pettigrew (1976), Orfield (1976), Farley (1977), Rossell (1978), and Cunningham and Husk (1980) are but a few who have written extensively about the resegregation of once desegregated school communities due to the outward migration of the white population. A detailed discussion of "white flight" or any reason for the resegregation of desegregated communities is beyond the scope of this chapter. We shall instead focus on the relationships of significant groups in desegregating and resegregating school communities. Those relationships will be discussed from the perspective of (1) minority and majority students, (2) administrative and staff behavior, and (3) parent and community involvement in the school program.

Minority and Majority Student Relationships

Before discussing relationships within the context of desegregation, the semantics of desegregation and integration should be clarified. Gordon (1976) defined *desegregation* as the physical mixing of the races without regard to the relative statuses among the groups, and *integration* as the interaction of races based on mutual respect and equal status among them. Nevas (1977) asserted that integration "is ultimately realized when the targets of the effort, the children, interact positively" (p. 1). We support the Nevas meaning of desegregation as a goal rather than in terms of the ratio of different races in schools—most commonly, the mixture of black and white students. Although relationships within the context of desegregation will be discussed, the focus of this writing is on the objectives of integration—positive interaction among races rather than merely the mixing of the races.

Majority and minority relationships in desegregation must be viewed in terms of past experiences as well as existing conditions. In many cases, by the time schools are desegregated, there have already been several conflicts and confrontations at various levels. Conflicts have been led by adult citizens in the community. Students, especially those in upper grades, are frequently aware of those developments.

Naturally, that awareness can and does affect the relationships between both majority and minority students. Examination of the activities preceding the desegregation of schools may provide some clues to the types of opposing forces, the intensity of interaction between those forces, and other information about the desegregation that may be useful in understanding and dealing with majority-minority student relationships. Interpersonal and group activities are usually focused at various levels of desegregation decision making. Important desegregation decisions are made by courts, federal and state agencies, boards of education, school administrations, and teachers. Those for and against integration, militant and various other community groups, and opponents and supporters of desegregation are frequently active in efforts to influence desegregation decisions at the various levels (Sommerville, 1980). We therefore encourage a review of the developments at various levels of decision making. Frequently, that review aids in the identification of resource persons who will be helpful in improving majority-minority student relationships.

Student Interaction

The socialization between majority and minority group students often mystifies school personnel. When students have opportunities for voluntary interaction in the classroom, in the lunchroom, on the playground, and in extracurricular activities, they frequently segregate themselves. It is quite common to see all black tables in the lunchroom or all white or black subgroups in situations when students may freely interact. Naturally, minority and majority student relationships and understanding of each other are not enhanced by such separations. However, many administrators in our study reported successes in facilitating positive relationships and understanding by organizing student interaction during lunch period and after school (Sommerville, 1981, p. 24).

Even though it is understood that student relationships in a desegregating school situation are sometimes governed negatively by external individuals and groups, school personnel can play a vital role in improving those relationships. Bringing segments of conflicting groups together by focusing on areas of common interest and cooperation is a well-known strategy in group dynamics. In other words, structuring activities in which minority and majority students may work cooperatively to complete a single task, such as a school beautification project, often influences positive interaction between the groups. A primary objective of the activity should be to facilitate changes in attitudes and opinions about each other. The attitudes and reactions of persons unaccustomed to positive racial reactions are important factors in desegregation (Smith, 1974, pp. 14, 28-29).

Students often share information about positive and negative interaction in desegregation with their parents. Positive experiences of students frequently serve as a stimulus for interaction between parents of minority and majority parents. As a parent who has had two boys who attended integrated schools, this writer is acquainted with several minority and majority group parents who were specifically introduced because of positive experiences our children had. Parents of students who have had positive experiences in a desegregated situation are often excellent resource persons for the school-community relations program. As a follow-up of student experiences, school administrators should work with other key persons in the school setting in structuring parent activities (PTA, PTO's, school projects, and parent councils) in which majority and minority parents focus on a common task so that they too may have an opportunity for cooperative positive interaction. Improving majority and minority group relationships and school-community relations programs should not be left to chance. The effective leadership of the school administrator and other school personnel is essential in the process.

Facilitating Interracial Interaction

Structured small group interaction of majority and minority students is recommended to promote our definition of integration. Several researchers—Slavin and Madden (1979), Garbaldi (1979), and Sharan (1980)—have reported success with the small group racial interaction process. After a survey of conditions and processes of effective school desegregation in ninety-four elementary schools and sixty-eight high schools, Forehand and Ragosta (1976, p. 30) concluded that "when students are assigned to work together and play together they are more likely to have good racial attitudes." They thus suggested that teachers (1) "make student assignments affirmatively to promote interracial contact" and (2) "use small group projects as opportunities to promote interracial contact and multiethnic learning." Nickerson and Prawat (1981) reported a case study and observations of subgroups of students who interacted in racially diverse classrooms—one group under a teacher who structured interaction and the other group under a teacher who permitted students to group themselves. They revealed that more positive cross-racial interaction resulted between students who had been a part of the structured class subgroup setting than between those who had been members of voluntarily organized subgroups. These positive interactions between the races were observed in the lunchrooms and other places where students were free to mingle and socially set up their own subgroups. This type of positive informal interaction is often the aim of facilitators of effective desegregation.

Aronson et al. (1978, p. 26) described the jigsaw classroom technique as an effective instructional strategy and a way to integrate schools. They explained that the basic classroom structure of one expert and thirty listeners was changed by placing students in small groups of about six. The role of the teacher was changed so that he or she was no longer the major resource for each learning group. Instead, the process made it imperative that the children treat each other as resources. The technique is based on the principle of team building and cooperation rather than competition in the classroom. Aronson et al. pointed out that though the jigsaw technique was developed as an attempt to bridge the gap between different ethnic groups, its function is not limited to multiracial situations. The goal is to curb undesirable aspects of excessive competition and increase the excitement children find in cooperating with each other. They instituted the jigsaw technique in several classrooms for various extended periods of time. The performance of children in the jigsaw classrooms was compared with the performance of children in more competitive classrooms that were taught by effective teachers. Comparing the control groups with their experimental jigsaw classroom group, we find the major results as follows:

Students in jigsaw classrooms increased their liking for their mates without decreasing their liking for others in the classroom.

Students in jigsaw classrooms tended to increase their liking for school to a greater extent than children in nonjigsaw classrooms.

Students in jigsaw classrooms increased in self-esteem, decreased in competitiveness, and viewed their classmates as learning resources in relation to students in nonjigsaw classrooms.

Black and Mexican-American students in jigsaw classrooms learned the material

significantly better than black and Mexican-American students in nonjigsaw classrooms (as measured by objective test results).

Anglo students performed as well in the jigsaw group as in the nonjigsaw groups.

Children in jigsaw classrooms (compared with children in competitive classrooms)
showed a greater ability to put themselves in the role of another person even
outside of the school environment. (ibid., pp. 120-21)

The studies of Forehand and Ragosta (1976), Nickerson and Prawat
(1981), and Aronson et al. (1978)—briefly described above—strongly
indicate that structured cooperative interaction between majority and
minority students is a fruitful strategy for improving attitudes and
relationships. However, if that interaction is to occur to any appre-
ciable degree, it will require the effective involvement of students,
parents, and especially the staff in the school program. The leadership of the administrators and the cooperation of the faculty are
pivotal variables for facilitating the effective involvement and attaining
success in desegregation.

Administrator and Staff Behavior

To say that school administrators and the faculty play a major role
in desegregation is almost an understatement. Researchers have
repeatedly found that the behavior of the school adminstration tends
to influence the behavior of their subordinates in the school setting.
Gross and Herriott (1965), in their classic study of executive leadership behavior, found that the leadership behavior of the principal was
positively related to the executive professional behavior of the
principal's immediate superior. In turn, teachers' behavior was
influenced by the behavior of the principal. Similarly, Forehand and
others (1976), in their study of 168 schools, found that the principal's
racial attitudes had a direct influence on the attitudes of teachers and
that teachers' attitudes subsequently had a direct effect on the attitudes of white students in both elementary and secondary schools.
Goodlad (1979) concluded that in schools effecting integration with
success, almost invariably the principal was identified as the key
person. In the study of the behavior of 107 top-level administrators
throughout the nation (Sommerville, 1981), the building administrator's action or failure to act at the proper time was found to be a
critical variable in desegregation conflicts and crises. In other words,
problems evolved both from school officials' precipitous action and
from their failure to act when action was warranted. There is little

doubt that school personnel can and must play critical roles as regulators and influencers of the school climate, which in turn naturally affects school-community relations.

The role of the teacher as a coordinator of small group interaction between diverse racial groups has already been discussed. The teacher in that role, and by virtue of his/her designated function in the school, is the major regulator of the climate in the classroom. Thus, the behavior of both the principal and teacher should be a prime focus and given special attention in desegregation change situations. Students who have been traditionally separated by cultural, racial, and socioeconomic barriers frequently develop a mistrust and a fear of the unknown, which is not conducive to wholesome relationships. A potent force in allaying those fears and building mutual trust is often the authority figure of the school, the principal and/or the teacher. It is thus important that the school officials remain sensitive to and aware of the potential impact of their personal behavior on the school climate and the interpersonal relationship of students.

Our studies of desegregation indicate that generally school personnel have not adequately planned, designed, and implemented activities to facilitate a smooth transition of students into newly desegregated school settings. Students with significantly different backgrounds than those who previously attended the school have been expected to "fall in line" with traditional practices. Few, if any, changes in the school curriculum and environment, and in instructional and interpersonal approaches, were made. As a result, too often school people expend much energy "putting out the fire" of conflict. They develop plans to deal with the problem after it develops. Granted, those plans are needed to deal with conflict. However, the barriers and "scars" resulting from conflicts often serve as obstacles to planning and implementing other activities for attaining the goals of desegregation. School personnel are therefore urged to demonstrate diligence in effectively involving the community, especially parents, in preplanning and implementing the changes necessary to meet the challenge of desegregation in their unique school setting.

Parent and Community Involvement

Whether the decision makers want community involvement or not, segments of the community will become involved in the often-emotional desegregation struggle. The reactions of parental and community groups to desegregation decisions often contribute to a widening chasm between minority and majority parents. The massive struggle to desegregate Central High School in Little Rock in 1957, the major conflict stimulated by the effort to desegregate schools in Boston in 1976, and the parent boycott about efforts to desegregate two schools in Chicago in 1981 are but three of the many desegregation struggles that have received the attention of our nation's mass media. In almost all of the situations, the community and often outside groups were directly involved in the struggle. The point we wish to make is that parents and the community are often involved in desegregation struggles in negative ways, outside the formal school-community linkage structure, and that involvement frequently becomes news headlines. We suggest that much of that involvement can and should take place within the framework of a formal school-community relations program.

Approaches to Community Involvement

The literature and the respondents in our study agree that involvement of and communication with the community and parents are very important facets of the desegregation process (Sommerville, "Leadership," 1980). However, major questions and challenges regarding community involvement usually center around timing, techniques, and strategies. Our investigation seems to indicate that school administrators raise process kinds of questions. That is, should only those who are generally supportive of the desegregation plan be involved in the planning implementation? Should the plan be developed in its entirety before seeking external (community) involvement? Should a decision to desegregate following a specific pattern remain firm in spite of emotional opposition? In most situations the answer to those three questions would be no! However, a better answer can be given within the context of the unique school community situation. In other words, there is no one best strategy or approach for all school districts and situations. It is, however, strongly recommended that the community be effectively involved in the planning, implementing, and evaluating efforts to attain the goals of desegregation.

Tompkins (1978) criticized the focus of community preparation for school desegregation. She asserted that community preparation, whether undertaken by school officials or community organizations, tended to "focus on compliance with the law and avoidance of violence" (p. 108). She indicated that little attention is paid to possibilities for new educational programs, increased parent involvement, or renewed investment of community resources, and she suggested that effort should be in the direction of creative responses and desegregation decisions. Those responses may be stimulated by effectively using community resources through small group interaction. Community input and direct involvement in each phase of the process are suggested. Brainstorming and the procedures discussed by Delbecq et al. (1975)—the Nominal Group Technique (pp. 40-82) and the Delphi Technique (pp. 83-106)—are but a few facilitating processes by which input from diverse personalities may become a part of group decisions. If the persons who are charged with the responsibility of facilitating effective desegregation do not possess the skills needed to effectively coordinate cooperative and collective input from diverse persons and groups, competent assistance should be secured.

Facilitating Community Involvement

The involvement of the community should occur early in the planning stage of the desegregation process. That involvement should influence what actually takes place in the operation of the school program. D. Bennett (1979, p. 21), in a report on desegregation in the Milwaukee schools, asserted that "participation must be legitimate; the only way administration can demonstrate the legitimacy of the involvement process is to adopt the majority of the recommendations it receives from the community." Though we support the need for legitimacy of involvement, we suggest caution about the representativeness of some community groups and the importance of weighing relevant factors and information regarding the adoption of a community subgroup's recommendations as reflective of the total community. If, however, after considering relevant factors and information a community group's recommendation is not adopted, the rationale for rejection should be clearly articulated for the group.

Sobol and Beck (1980) strongly recommended that school leaders assess the perceptions of parents and students prior to desegregation. They suggested that perceptions especially of minorities can be helpful for educators planning school programs, social reformers, and researchers. Many of the respondents in our investigation identified minority church organizations and ministers, ghetto residents, parents, staff personnel, and traditionally nonelitist groups as most helpful in the desegregation of their districts (Sommerville, "Leadership," 1980, pp. 624-25). The opinion of parents, the community, and other groups should be sought, utilizing approaches— such as surveys, forums, informal discussions, representative advisory committees, task forces—that are appropriate for the community and situation.

While the initial focus of efforts for involvement may be on desegregation, it is quite common for special interest groups to introduce other issues. The concerns of the bilingual community, handicapped, religious, and other special interest groups in the community are frequently raised. In his report on the impact of court-ordered desegregation, D. Bennett (1979) indicated:

Since the desegregation process assumes the center ring, other special interest groups in the community have problems finding the attention and advocates they think they deserve. Members of these special interest groups attempt to accommodate this problem in two ways—they either raise the decibel level and frequency of their complaints or try to ride the coattails of desegregation, even if their cause and desegregation results in a curious juxtaposition of alien elements. Some of these special interest group representatives have great success in working out their agenda under the rubric of desegregation. The leadership of the school system should expect and understand this phenomenon. (p. 23)

There will obviously be concerns in the community other than those which a school system may be focusing on at any given time. The opening up of a communication forum with the community provides opportunities for expression of those concerns even when the expression tends to be opposed to the specified objective of the forum. The school should plan and clearly outline how it will deal with expressed concerns. Empathetically acknowledging and addressing those concerns when appropriate are suggested. The way the school system or group leaders handle the expression of extraneous (at that time) but sincere concerns of individuals can be an important factor in promoting positive or negative school-community relations. Effectively listening to diverse groups even when their views may be antithetical to those of the school leaders is encouraged. After groups are given the opportunity to express their concerns or opposition directly to school authorities, many are willing and sometimes eager to support the school program. Involvement and communication with community and parents are complex and ongoing processes. School leaders and others must regularly plan, implement, and evaluate the strategies and approaches employed in those processes if effective school-community relations are to be developed and maintained.

Contemporary Desegregation Developments

Though in the eighties desegregation appears to be receiving less attention, it is far from resolved. *Brown* v. *Board of Education* (1954) is still the law of the land. Yet schools continue to exist in which students appear to have been segregated on the basis of race. It is apparent that the process of desegregation is incomplete. Discussion about its effects on student achievement and its relationship to forced busing is ongoing. The politician and others have succeeded in making forced busing instead of desegregation a major issue. Though a detailed discussion of desegregation as it relates to the achievement and busing issues is beyond our scope, we shall discuss briefly a few important related developments that have implications for school-community relations.

Willis Hawley (1981), director of a seven-year national study, reported that "desegregation seems to have positive effects on children, particularly minority children." That report was based on analyses of more than 1,000 studies, ten court cases, 170 interviews with experts, and the desegregation strategies of sixteen school districts around the country. He further indicated that public school desegregation seems to improve minority student performance without hurting white student performance. Similarly positive effects on minority achievement were reported by Crain and Mahard (1981). The U.S. Commission on Civil Rights (1981) also reported that "research evidence clearly demonstrates that school desegregation results in improvements in achievement for minority students and majority students hold their own academically" (p. 41). In addition, the commission reported: "Research indicates that desegregated elementary and secondary education has positive effects on long-term aspirations of black students and promotes interracial relationships" (ibid.).

Arthur Flemming (1982) stated that desegregation of schools has brought many very positive relationships between racial groups in several communities throughout the nation. The Charlotte Mecklenberg County, North Carolina, community was cited as an example.

After substantial opposition to desegregation in 1971, ten years later, in June 1981, an impressive cross-section of the Charlotte Mecklenberg community turned out to celebrate the tenth anniversary of the desegregation decision and to honor key decision makers (U.S. Commission on Civil Rights, 1981). Though there have been recent reports with differing points of view—the Coleman (1981) report most notably—our search indicates that the vast majority of the literature reports very positive outcomes, especially for minority students, from the desegregation of schools.

In the 1978-1979 school year, 6,218,025 minority students (60.2 percent) attended schools that were at least 50 percent minority, and 37 percent attended schools that were at least 80 percent minority (U.S. Commission on Civil Rights, 1981). The percentage of minorities in many large city school districts—Chicago and Philadelphia, for example—has steadily increased until today the whites are a relatively small percentage of the school population. The common trend in many urban areas where the majority race has become the minority population in public schools has many implications for school-community relations. Those interested in improving relationships should be reminded that the strategies discussed in this chapter for building positive relationships are applicable regardless of which race of students is in the majority.

With a primary focus on forced busing and led by the actions of the Reagan administration, there is much evidence that the current executive branch has assumed a weakened enforcement posture and that it intends to leave much of the enforcement and implementation of desegregation to the states and local communities. Congress has also passed amendments to curb forced busing to achieve desegregation. In addition, throughout the early eighties the courts have been relatively inactive in surrendering desegregation decisions. These actions by the supreme bodies of the nation have many implications for the local school communities. Without the clout of the federal government, it becomes increasingly important that the community become involved early and in every aspect of what may now be an almost exclusively voluntary desegregation process.

School communities are constantly changing. Whether by desegregation or general population mobility, those changes seem to offer a special challenge to those charged with the responsibility of improving school-community relations. Meeting that challenge will require special attention from school personnel and the effective involvement of the community in every phase of the school program.

MULTICULTURAL AND BILINGUAL SCHOOL COMMUNITIES

The increased attention focused on multicultural and bilingual education presents a special challenge for school personnel, especially the school administrator. That challenge is somewhat analogous to the challenge presented by the desegregation thrust in that the expressed aim in each situation is to equalize educational opportunity for a racially, culturally, or linguistically diverse student population. Communities expect school personnel, led by the school administrator, to facilitate the changes necessary to equalize those educational opportunities. Whereas the desegregation focus is frequently on the number and ratio of ethnic individuals in a school, the multicultural and bilingual education focus is usually on the curriculum and its supportive environment. However similar to desegregation, changes in multicultural and bilingual education have been stimulated by the collective action of citizens followed by legislative and court decisions. Questions of propriety relating to the Constitution, tradition, limited resources, use of resources, and guidelines for school district action are frequently raised. Many of these questions relate to administrative behavior in the process of change designed to upgrade multicultural and bilingual education. Administrative behavior that appropriately facilitates those changes, with a focus on improvements in school community relations, will be discussed.

Several important developments have provided impetus to the current focus on multicultural and bilingual education. Aspects of the civil rights movement in which "black pride" was emphasized, the acceptance by the federal government of the policy of self-determination of Indians, the Indian Education Act of 1972, the Bilingual Education Act, and the *Lau* v. *Nichols* (1974) Supreme Court decision are but a few factors which have stimulated changes in emphasis on multicultural and bilingual education.

The evolution of the focus on bilingual and multicultural education has implications for strategies and approaches that school administrators use. With past developments as a point of reference and with a focus on improvement in school-community relations in this section, we shall examine multicultural and bilingual education from the perspective of administrative behavior as it relates to (1) barriers to communication with parents and their community, (2) strategies for involving parents in curriculum development and in decisions about the school program, and (3) controversy about program support and implementation.

Barriers to Communication

Though many school districts have identifiable cultural and ethnic subcommunities, these subcommunities are often separated from the mainstream of school participation and communication by the constraints of culture and language. Those constraints may be manifested in terms of fear, mistrust, feelings of inadequacy, feelings of not belonging, unwillingness or inability to follow bureaucratic procedures, and other barriers. Administrators need to facilitate an assessment of constraints to subcommunity participation as an initial step in addressing the problems of communication. Obviously, educators should attempt to be responsive to the particular community they serve. Those efforts must be specific for distinct subcommunities as well as for the community as a whole.

We agree with the premise advanced by the Education Commission of the States (1981) that it is necessary to assess the unique needs of the group to be served. The commission authorized the writing of six papers by experts on the special needs of minority students (Asians, blacks, Cubans, Indians, Mexican-Americans, and Puerto Ricans). All six of the authors emphasized the need for parent education and involvement as a means of improving educational opportunity. Parent involvement was considered vital for formulating education programs that were accepting and responsive to different cultural groups. Although writers continue to emphasize the need for parental and community involvement in school programs, few focus on strategies that the administrator may use to remove barriers and facilitate communication.

Strategies for Enhancing Participation

Bequer and Bequer (1978) presented three examples of parental overprotection of students that we think are useful in a discussion of administrative strategies. The examples were descriptions of (1) a new business consisting of a large fleet of privately owned "minibuses" used to transport Hispanic children—who live less than the two-mile limit required by law for students to receive free transportation—to schools; (2) groups of Spanish mothers or grandmothers waiting outside buildings each day for elementary children and junior high students to leave school; and (3) night conferences held by one of the authors with parents twice a week on a one-to-one basis, during which an average of five different parents per night discussed their children's problems (p. 86). The authors indicated that valuable information was exchanged and insights about the community obtained. Bequer and Bequer also emphasized that "Educators must learn that Latino parent participation can be increased by making the method of participation comfortable and personal, attuned to the mores and habits of these parents" (ibid.). Accordingly, we suggest some considerations for enhancing parent participation with this subgroup and for improving school-community relations.

As a response to example one (the "minibus"), the administrator may organize a liaison and communication link between the school and "minibus" system. School representatives who are skilled in communicating with the Latino community may meet with the program coordinators to assess barriers to communication and to facilitate cooperation in establishing an ongoing communication link with the group. In example two (the waiting parents) parental participation and communication may be enhanced by school personnel going outside and talking informally with the waiting mothers and grandmothers and inviting them into the school for comfort and for informal discussion of their concerns while they wait. In example three (the night conference), though it may be unrealistic to hold night conferences twice a week as discussed, the administrator and others may facilitate the organization of coffee klatches, small group sessions (both in the school and in the community), and one-on-one conferences that are scheduled at a time that is mutually agreeable with the parent and school representative.

Many community relations writers (Bequer and Bequer, 1978; Ratliff, 1980; Sitton, 1980) advocate use of the community as a resource for learning. They encourage the use of persons from ethnic communities as resources for the classroom and the use of events and activities in those communities as supplements to the formal curriculum. They stress the importance of experiential learning through direct contacts with ethnic groups. Ratliff (1980) emphasized that rather than textbooks, students should analyze data about conflicts and events involving their own ethnic groups, those ethnic groups in their communities, or groups that they identify with in other parts of the world (p. 51).

We agree that the ethnic communities and activities are excellent learning resources. They should be an integral part of every school's curriculum and used effectively in the school-community relations program. School administrators and other personnel must, however, carefully plan and organize for positive rather than negative interaction with these communities. A well-planned orientation for school personnel and students regarding community idiosyncrasies, sensitivities, and expectations is encouraged. Educators must be aware of their own behavior that may inhibit communication. The tendency to judge cultural and ethnic groups from the perspective of one's own values is perhaps the greatest barrier. Although minority cultural and ethnic groups may welcome empathy, they often resent sympathy. Schools should strive for empathetic understanding of an interaction with ethnic groups in the continuing effort to improve school-community relations.

Strategies for Parental and Community Involvement

Often school districts make decisions that directly affect a minority community that was not appropriately involved in decision making. Such decisions may cause negative reactions that affect the entire district. To demonstrate this possibility, consider the school closing issue relating to the Chicano community in Santa Barbara, California (Valencia, 1980). Because of declining enrollment and related financial losses, the Santa Barbara school district decided to close three schools. The buildings proposed for closing happened to be schools serving the predominantly Chicano low-income population. The decision "set in motion a school boycott, charges of discrimination, and a lawsuit by Mexican-American parents" (p. 6). It became clear after the district decided to close the schools that the decision had profound implications for the Chicano subcommunity. The question needs to be asked: was the district aware of those implications and the probable negative reactions prior to that decision? We are aware of countless instances in which school administrators characterized parent groups and subcommunities as apathetic until school decisions with which group members did not agree were made which stimulated emotional and collective reactions. Those same so-called apathetic citizens often marshaled a great deal of support for their position. Clearly, it is better to stimulate responses and explore strategies for influencing the participation of significant groups that appear to be apathetic *before* rather than *after* making decisions that affect them.

Although the administrator may not leave the making of decisions for which he or she is responsible to community groups, these groups contribute to the quality of the decisions. Parental involvement appears to be of special value in multicultural and bilingual education. Those parents can provide a valuable resource to educators unfamiliar with the culture and idiosyncrasies of ethnic groups in the community. However, if those resources are to be effectively utilized, an effective communication link should be established through direct involvement of parents in the school program, active advisory committees, and other ongoing organizations designed to facilitate two-way interaction between the school and community.

Davies (1981) suggested that "criteria are needed to help think clearly about the vast array of activities and events in a field characterized by polemics, inflated claims and conflicting goals" (p. 87). He delineated six criteria for judging citizen participation. Of those, criterion two, more equitable distribution of power, seems targeted as a major challenge for the school administrator. The primary question asked is: does the policy or activity contribute to increasing access to power for those now least powerful—the poor, the working class, and members of racial and ethnic minority groups? We strongly agree that the question should be used as a measure of the effectiveness of citizen participation. Also, many community subgroups ask the same question. If the response is positive, that serves as an incentive for further participation. If it is negative, important groups eventually feel that interacting with school personnel is a waste of time. In other words, the bottom line is that participation by cultural, racial, and ethnic minority groups must have an impact on important decisions. And that impact should be readily evident, especially when those decisions specifically relate to the community the groups represent.

Gay (1981) described a good multicultural program as one that "addresses many different ethnic groups, includes both historical and contemporary perspectives, and focuses on variations and similarities within and among different ethnic groups. School nutritionists and planners of assembly programs are as responsible for ethnic diversity and cultural pluralism as are the social studies teachers. In short, the program is comprehensive, integrative, and systematic" (p. 188). We accept Gay's description of multicultural education and contend that good programs must be directed and coordinated by committed school administrators. If the elements of the program (different ethnic groups, community, faculty, and staff members) are to function as a unit, skilled leadership of the administrator is essential.

Most evaluative criteria for school programs have a multicultural component. Institutions continue to delineate how they are meeting the multicultural criterion by identifying activities they have had during Brotherhood Week and other special times or units they covered as a small component of the total curriculum. However, other aspects of the school operation convey the message to all students that there is only one culture, that of white, middle-class America. The message is evident in many schools as students observe principals, teachers, characters in textbooks and instructional materials used, nonteaching personnel, and displays. *The point we wish to make is that representatives of minority cultures and role models for minority students are often not an integral part of the internal school environment and daily operation at the school.* We believe that they should be, and the school administrator is the key agent of the change process by which multiculturalism may become evident in the various aspects of the school program and operation.

Bilingual and Multicultural Issues

Changes in the schools' ethnic population and community and in the nation's focus on bilingual and multicultural education have stimulated controversy about the emphasis and implementation of school programs. Naturally there are persons and sometimes activist groups in the community who take opposing positions regarding multicultural issues. The resulting conflict and controversy have many implications for bilingual and multicultural education and school-community relations. Persons who are charged with the responsibility of program planning need to be aware of and sensitive to evolving issues that signify the need for (1) changes in administrative behavior and leadership strategies, and (2) increases in the dissemination of accurate information to counteract the potentially negative impact on program development and implementation. Though there are no doubt many other issues that deserve the attention of school leaders, three surfaced repeatedly in our review of the literature and experiences. They are: (1) the staffing of the school for bilingual and multicultural education, (2) the uncertainty and controversy about federal government support of bilingual education, and (3) conflicting views regarding the value of bilingualism and the future impact of pluralism in America.

The controversy over whether a person can effectively teach or administer a program and interpret a culture he or she has not experienced has been with us for some time. The controversy was highlighted in the early sixties when the civil rights movement was at its peak and occupied the daily news headlines. Feinberg et al. (1978, p. 54), in their discussion of staff development, emphasized that bilingual teachers must be able to interpret culture and languages and should be familiar with the culture and background of the students served. Many ethnic groups advocate a need for teachers and other school personnel who are members of the specified ethnic group. Whether right or not, they often maintain that qualified members of the same ethnic group are generally better prepared by experiences and exhibit a greater understanding of their children than staff personnel who are not members of that group. Though there are many exceptions to their contention, we affirm that qualified members of the same ethnic groups who hold key instructional and leadership positions frequently serve as valuable role models for students and vital communication links between the school and sub-communities.

The rapid expansion of bilingual and multicultural education programs has placed a strain on the limited supply of qualified personnel to staff those programs. Securing qualified personnel has become a major problem. Washburn (1982) surveyed 3,038 post-secondary institutions in an effort to identify those that offered a major, a minor, or a concentration in bilingual or multicultural education. He found that programs with that focus are of recent development, not fully developed, and touched only a small number of prospective teachers. These results seem to indicate that school districts need to devote additional attention and resources to bilingual and multicultural training since there is little indication that staffing needs are likely to be met through preservice training institutions. Research data of that nature may be very useful in efforts to influence community group support for the funds needed for program development and implementation.

The position of the Reagan administration to diminish the role the federal government plays in operating schools has created uncertainty about the funding of programs. A decision memorandum by the Education Department would change the statutory definition of bilingual education to limit the number of children eligible for federal bilingual programs ("Policy Reversal," 1982, p. 1). The controversy over funding has continued with key members of Congress, the administration, and special interest groups arguing for and against federal government support of programs ("Bell Lobbies," 1982, pp. 7-8). However, the trend is toward less federal and more local control. Thus, school administrators are encouraged to facilitate informed interaction among diverse school and community groups in an effort to upgrade local program. At the same time, they must keep informed about developments, at the state and national levels, which may impact on local efforts.

Support for bilingual and multicultural education is far from unanimous. Yaffe (1981) discussed many problems in the interpretation of the *Lau* decision. She also highlighted debates between opponents and supporters of bilingual/bicultural education programs. Glazer (1981) raised some hard questions about ethnicity and education. He expressed fear that America's new emphasis on ethnicity "is undermining what has been, on the whole, a great success in schooling and nation building" (p. 386). Similarly, Thomas (1981) argued that pluralism has the potential to diminish the effectiveness of schools (p. 591). Conversely, C. Bennett (1981) and Foster (1982) strongly supported pluralism and bilingualism in education. We have already discussed many other writers who have supported and advocated bilingual and multicultural education. The point to be made here is that there are conflicting views about bilingual and multicultural education. The school administrator should know this in order to (1) respond intelligently to questions and (2) provide leadership for meaningful school-community interaction, a necessity if the needed improvement in the school's bilingual and multicultural education program is to become a reality.

SPECIAL PROGRAMS AND THE COMMUNITY

Special programs are commonly identified as those nontraditional curricula designed to meet the needs of specific segments of the school population. These programs often serve students from several school attendance areas. Special programs for the disadvantaged and gifted and specialized schools within a district (magnet, vocational, alternative schools) and others are found in many school systems throughout America. However, Public Law 94-142 requires that all school districts support special education programming for all handicapped students who need it (Ballard and Zettel, 1977, p. 177). Thus, though programs for the disadvantaged and gifted, specialized vocational, and magnet schools will be discussed briefly in this section, the primary focus will be on special education programs as they affect school-community relations. Special attention will be given to the implications of special program development and implementation for administrative behavior.

Similar to desegregation and multicultural education, the aim of special programs is to upgrade educational opportunities for special classes of students. Differences exist, however, in (1) the student groups targeted for service, (2) the parental and community support groups, and (3) the politics of interaction between and among groups that support or oppose the special programs. Competition, cooperation and/or conflicts among community subgroups have implications for school-community relations and for the actions of the school administrator. We shall review several of those developments.

Programs for the Disadvantaged

Programs for the disadvantaged are found in many school districts, especially in urban areas. Most often the focus is on remedial reading or mathematics and enrichment in art and music. Though the programs are usually externally funded and must be operated within the framework of the guidelines provided by the funding agency, schools are criticized by persons and groups in the community for serving a selected group of students while excluding others. Some programs have supported and mandated parental assistance. Title I programs, for several years, required the establishment of ongoing advisory councils. Since 1974, the Toledo public school system has operated a program in which some parents work in the homes of students who have special needs (*Parent Partners,* 1981). These parents are paid for their services. In addition, the Title I program pays transportation and babysitting expenses for parents to attend the advisory council meeting. Based on family income, many of the students are served free breakfast and lunch. All of these programs (often called "special plums") for disadvantaged parents and students sometimes stimulate resentment, conflict, and misunderstandings among parental groups in the community.

Special programs for the disadvantaged can introduce variables in school operation that lead to interpersonal conflicts about resources and program management. These frequently have negative implications for school-community relations. The administrator must provide leadership to establish effective communication with and among segments of the community regarding the goals of the program, sources of funding, and specific guidelines for operation. Effectively utilizing internally developed written communication (school newspapers, newsletters, bulletins), the mass media, and meeting and communicating with a representative group of parents are obvious first steps in communication.

Programs for the Gifted

The selection and operation of programs for the gifted also affect community relations. While the common aim of the programs—to meet the needs of the academically talented—is noble, the negative reactions from teachers, students, and the community have influenced many school districts to discontinue efforts to establish special programs to serve the gifted and talented. Such programs have usually been poorly conceived and not well organized; and accurate information about them has not been sufficiently disseminated. However, Renzulli et al. (1981) have delineated a new approach to giftedness: the revolving door model. It allows students to move into and out of special programs and opens these programs to new clients (p. 648). The model is designed to increase substantially the number of students receiving services for the gifted.

Because of the usual prestige and positive image often associated with being talented and gifted, many parents of students of average or below-average ability seek to have their children included in these types of special programs. Relationships between school and community will be damaged unless there are clear and defensible criteria for choosing the students to participate in the special program. Whether a school uses the revolving door or some other model, the criteria for student selection must be sound, clearly articulated, and effectively presented for parents of both participating and non-participating students.

Vocational Education Schools

Special programs of vocational schools often serve students from several communities within a school district as well as communities in multiple school districts. In Toledo, specialized skill training programs—mechanics, broadcasting, printing, business technology, etc.—are distributed among seven high schools so that each school houses a particular skill training program. All students—regardless of the school attendance area in which they live—who wish to acquire a specific skill training must travel to the school in which the program is housed. Vocational schools have been established to serve several school districts. Administrators of special programs that serve students from diverse communities face a special and difficult task of building and maintaining a good school-community relations program since the allegiance of the students and parents is often with the home school rather than with the vocational school they are attending.

Although there is no one strategy that will work in every situation, several schools have reported success with a few approaches. In each, the principal or superintendent took the initiative in structuring and implementing a procedure for two-way communication between parents and citizens of the students' home community and the vocational school. Thus, in an effort to improve school-community relations of vocational education schools, the following approaches are suggested:

1. Organize a team including teacher, student, parent, and administrative representatives to orient students and parents about the special program prior to the time of decision making about their enrollment in the program.
2. Involve representatives from selected business and industrial operations and key citizens from diverse communities in an ongoing advisory council regarding program planning, operation, and evaluation.
3. Establish a school-community relations council consisting of representatives from the various home schools and communities that will focus primarily on the communication network between the vocational school and the schools and communities served by it.

4. Encourage two-way communication by establishing convenient non-threatening ways (anonymous questionnaires, informal person-to-person sessions, suggestion boxes, etc.) for parents, students, and other citizens to express their concerns and provide feedback regarding program operation.
5. Exhibit a sincere interest in securing parent, student, teacher, and citizen input, and show that you have carefully considered it in the process of decision-making.

There are other factors which affect the school-community relations program. However, developing effective procedures for two-way communication is an essential element in such situations.

Magnet Schools

Most of the recent attention given to magnet schools has been associated with school integration. The magnet principle, that of providing unique programs to serve and attract students from diverse school attendance areas, is similar to the principle of vocational schools discussed above. Thus, many of the same approaches and techniques for promoting two-way communication between school and community are indicated. In providing leadership for change to magnet schools, it is important that special consideration is given to such emotional issues as busing, racial and ethnic diversity, and the climate for change. Attention should be given not only to the quality of the magnet school but also to the quality of the former home schools of the students. Many of the successes of the magnet school are often diminished when negative ramifications of such design are not carefully considered (Warren, 1978). Thus, parents and the community should be strategically and cooperatively involved in planning, implementing, and evaluating the magnet school and in minimizing the negative ramifications. We shall discuss techniques for that strategic and cooperative involvement in the special education section that follows.

SPECIAL EDUCATION DEVELOPMENTS AND COMMUNITIES

Though special education programs have been an integral part of the curriculum for some time, federal legislation of the seventies—namely, Section 504 enacted through (1) Public Law (P.L.) 93-112 (1973) that mandated an appropriate special education and regular accessibility, (2) P.L. 93-380 (1974) that guaranteed due process procedures and the assurance of education in the "least restrictive environment," and (3) the comprehensive P.L. 94-142 (1975) that guaranteed special education to handicapped children who needed it (Ballard and Zettel, 1977)—provided a new thrust for program implementation and new problems for school and community relationships. Each of the provisions of P.L. 94-142—specifically the assurance and guarantee of (1) free and appropriate education, (2) individualized education programs, (3) complete due process safeguards, (4) special education provided in the "least restrictive environment," (5) nondiscriminatory testing and evaluation, (6) policies and procedures to protect the confidentiality of data and information, and (7) appropriate public education at no cost to parents for all handicapped children—indicates a need for administrative actions that will often affect school-community relations.

As a result of recent statutes, schools are serving many more special education students and, of course, a more diverse population. Students from wide geographic areas—within and frequently outside a district—are brought together in special education centers designed to meet the needs of particular handicapped students. Atkins et al. (1980) discussed how P.L. 94-142 has affected local district governance and fostered cooperation between districts in serving the deaf, blind, and others. They emphasized that data seem to indicate that a student population of 5,000 or more is required to provide cost-effective programs for handicapped students with special needs. Some programs such as those for deaf and/or blind students require even larger populations.

Efforts to serve students with similar special education needs in a central location have brought together parents from dissimilar school communities who have a common focus, the education of their children. Through these parents, school administrators must relate to disparate and often competing communities. Mayer (1982) indicated that the parents of handicapped students are frequently the most active supporters of school programs and that they have been very active and very successful in political activities (pp. 24-25). The strategy and techniques used by the administrator in relating to those groups sometimes serve to broaden school-community divisions and intensify competition between those parents who represent the school's subcommunities, or sometimes they foster their cooperative interaction with each other and the school. The latter outcome is the goal.

Recognizing that the parents of special students come from many different subcommunities, school administrators can foster cooperation by coordinating the assignments or appointments of persons from diverse communities to common tasks. Committee assignments, school job appointments, and the election of officers for organizations within the school should be made after giving consideration to socioeconomic, racial, ethnic, and community differences. Special efforts should be made to include appropriate representatives of all groups in decision making. Persons in key positions need to be sensitive to diversity among groups served by the schools. That awareness and sensitivity should be evident by the school leader's actions to reconcile differences and influence cooperation among subgroups within the community.

Strategies for Working with Diverse Parental Groups

It is important to accept diversity in parental groups and to recognize that parents of students with different kinds of handicaps have different kinds of concerns about their children. Marion (1981) delineated some of the common concerns of parents of: (1) educationally mentally retarded, (2) learning disabled, (3) multihandicapped, (4) behaviorally disordered, (5) abused and neglected, and (6) minority children. He suggested techniques educators may use to effectively involve parents of exceptional children in the school program. The key element in each technique was the educator's acceptance and understanding of the feelings parents may have about the school and its program. Marion agreed with other writers—Kroth (1975), Evans (1980), Michaelis (1980), and Mayer (1982) who focused on strategies for working with parents of exceptional children—that educators must develop a sensitivity to the feelings that parents may have about their handicapped children. Employment of the skill of effective listening is essential in the development of that sensitivity and in the process of establishing rapport with parents. School administrators are thus urged to facilitate an assessment of administrative, faculty, and student interpersonal interactions—nonacceptance of the handicapped, failure to effectively listen, nonverbal behavior that is inconsistent with verbal behavior—which serve as barriers to communication and to the development of a wholesome relationship with exceptional children and their parents. The needs indicated by that assessment should be promptly addressed through effective in-service training for school personnel and in orientations for students.

A tested strategy for facilitating cooperation among different groups is that of bringing various groups' resources to bear on the needs of one group or another. If parents of the orthopedically handicapped express a concern or need, the resources of the parents of the blind, learning disabled, mentally retarded, multihandicapped, and regular students may be coordinated in an effort to address the concern or need. A similar cooperative effort may be marshaled to address total school needs for students rather than adhering only to subunit needs and concerns. For example, Joseph Sansbury, principal of Toledo's Oakdale School—in which severely handicapped students from that and surrounding districts are served—indicated that he frequently seeks and gets the cooperation of parental advocacy groups for handicapped students in total school improvement efforts. "One way to ensure the success of mainstreaming special education pupils may be to 'mainstream' their parents" (Mayer 1982, p. 251).

Some suggested guidelines for securing cooperation among groups are:

1. Promote a school climate in which subgroup and subunit problems are, when appropriate, presented and accepted as total school problems.
2. Take adequate time and use the appropriate resource personnel to clarify and make sure that there is a mutual understanding of the problem.
3. Carefully analyze the constraints or barriers that may be blocking a solution to the problem.
4. Survey the available resources, including those of each subunit, which may serve to remove the barriers to a solution and attain the objective.
5. Examine alternative approaches and the potential consequences of any alternative selected.
6. Plan and implement a solution strategy and an effective evaluation procedure.
7. Foster total school acceptance, recognition, and responsibility for the outcome.
8. Facilitate the shared use of resources, reciprocity, and a continuous cooperative relationship among subgroups.

Implementation of P.L. 94-142 and School Personnel

As facilitators of the implementation of P.L. 94-142, school personnel should seek ways to break down many traditional barriers to meaningful interaction between parents of handicapped children and the school. Several of today's barriers evolved from past practices.

For many years, schools refused to serve severely handicapped students. And today, many parents feel that their handicapped children are not welcome or adequately served by the school. Allaying that feeling through demonstrated action is a primary challenge for the school administrator.

If there is one thing that most current special education authorities seem to agree on, it is the need for school personnel to promote a school-community relationship in which parents occupy a major role in decision making regarding the child's education. Robson and Carpenter (1980) reported that there is a lack of congruence between the expectation of the service deliverers (school people) and service recipients (students and parents). They suggested a need for additional attention to and consideration of modern communication techniques for the dissemination of information and program implementation. Davies (1980) discussed co-production as a partnership between the professionals (delivering services) and the direct consumers (the students) and indirect consumers (the parents). Key features of co-production are a focus on (1) the core of the school's program, (2) collaborative planning between the professionals and consumers, (3) shared responsibility, (4) shared power, and (5) collaborative assessment of the process. Marion (1981) emphasized that to carry out the intent of P.L. 94-142, parents must be considered as equal partners with the professionals in the implementation of the school program. Marion encouraged educators to establish a helping relationship with parents in pursuit of needed services for handicapped students. Chapman (1981) urged administrators to initiate communication with and use advocacy groups for handicapped children in the school program (p. 7). Henley (1981) warned school administrators to change the "tough guy" image and to develop an attitude of trust in parents by providing needed services for handicapped students before they are mandated by the courts (p. 7). A central point advanced by these writers, and by most contemporary special education authorities, is that there is a need to establish a climate in which the professional works with rather than directs parents in ongoing efforts to improve opportunities for handicapped children.

Coordinating the School's Program

If parents and the community are to contribute and share in the school's decision making and operation, they need to have accurate and adequate information. Though positive person-to-person contacts are highly recommended in the process of improving school-community relations, administrators must not underestimate the importance of written communication. Kroth (1975) emphasized that the "special education teachers should think in terms of developing special handbooks and handouts that are directly relevant to the parents of children in their classes" (p. 72). They should be short and attractive and written at the reading level of parents. The handbooks should include names and phone numbers of key personnel, unique procedures, techniques they used, information on transportation, a list of special material needed by the child, and additional information for the population served (ibid.).

The Sandusky (Ohio) public schools developed a handbook entitled *Parents and Schools: Partners in Special Education* (1980). A key feature of the handbook is a clear delineation of provisions of P.L. 94-142 (federal) and House Bill 455 (state). Parents' and childrens' rights are clearly delineated. The handbook clarifies the provisions of P.L. 94-142 in layman's language and includes little educational jargon or legal terminology.

Marion (1981) indicated that successful program coordinators (the professionals) usually carry out a well-articulated public relations campaign. He stressed public relations as a function of the professional and pinpointed handbooks, newsletters, notes, and informal contacts as means to keep parents informed and to reduce conflict. He suggested the use of these avenues to answer the following questions:

1. Why does the program exist?
2. What is the source of funding?
3. What ages and types of children are served?
4. What are the program's beliefs toward the rights and needs of handicapped children?
5. Is information available about transportation registration, health, safety, and other special considerations (parking, pickup regulations)?
6. Are parents allowed to visit classrooms?
7. How are parents involved in the decision making, program planning, and evaluation? (p. 35)

It should be emphasized that the written communication must be well organized, clearly presented, and updated at regular intervals if it is to be an effective tool in improving school-community relations.

Personalized contacts and empathetic consideration of individual problems—whether they are those of the teacher, student, parent, or citizen—are important. The administrator sets the tone for an effective program by his or her personal behavior and by coordinating a cooperative program and providing support for the staff in program implementation.

McCoy (1981) suggested that the principal has the primary responsibility for assuring the quality of education of the handicapped and nonhandicapped. His acceptance of handicapped children will influence the acceptance by others (teachers, students, and nonteaching personnel). The integration of handicapped and nonhandicapped children must not be left to chance (Guinagh, 1980). Increased coordination and communication are essential since providing the mandated special education calls for greater interaction of the regular and special teacher (Oliver, 1982).

In a workshop for elementary school principals on the implementation of P.L. 94-142, principals identified most frequently conflicts between regular and special teachers regarding student mainstreaming as the major problem in implementation (Sommerville, "Summary," 1980). Many of those conflicts had obvious implications for the school-community relations program. And they evolved from a lack of effective planning, coordination, communication, and involvement of key people in the implementation of the provision.

In summation, because of the proliferation of special programs spurred by the passage of P.L. 94-142, many diverse communities are being brought together as school units. Clouded by past experiences and the uniqueness of student needs and the concerns expressed by parents, conflicts and competition between groups will serve as major barriers to positive school-community relations unless school administrators take leadership in (1) recognizing and reconciling differences and (2) promoting a partnership between school and parents and between diverse subgroups within the school-community unit.

SUMMARY

In this chapter, we have discussed several factors that contribute to changing and multiple school populations and communities. School desegregation, multicultural and bilingual education, and special programs with an emphasis on special education were indicated as major developments in education that have given impetus to new school subcommunities. School administrators and other school personnel are urged to take the initiative in structuring situations and experiences for positive interactions between diverse groups and between the school and each of its subcommunities. Administrative behavior was delineated as the key variable in efforts to improve relationships between the school and multiple communities. Accordingly, school administrators are encouraged to provide skillful leadership for involving subcommunities in planning, implementing, and evaluating the school's activities and in its community relations program.

Exercise 6.1
ADVOCACY CONFRONTATION

Because of the pressure from two parent advocacy groups for handicapped children regarding overcrowded conditions and building barriers at Graymont School, at the end of the school year the Board of Education voted to reassign two classes (the orthopedically and multihandicapped) to another school in the district. Since West Point Elementary School was below capacity and much more accessible, they were assigned to that building. As principal of West Point and since room assignments for the new school year had already been made, you assigned the classes to the two vacant rooms, which are in an isolated section of the building.

In October, after a mild reaction from two or three parents about isolating their children from others in the building, the full force of the politically powerful parent advocacy groups was turned on you with charges that you are prejudiced and did not want their children in the building, kept them away from the mainstream of activity, and assigned them to the most remote place on campus. The groups have already gone to the media with their protest. Your exploratory inquiries about exchanging classrooms have been met with teacher and student resistance.

As the school leader who wishes to build a good school-community relations program, what strategy will you use to resolve this problem?

Specifically:
1. How will you respond to the media inquiry?
2. What will be your reaction to the protest group?
3. What techniques will you employ to utilize the resources of those advocacy groups as well as others in the school's community relations program?

What approaches do you recommend to principals for avoiding or minimizing problems in a similar situation?

Exercise 6.2
MINORITY GROUP RELATIONSHIPS

Situation. Several minority group parents complained about the absence of minority group representation in displays in the classroom and in other areas of the school as well as in the various resources used by students. As principal of this school, which has an approximately 30 percent minority population, you investigated and confirmed the validity of their complaint.

Directions. Meet in a subgroup with two to five other members of your class and decide how the school administrator should:

1. Respond to the parents regarding their complaint.
2. Facilitate improvements in multiculturalism in the specified school environment.
3. Enhance communication with the concerned parents and the community regarding the improvements after they have been made.

SUGGESTED ACTIVITIES

1. Identify the school in your area that has had the largest change in its racial or ethnic student population during the past few years. Approximately what was the racial or ethnic ratio prior to the change and what is it today? Interview the principal or any other knowledgeable school staff member to find out:

    a. the general reaction of the school and community to the change;

    b. the kind of school-community relations challenges or problems the change has presented or is presenting for the administration and school staff; and

    c. what changes have occurred in the school's public and/or community relations program.

    Share your findings with colleagues and together outline the school-community relations strategies that you recommend the administrator use prior to, during, and after the above-described or similar change in the student population.

2. Ask two different school principals to:

    a. identify at least two distinct subgroups (racial, ethnic, handicapped) that attend his/her school;

    b. describe any differences noted in the disciplinary behavior between the groups, especially the kinds of challenges they present for the faculty and administration; and

    c. delineate any strategies the school uses to promote positive interaction between the groups. Now outline strategies you would use to promote positive interaction between the subgroups and the school and between the subgroups' communities and the school.

SUGGESTED READINGS

Davies, Don, ed. *Communities and Their Schools*. New York: McGraw-Hill, 1981, Chs. 4, 8, 10, 11.

Evans, Joyce. *Working with Parents of Handicapped Children*. Austin, Tex.: Southwest Education Development Laboratory, 1980.

Forehand, Garlie H., and Ragosta, Marjorie. *A Handbook for Integrated Schooling*. Princeton: Educational Testing Service, July 1976.

Marburger, Carl. *Who Controls the Schools*. Columbia, Md.: National Committee for Citizens in Education, 1978.

Marion, Robert L. *Educators, Parents, and Exceptional Children*. Rockville, Md.: Aspen Systems Corporation, 1981.

Mayer, C. Lamar. *Educational Administration and Special Education: A Handbook for School Administrators*. Boston: Allyn & Bacon, 1982.

Michaelis, Carol T. *Home and School Partnerships in Exceptional Education*. Rockville, Md.: Aspen Systems Corporation, 1980.

National School Public Relations Association. *Linking Schools and the Community*. Arlington, Va.: NSPRA, 1977.

U.S. Commission on Civil Rights. *Fulfilling the Letter of the Law*. Washington, D.C.: U.S. Government Printing Office, August 1976.

_____. *With All Deliberate Speed: 1954-19??* Washington, D.C.: U.S. Government Printing Office, Clearinghouse Publication 69, November 1981.

Valverde, Leonard, ed. *Bilingual Education for Latinos*. Washington, D.C.: Association for Supervision and Curriculum Development, 1978.

REFERENCES

Aronson, Eliott, et al. *The Jigsaw Classroom*. Beverly Hills, Cal.: Sage Publications, 1978.

Atkins, Roger; Allen, Connie I.; and Wachter, Donald H. H. "94-142 and Local District Governance." *Educational Leadership* 38 (2) (November 1980):120-21.

Ballard, Joseph, and Zettel, Jeffrey. "Public Law 94-142 and Section 504: What They Say About Rights and Protections." *Exceptional Children* 48 (3) (November 1977):177-84.

"Bell Lobbies for 'Local Choice' Bilingual Education Bills." *School Law News,* May 7, 1982, pp. 7-8.

Bennett, Christine. "A Case for Pluralism in the Schools." *Phi Delta Kappan* 62 (8) (April 1981):589-91.

Bennett, David A. *The Impact of Court-Ordered Desegregation: A Defendant's View*. Monograph. Milwaukee: Milwaukee Public Schools, April 1979.

Bequer, Marta M., and Bequer, John. "Communication Involvement: A Rich Resource." In *Bilingual Education for Latinos*. Ed. Leonard A. Valverde. Washington, D.C.: Association for Supervision and Curriculum Development, 1978, pp. 81-95.

Brown v. *Board of Education,* 347 U.S. 483 (1954).

Chapman, Randy, director of litigation for Legal Center for Handicapped Children. "Administrators' Attitudes Make a Big Difference." In *School Law News*, November 20, 1981, p. 7.

Coleman, James S.; Hofter, Thomas; and Kilgare, Sally. *Public and Private Schools*. Report to the National Center for Educational Statistics Under Contract No. 300-78-0208, Chicago, Ill.: National Opinion Research Center, University of Chicago, March 1981.

Coleman, James S.; Kelly, S.D.; and Moose, J.H. *Trends in School Desegregation, 1968-73*. Washington, D.C.: Urban Institutes, 1975.

Crain, Robert L., and Mahard, Rita. *Some Policy Implications of the Desegregation Minority Achievement Literature*. Baltimore: Center for the Social Organization of Schools, April 1981.

Cunningham, George K., and Husk, William L. "White Flight: A Closer Look at the Assumptions." *Urban Review* 12 (1) (Spring 1980):23-30.

Davies, Don. "School Councils: Partners or Watchdogs?" *Citizen Action in Education* 7 (2) (November 1980):1, 5-6.

_____ . "Citizen Participation in Decision-Making in the Schools." In *Communities and Their Schools*. New York: McGraw-Hill, 1981.

Delbecq, Andre L.; Van de Ven, Andrew H.; and Gustafson, David A. *Group Techniques for Program Planning*. Glenview, Ill.: Scott, Foresman, 1975.

Education Commission of the States. "Special Needs of Students: Essential for State Planning." Denver, Summer 1981, pp. 4-16.

Evans, Joyce. *Working with Parents of Handicapped Children*. Austin, Tex.: Southwest Education Development Laboratory, 1980.

Farley, R. "Integrating Residential Neighborhoods." *Society* 14(4) (May-June 1977):38-41.

Feinberg, Fusa Castro; Cuevas, Gilbert J.; and Perez, Carmen. "Staff Development: The Selection and Training of Instructional Personnel for Bilingual Education Programs." In *Bilingual Education for Latinos*. Ed. Leonard A. Valverde. Washington, D. C.: Association for Supervision and Curriculum Development, 1978, pp. 51-63.

Flemming, Arthur S. "Description for Equality." Address presented at Advocacy Training Workshop, University of Toledo, Law Center, January 30, 1982.

Forehand, Garlie, and Ragosta, Marjorie. *A Handbook for Integrated Schooling*. Washington, D.C.: U.S. Department of HEW, Contract H-OEC-73-6341, July 1976.

Forehand, Garlie; Ragosta, Marjorie; and Rock, D.A. *Conditions and Processes of Effective School Desegregation*. Final Technical Report for U.S. Office of Education, Contract OEC-0-73-6341. Princeton: Educational Testing Service, 1976. ED 131 155.

Foster, Charles R. "Defusing the Issues in Bilingualism and Bilingual Education." *Phi Delta Kappan* 65 (5) (January 1982): 342-44.

Garbaldi, A.M. "Affective Contributions of Cooperative and Group Goal Structures," *Journal of Educational Psychology* 71 (6) (1979):788-94.

Gay, Geneva. "What Is Your MEQ?" *Educational Leadership* 39 (3) (December 1981):487-89.

Glazer, Nathan. "Ethnicity and Education: Some Hard Questions." *Phi Delta Kappan* 62(5) (January 1981):386-89.

Goodlad, John I. "Can Our Schools Get Better?" *Phi Delta Kappan* 60(6) (January 1979):342-47.

Gordon, Edmund W. *A Comparative Study of Quality Integrated Education.* Final Report for National Institute of Education. New York: Institute for Urban and Minority Education, Teachers College, Columbia University, 1976.

Green, R. L., and T. F. Pettigrew. "Urban Desegregation and White Flight: A Response to Coleman." *Phi Delta Kappan* 57(6) (February 1976):399-402.

Gross, Neal, and Herriott, Robert E. *Staff Leadership in Public Schools.* New York: Wiley, 1965.

Guinagh, Barry. "The Social Integration of Handicapped Children. *Phi Delta Kappan* 62(1) (September 1980):27-29.

Hawley, Willis. "Integration Seek Aiding Minority Students." *Toledo Blade*, September 16, 1981, p. 19.

Henley, Robert, Superintendent of the Independence, Missouri Schools. "Administrators' Attitudes Make a Big Difference." In *School Law News,* November 20, 1981, p. 7.

Kroth, Roger L. *Communication with Parents of Exceptional Children*. Denver: Love Publishing Co., 1975.

Marion, Robert L. *Educators, Parents, and Exceptional Children*. Rockville, Md.: Aspen Systems Corporation, 1981.

Mayer, C. Lamar. *Educational Administration and Special Education: A Handbook for School Administrators*. Boston: Allyn & Bacon, 1982.

McCoy, Kathleen. "Interest, Leadership, and Implementation: Views on the Role of the Mainstream Principal." *Education* 102 (2) (Winter 1981):165-69.

Michaelis, Carol T. *Home and School Partnerships in Exceptional Education*. Rockville, Md.: Aspen Systems Corporation, 1980.

Nevas, Susan R. "Factors in Desegregation and Integration." *Equal Opportunity Review*. Institute for Urban and Minority Education, Teachers College, Columbia University, Fall 1977.

Nickerson, Jacquelyn R., and Prawat, Richard S. "Affective Interactions in Racially Diverse Classrooms: A Case Study." *Elementary School Journal* 81(5) (May 1981):291-303.

Oliver, Thomas E. "Administrative Systems for Service Delivery." In *Administrator's Handbook on Integrating America's Mildly Handicapped Students*. Ed. R. Talley and J. Burnette. Reston, Va.: Council for Exceptional Children, 1982.

Orfield, Gary. "Is Coleman Right?" *Social Policy* 6(4) (January-February 1976):24-31.

Parent Partners Title I. Toledo, Ohio: Toledo Public Schools, 1981.

"Policy Reversal on Bilingual Efforts Charted in Memo." *Education Week*. 120 (February 10, 1982):1.

Ratliff, Roosevelt. "Ethnicity in Citizenship Education." *Educational Leadership* 58(1) (October 1980):50-51.

Renzulli, Joseph S.; Reis, Sally M.; and Smith, Linda H. "The Revolving Door Model: A New Way of Identifying the Gifted." *Phi Delta Kappan* 62(9) (May 1981):648-49.

Robson, Donald, and Carpenter, Robert L. "P.L. 94-142: Legislating Educational Change in Handicapped Service Delivery." *Planning and Changing* 11(4) (Winter 1980):203-13.

Rossell, Christine H. "The Effect of Community Leadership and Media on Public Behavior." *Theory into Practice* 17(2) (April 1978):131-39.

Sandusky Public Schools. *Parents and Schools: Partners in Special Education*. Sandusky, Ohio, 1980.

Sharan, S. "Cooperative Learning in Small Groups: Recent Methods and Effects on Achievement, Attitudes, and Ethnic Relations." *Review of Educational Research* 50(2) (1980):241-71.

Sitton, Thad. "Bridging The School-Community Gap: The Lessons of Foxfire." *Educational Leadership* 38(3) (December 1980): 248-50.

Slavin, R.E., and Madden, N. "School Practices That Improve Race Relations." *American Education Research Journal* 16(2) (1979):169-80.

Smith, Kathleen, ed. *Desegregation/Integration: Planning for Social Change*. Washington, D.C.: National Education Association, 1974.

Sobol, Marion G., and Beck, William W. "Phenomenological Influences in Minority Attitudes Toward School Desegregation." *Urban Review* 12(1) (Spring 1980):31-41.

Sommerville, Joseph C. "Leadership for Successful School Desegregation." *Educational Leadership* 37(8) (May 1980):622-26.

_____ . "Summary of Participants' Backhome Problems and Objectives." Mimeo. Toledo, Ohio: University of Toledo, 1980.

_____ . "Actions of School Administrations in Desegregation." *Integrateducation* 18(1-4) (Spring 1981):21-25.

Thomas, M. Donald. "The Limits of Pluralism." *Phi Delta Kappan* 62(8) (April 1981):589, 591.

Tompkins, Rachel B. "Preparing Communities for School Desegregation." *Theory Into Practice* 17(2) (April 1978):107-14.

U.S. Commission on Civil Rights. *With All Deliberate Speed: 1954-19??* Washington, D.C.: U.S. Government Printing Office, Clearinghouse Publication 69, November 1981.

Valencia, Richard R. "The School Closure Issue and the Chicano Community." *Urban Review* 12(1) (Spring 1980):5-22.

Warren, Constancia. "The Magnet School Boom: Implications for Desegregation." *Equal Opportunity Review*. New York: Institute for Urban and Minority Education, Teachers College, Columbia University, Spring 1978.

Washburn, David E. "Cultural Pluralism: Are Teachers Prepared? *Phi Delta Kappan* 63(7) (March 1982):493-95.

Yaffe, Elaine. "Colorado Springs Wrestles with Law: A Case in Federal Intervention." *Phi Delta Kappan* 60(1) (1978):51-54.

_____ . "Ambiguous Laws Fuel Debate on Bilingual Education." *Phi Delta Kappan* 62(10) (June 1981):740-41.

7

COURTS, LEGISLATURES, AND THE SCHOOL COMMUNITY

by

David S. Rosenberger

Good laws lead to the making of better ones: bad ones bring about worse. As soon as any man says of the affairs of state, "What does it matter to me?", the state may be given up for lost.

(Jean-Jacques Rousseau, 1762)

The impact of national and state events upon school-community relations has been noted in our introduction. Seldom do events in a community occur in isolation. Indeed, the local scene is frequently defined by influences beyond its borders. An important aspect of these influences is the decisions made by courts and legislatures on both the state and national levels.

Although our nation has a strong tradition of local control of schools (Campbell, 1959), and the roots of this tradition run deep in the thinking of our citizenry, nevertheless, the legal framework for education is determined outside individual school communities. Since the federal Constitution is silent on the matter of education, basic control of schools is placed with the states. The constitution of each state accepts authority for the conduct of schools, frequently referred to as a "system of common schools." State legislatures are designated as the major controlling bodies of the educational enterprise. Generally, school districts have only those powers expressly granted by the legislature plus those necessarily implied by the basic grant of power (Bolmeier, 1973). School districts are often referred to as "creatures of the legislature." State courts have the role of deter-

163

mining the constitutionality of laws passed by the legislature as well as interpreting those laws and settling disputes.

The fact that the U.S. Constitution is silent on education does not mean there is no role for the federal government. Congress is empowered to "make needful rules and regulations respecting the territory or other property belonging to the United States" (Article IV, Section 3.2) as well as to "lay and collect taxes" and to "provide for the common defense and general welfare of the United States" (Article I, Section 8). These and other parts of the Constitution have been interpreted as giving the federal government broad powers, especially to use education as a means of solving societal problems even though it does not have basic control.

Federal courts are charged with duties similar to those of state courts and have made decisions having strong impact upon school operations, especially when they have judged school district actions against the criteria presented by several amendments to the Constitution. In the hierarchy of laws, the federal level stands highest, so actions at the state and local levels cannot be in conflict.

This chapter will describe decisions affecting education made by legislatures and courts at the federal and state levels. This description can only be illustrative of the multitude of issues that become the subjects of statutes and court decisions. *One might conclude that almost every time a law is passed or a court makes a decision, an area of decision making about schools is removed from local control.*

The second part of this chapter arises from the importance of the impact of state and federal actions upon local school governance. School-community relations are a part of local school governance, and there are increasing attempts to have influence flow from the local school to power centers at state and national levels. If decisions made in these power centers are so important at the local level, it becomes logical that educators and citizens in school communities attempt to influence legislation and argue in courts for majority opinions favorable to their interests. Increasingly, the broad perspective of school-community relations will go beyond matters of purely local concern to those issues which have local impact but also impinge upon a large number of schools.

SALIENT NATIONAL EVENTS

Legislative

Historically, a federal role in education predates the U.S. Constitution. In 1785, Congress under the Articles of Confederation passed the Land Ordinance, which dealt with the Northwest Territory. Section 16 of each township was reserved for schools. As westward movement continued, additional sections were set aside to support the educational enterprise in newly developed areas. As the years went on, other types of land, such as salt, swamp, and grazing lands, were devoted to education either through the proceeds of sales or revenues from use.

From these beginnings the federal role has developed. For elementary and secondary education, it can be said that the national government had little impact until the passage of the Smith-Hughes Act in 1917. Reacting to World War I food shortages, Congress set out to solve this societal problem by helping to finance instruction in agriculture and home economics. Vocational education was "born" and subsequently grew to encompass many skill areas and to involve huge federal financial support in the 1960s and 1970s. Local schools added these subjects to their curriculum or combined with other districts to provide centers for teaching vocational subjects. As with most federal programs that followed, the stimulus of shared financing caused school communities to make this decision.

During the Great Depression of the 1930s, many federal financial stimuli impinged upon schools. Programs to pay student workers, to provide part of the cost of new buildings, and to give food for lunches came in quick succession. The federal government adopted these programs to stimulate a badly lagging economy. Again, schools were seen as a means of helping solve societal problems.

World War II stimulated additional programs that influenced local school districts. Characteristic of these war years were financial assistance to districts having military or other federal installations and a high percentage of the population employed by the national government, eligibility for surplus property, and a continuation of school lunch support.

During the 1950s Congress expanded its influence into curricular areas beyond vocational courses. The creation of the National Science Foundation and, later, passage of the National Defense Education Act were reactions to the international situation. The growing ideological and technical competition with the USSR resulted in substantial infusions of money into science, mathematics, and foreign language instruction during this decade. Again, schools were seen as a means of dealing with societal problems.

The attention of the nation in the 1960s and 1970s was focused upon the disadvantaged members of society. The Elementary and Secondary Education Act, the Civil Rights Act, the Education Professions Development Act, and the Education for All Handicapped Children Act are all examples of Congress's attempt to deal with this important problem area. Again, local schools were a central part of the attempt to assist numerous members of society to attain better status socially, economically, and politically. Federal financial participation in education reached all-time high levels.

The early years of the 1980s indicate new directions of national concern as attention is drawn to economic conditions. Reduced federal spending in most nondefense areas brings about new adjustments to a change in federal policy by local school communities. Just how schools will fit into attacks upon newly identified societal problems remains to be seen. The probability is high that in the future local schools will be enlisted in the attempts to solve them.

An Illustration

One national event stands out as illustrative of the past emphasis that was placed upon education by the federal government. On July 28, 1964, President Lyndon B. Johnson spoke of the needs of the nation:

If we are learning anything from our experiences, we are learning that it is time for us to go to work, and the first work of these times and the first work of our society is education. ("First Work," April 1965)

In 1965, Congress passed an act to strengthen and improve educational quality and educational opportunities in the nation's elementary and secondary schools. President Johnson then signed the Elementary and Secondary Education Act (ESEA) of 1965 (P.L. 89-10), which signified a revolutionary change in the role of the federal government in education. According to many observers, the "carrot" of federal money led schools into paths that they otherwise would not have followed. Local schools were induced by federal largess to undertake new curricula and new programs in conformance with nation-ally rather than locally determined priorities (Bailey and Mosher, 1968).

The major target of the act was the education of children in culturally deprived areas. A yardstick of poverty was applied to the states as well as to districts and buildings within the states. Title I of the act required school districts to establish eligibility for funds on the basis of the number of low-income children residing in the districts, but the programs financed by these grants were open to all students whose achievement levels fell below that "appropriate for their age" even if they were not poor. Within a few years, nearly two-thirds of all school districts and some 9 million students in both public and private schools participated in Title I programs (Yudof, 1969).

One of the things the framers of Title I sought was the involvement of parents and other citizens in its programs and projects. At first, local school officials were urged to bring about this involvement, and in 1970 such involvement became a legal mandate. Warning that "paper" or "figurehead" involvement would only serve to increase public distrust of the school systems, the resultant regulations advised an effective partnership between home and school that would result in a more relevant school program, greater community support for schools, and a more comfortable relationship between teachers and parents, school officials, and the community (U.S. Department of HEW, *Parental Involvement,* 1972). Subsequent revisions of the law applied the requirement to both the district and project area or school level and provided detailed requirements governing membership selection and involvement (Brown, 1980).

In spite of the clarification and strengthening of the involvement requirements, noncompliance with both the letter and the spirit of Title I were described as being pervasive. Complaint procedures instituted in 1978 provided a specific mechanism for appeal to the federal level. States had been required since 1974 to develop com-plaint procedures, but most did not do so. The record on complaints at the federal level center upon not having access to information, being plagued with membership election irregularities, and having difficulties with meeting times, places, agendas, and decision-making procedures. School officials were criticized for not perceiving partici-pants as capable of understanding the educational process and ignoring or giving them very low priority with a consequent lack of leadership for the involvement. Recommendations for dealing with these complaints included increased reporting, monitoring, and assistance to school districts so that compliance could be achieved. In addition, further research in the best ways of increasing the positive impact of federal and state leadership was recommended. The views expressed here were those of the director of the Federal Education Project, begun in 1975, to assist parents and advisory council members with filing complaints and having them satisfactorily resolved (Brown, 1980).

The pendulum has now moved in the opposite direction. In 1981, the ESEA was replaced with the Education Consolidation and Improvement Act. Effective in July 1982, the mandated involvement of citizens was eliminated, except that school districts must provide assurances that programs to be funded are designed and implemented in consultation with parents. School districts may choose to keep advisory councils, and many probably will. Others certainly will not (Citizen's Council for Ohio Schools, 1982). The new law repeals complaint procedures, however, and states and local districts may choose to continue orderly complaint procedures.

Since the thrust of this chapter is the impact of federal law upon school-community relations, emphasis has been given to one aspect of Title I. Other aspects of the title will not be reviewed here nor will the details of other titles of the ESEA. Other titles authorized funds for acquisition of library resources and other learning materials, for supplementary education centers established in cooperation with other educational and cultural interests in the community, for research and training facilities, for strengthening state departments of education, for creating a bureau in the Office of Education to deal with education training and research affecting handicapped children, and for dissemination of information—advice, counsel, technical assistance, demonstrations—to states or local agencies requesting it ("What's New," 1967). The facts are not yet in on the total impact the ESEA has had. Surely all titles in some way had their effect on school-community relations.

Courts

The federal courts have been as active as Congress and the executive branch in influencing local school-community relations. A rapidly increasing volume of litigation starting in the 1950s has found these courts ruling on such matters as desegregation, loyalty oaths, sex education, hair length, corporal punishment, student publication censorship, library censorship, rights of pregnant students and teachers, teacher contract rights, school finance programs, voting and representation standards, teaching of evolution, prayer and religious observances in public schools, public funds and private schools, and even the catheterization of handicapped pupils by school employees. Many citizens could add to this list just from general knowledge gained in reading newspapers. Few areas of local school operation are untouched by rulings of the courts. Volumes would be needed to review the decisions encompassed in the topics mentioned above, and it cannot be assumed that there is agreement among courts with regard to the topics. Indeed, lower courts with differing geographical jurisdictions disagree, as do appellate courts with trial courts and as does the Supreme Court with the courts from which its cases come. Most aspects of some topics are settled by higher courts. Others continue to be "gray" areas, subject to further litigation. Case law, like other aspects of law, is constantly changing as indeed our society and its governmental forms are changing. Both educators and citizens are caught up in the necessity to stay current and to attempt the revision of their actions to conform to the laws.

There are conflicting views about the role of the federal courts in our society. On one hand, advocates of societal changes have used the courts to forward their causes. Civil rights groups, parents of special children, advocates of church-state separation, gay liberation groups, professional associations, and individual citizens have paid substantial sums of money to finance court tests of certain principles. Those who have won their cases are happy with the outcomes, and many are engaged in collecting more money from adherents to finance further challenges.

Reacting to the decisions rendered as a result of these actions, a cry of anguish has arisen against "faceless men in black robes" who speak in a tongue that laymen find baffling. Critics complain that these judges are given license by a vague Constitution and malleable laws, so they are roving all over the lot: into school desegregation, voting rights, sex, mental health, the environment—the list goes on and on. As specific examples touching schools, critics point to the federal judge who overruled a school board ban on the publication of a high school poll on birth control, and another who, when Boston's duly

elected school committee refused to bus school children, did it himself, right down to approving the bus routes ("Essay," 1979).

An Illustration

In 1975, the U.S. Supreme Court in *Goss* v. *Lopez* was called upon to
decide the appeal of students who had been suspended from school
for alleged misconduct. The decision of the Court was made by a
majority of five justices with four dissenting. The issues involved a
definition of rights of students as well as the role of the courts in
defining local school operation.

The majority of the judges stated that students have both liberty and
property interests in public education and that there can be no
arbitrary deprivation of these rights. Therefore, the minimal requirements of the due process clause of the Constitution must be met when
a ten-day suspension is imposed. Such suspension, if sustained and
recorded, could seriously damage the students' standing with their
fellow students and teachers and interfere with opportunities for
higher education and employment. Students facing suspension must
be given some kind of notice and some kind of hearing. Disciplin-
arians, although proceeding in utmost good faith, frequently act on
the reports and advice of others, and the controlling facts and nature
of the conduct under challenge are often disputed. The risk of error is
not at all trivial, and should be guarded against if this may be done
without prohibitive cost or interference in the educational process.
The requirements of a notice and hearing are, if anything, less than a
fair-minded school principal should observe.

The dissenting judges' opinion said that the decision of the majority
opened avenues for judicial intervention in the operation of public
schools that may affect adversely the quality of education. According
to the dissenting members, the Court held for the first time that the
federal courts, rather than educational officials and state legislatures,
had the authority to determine the rules applicable to routine classroom discipline of children and teenagers in the public schools. The
minority opinion was that the teacher must be free to discipline
without frustrating formalities. We have relied for generations,
according to these four jurists, upon the experience, good faith, and
dedication of those who staff the public schools. Finally, the dissenters
said they could only speculate as to the extent to which public education would be disrupted by giving every school child the power to

contest in court any decision made by his teacher that arguably infringes the state-conferred right to education.

As many teachers and administrators would testify, pupil discipline is a major issue over which schools and communities interact. Traditionally, communities have directly or indirectly set the standards by which students shall conduct themselves. Reputations of both teachers and administrators are sometimes made or broken in this arena of activity. Consequently, this case has substantial implications for school-community relations, and the close vote of the justices is most likely representative of divided opinions on these issues in our society. The majority opinion does remove one area of state and local decision making. No longer does the decision whether or not to grant due process before suspension rest at those levels. The decision has been made at the federal level.

Interrelationships

There are many interrelationships between the federal courts and federal legislation. Actual cause-and-effect relationships probably can only be surmised, yet the precedent of one seems to influence the other. Two examples will serve to illustrate this phenomenon.

In 1972 a federal court in *Mills* v. *Board of Education* upheld individuals who alleged that, although they can profit from an education either in regular classrooms with supportive services or in special classes adopted to their needs, they have been labeled as behavior problems, mentally retarded, emotionally disturbed, or hyperactive and denied admission to public schools or ejected therefrom after admission, with no provisions for alternative educational placement or periodical review. The Court held that the school district is required to provide a publicly supported education for these "exceptional children." Its failure to fulfill this clear duty to include and to retain these children, or otherwise provide them with publicly supported education, and the failure to afford them a due process hearing and periodic review, cannot be excused by the claim that there are insufficient funds.

In 1971 another federal court in *Pennsylvania Association for Retarded Children* v. *Commonwealth* ordered a state to provide a free, public program of education and training appropriate to the child's capacity. In November 1975, Congress passed the Education for All Handicapped Children Act (P.L. 94-142). This act, sometimes called the "bill of rights for handicapped children," represents a sweeping federal mandate to school districts to provide a free and appropriate public education for these students. Its many provisions are designed to accomplish this goal. Although federal courts frequently interpret the Constitution, they also frequently interpret laws passed by Congress. The Education for All Handicapped Children Act has given rise to a flurry of litigation as has the Civil Rights Act of 1964. These provide further examples of the interrelationship between the legislature and the courts.

DEVELOPMENTS AT THE STATE LEVEL

Legislative

Primary legal responsibility for the conduct of education is in the hands of the states. State constitutions place this responsibility and authority in the hands of their legislatures, which have been thought of as "big school boards" because of their authority over the educational enterprise. Statutes passed by the legislature govern public schools. Schools have no inherent powers, and the authority to operate them must be found in either express or implied terms of statute (Alexander, 1980). One state supreme court specifically stated that boards of education must function within the limited powers granted them by statute (*Hartley et al.* v. *Berlin-Milan Local School District et al.*, 1982).

Specificity of statutes varies from state to state, but the framework for school operation is defined at the state level. The school district is a "creature of the state," and its board of education has only those powers granted by the legislature.

In most states, a number of laws concerning schools are passed at each session of the legislature. As previously mentioned, virtually each time the legislature passes a law, the options of local school district decision making are reduced. For example, a law requiring contracts with school employees to be written removes from the school board the option of not putting them in writing. It may seem wise to have such contracts in writing, but among hundreds of school districts in a state, some will elect to have oral agreements with employees if that option is open to them.

Among the kinds of local school actions governed by statute are the manner of raising money from local tax sources, the way in which school district boundaries are changed, the types of state-granted certificates needed by professional employees, the minimum salaries that can be paid to teachers, and the contractual arrangements (including tenure) under which teachers work. The list is almost endless. Board members are elected or appointed to their positions by procedures specified in statute, and their terms of office, conduct of meetings, means of recall or filling vacancies, and compensation (if any) are all matters of state determination.

Major areas of state legislation in recent years have to do with determining the formula by which schools receive state monies, framing laws by which collective negotiations are carried on in local districts, and determining procedures for suspension and expulsion of students. Again, these are only examples of the kinds of issues with which state legislatures deal.

The range of issues and problems dealt with by a legislature can be illustrated by this listing of the enactments of one state legislature from August 1979 to December 1980. A report of its actions shows, in part, the following table of contents under the heading "Education."

Prohibits school closings for financial reasons.
Tuition benefits for children of certain deceased law enforcement officers.
Out-of-state travel in school buses.
Employment of noncertificated coaches.
Bilingual multicultural education teaching certificates.
Makes the state a member of the Midwestern Education Compact.
Prohibits certain transfers of school district territory.
Notice of special education placement.
Cardiopulmonary resuscitation classes in public schools.
Provision and cost of special education for nonresidents of the state.
Rewards offered by boards of education.
Signature requirements for school district checks.
Employment of school administrators.
Issuance of age and schooling certificates.
Expansion of educational television law to include radio.
Lease purchase of office equipment by school boards.
School district competitive bidding and award procedures.
School district fiscal year and state aid.
Omnibus school discipline bill.
Make-up days for school closing due to strikes.
Provisions governing finances, city district status, and blind and deaf school employees. (Ohio Legislative Service Commission, 1981)

The list does not include those bills upon which much time and energy may have been spent but which were not passed by the legislature and signed by the governor. In addition, it does not include laws that affect school operation but that might be classified under headings such as elections, energy, financial institutions and insurance, health and safety, local government, state government, and taxation. Should the educator wish to identify the place where the action is—the one spot in which more decisions about schools are made than any other single place—the state legislature would probably be chosen.

Courts

State courts receive a continuous flow of cases that are related to the educational enterprise. Generally, these courts have three functions: they rule on the constitutionality of legislative enactments, they interpret laws, and they settle disputes (Bolmeier, 1973). While the names given at the various levels vary from state to state, the common arrangement is to have trial, appellate, and supreme court levels in the judicial system. As with the federal court system, higher courts sometimes uphold lower ones; other times they reverse them. It is important to know whether lower court decisions have been appealed and what the results of the appeal have been. Those who are responsible for school operation are called upon to keep track of decisions as they develop.

Sometimes state courts are asked to decide overarching issues that will have a substantial impact on many school districts. During the past decade, state systems of financing schools have been challenged in many states. We are in the midst of a rash of such litigation across the country since the U.S. Supreme Court decided not to get into the delicate and difficult questions of local taxation, fiscal planning, educational policy, and federalism; and thus the matter of a state's system of financing schools has been left up to state courts (*San Antonio Independent School District et al.* v. *Rodriguez et al.,* 1973).

As an illustration of state court activity following this U.S. Supreme Court decision, note that action was begun at the trial court level regarding the school finance system in Ohio. After long testimony, the trial court declared the finance system unconstitutional on the basis of two sections of the state constitution, namely, the "equal protection and benefit" clause and the "thorough and efficient" clause. The appellate court upheld the trial court in part, agreeing that the financing system did violate the "equal protection and benefit" clause but that the legislature, which is charged with providing a "thorough and efficient system of common schools throughout the state," had not abused its broad discretion in this matter.

The State Supreme Court held that the financing system did not violate either constitutional provision (*Board of Education* v. *Walter,* 1979). Thus, decisions relating to school finance were placed in the hands of the legislature, and changes, while they would be subject to court review if someone chose to start litigation, were also in the hands of the legislature and were to be worked out by those political forces and mechanisms at work in the state.

This type of decision may or may not be typical of the various states. New Jersey provides an example of the opposite result wherein the Supreme Court had a substantial impact upon changing the state's system of financing (*Robinson* v. *Cahill,* 1973). Certainly, interaction between the court system and the legislature is well illustrated by litigation regarding state school finance systems (see Lehne, 1978).

Another case illustrates the type of litigation found in state courts regarding the actions of a board of education. A tenured teacher allegedly had physical contact with a student in a study hall. The board held a hearing and decided that excessive and inappropriate force had been used on the student. A three-day suspension without pay was imposed on the teacher, who filed a complaint seeking that the court find that the board did not have authority to impose the suspension upon him. Both the trial court and the appellate court held that the board did not have the authority because state statute gives boards authority to suspend teachers only as a part of the process of termination (*Stewart* v. *Margaretta Board of Education et al.,* 1981). Court costs were assessed against the board of education. Prior to the appellate decision, the teacher resigned his position to become headmaster of a local private school. One might suspect that the case was attended by a certain amount of community interest and indeed by some school-community interaction.

Another illustrative area of litigation has to do with teacher contracts. U.S. Supreme Court decisions had established that teachers could acquire certain property and liberty interests to their public employment positions under certain conditions (*Roth* v. *Board of Regents,* 1972 and *Perry* v. *Sinderman,* 1972). Were these conditions met, the individual would be entitled to due process (charges and a hearing) prior to dismissal. A superintendent recommended the dismissal of a coach and the board accepted the recommendation. The Court thought it was unrealistic for a football coach with twenty years of experience to think that he had "reasonable expectation" of continued service (*Lukac* v. *Acocks*, 1972). The superintendent had won in court. Community opinion was divided, bumper stickers supporting the coach appeared on autos in the community, and the discussion continued. "Greener pastures" were sought and obtained by the superintendent, drawing the divisive issue to a close.

Courts certainly play a substantial role in defining issues, drawing guidelines, setting the limits of authority, and deciding which party will prevail in a dispute. The interaction between courts and the legislature and between both of these and the school community are illustrated by the examples of specific legislation and litigation reviewed here.

Impact on School-Community Relations

As suits are filed, newspaper stories are printed for all in the community to read. Those who have direct knowledge of the situation may form an opinion while others may form opinions from news accounts. One superintendent wrote a newsletter column to his community members in an attempt to explain the situation:

You may have read recently in the newspaper about our school district being a party to several pending suits that have been filed in the county court. Such suits against boards of education throughout the state are becoming more and more common.

Each suit is a complaint of an employee or his union against a specific action of the board of education. There is a definite difference between being dissatisfied with a board of education decision and the justification and legality of that decision.

When a dispute of this nature arises, any individual or his union can file a complaint against the board of education, and the paper, as a matter of course, reports such allegations that might be included in that claim. Seldom, if ever, is the reply to the court reported, let alone the court decision in favor of the board. In the past, the large majority of such suits filed against boards of education throughout the state were either dismissed or found in favor of the board of education when heard by the court.

Professionalism and ethics prevent boards of education from answering publicly such complaints that might be filed against them by individuals and unions; however, this is not to assume that such complaints have any substance or justification. (Tallman, 1981)

The point being made here is that the legal action *does not need to be complete in order to affect school-community relations.* The threat of action or initiation of action are sufficient to draw attention and perhaps stimulate conclusions in the minds of some people. The decision of the court may be a year away, yet lines are drawn and interaction is influenced.

Proposed legislation can have a similar effect. Reading about some of the hundreds of bills introduced into a session of the legislature may lead some readers to assume that they have passed or that they will pass, particularly if the report tells of passage by a committee or by one house of the legislature. Generally, a number of misunderstandings about the status of legislation exist in a community. Indeed, there is also a lack of knowledge and perhaps a feeling either of apathy or powerlessness.

Citizens generally do not respond to proposed legislation unless there is a "single interest" issue at stake—something about which the citizens feel strongly—or unless the citizens belong to an organization that urges them to make a contact with a legislator on a certain subject.

Legislation and litigation do affect school operation and school-community relations. School administrators cannot withdraw from these areas of activity if the best interests of their school districts are to be represented. They must take active roles in influencing both, through their own direct action and through marshaling action on the part of those specialists and citizens who can be of help.

TOWARD AN ENLIGHTENED ROLE
FOR ADMINISTRATORS

Vigilance is required of the school administrator in dealing with legislation and litigation. If decision-making bodies are to act on the basis of full information and knowledge, if the views of those affected by the decision are to be made known, then a proactive stance is necessary. One's time and energy cannot be completely consumed by immediate problems. Attention must be given to larger areas influencing school operation. These areas include the larger community, the state, and the nation. This discussion first considers various problems, procedures, and issues in dealing with the courts and then moves to consideration of the even greater concerns that are a part of dealing with the legislature.

Courts

A recent advertisement by a law publishing company contained these words in a bold print: "Warning! Every Action Your School Board Takes Is Subject to the Law." Beside the words was a picture of a robed judge pensively looking down from his bench (West Publishing Company, 1982). The purpose was to sell certain legal publications, but the message was applicable in a general sense as well. Schools are subject to courts in many ways. Some of the ways were illustrated earlier in this chapter. Indeed, we are becoming a "suing society."

Schools are spending increasing amounts on legal counsel. For the most part, such expenditures are wise, necessary, and often unavoidable. Legal counsel for school districts may be specified in a state law by the identification of a county or city official who is assigned the duty to provide legal services to the school districts. Generally, school districts have the option of using private law firms in addition to or instead of those designated. Larger school districts sometimes employ a full-time attorney to serve their many legal needs. Whatever the situation, the quality of legal counsel is crucial. Thorough investigation and study should precede selection of those who represent the district position. There are times when the choice of a law firm is in a real sense related to school-community relations. Local firms may be part of the power structure of the community, and the choice of legal counsel has repercussions within the community. In other instances, a firm possessing a given specialty but with headquarters in a distant city may be chosen. Sometimes, the choice of legal counsel may be dictated in part by the insurance carrier for the school district. Insurance companies often advocate the use of law firms that are well known to them and that specialize in areas of law related to the types of policies written for school districts.

Another source of legal assistance for school districts may be found on the staffs of national or state school board associations or organizations of administrators. These organizations sometimes employ attorneys whose major responsibility is keeping abreast of school law developments. In addition, such associations sometimes direct *amicus curiae* briefs to courts considering matters concerning one school district but which have implications for all districts. Such briefs spell out the position of the organization and argue points with legal precedent and documentation in a persuasive manner. This support can be very helpful to a school district involved in litigation.

As mentioned earlier, court cases sometimes involve community members. The interaction which takes place can be in an adversary relationship. Such litigation can be divisive, and there is the possibility of long-lasting animosities. Suits may involve individual parents or students, employee groups, pressure groups clustered around major issues, or a single citizen who challenges an action. The subject matter of the litigation can involve diverse matters such as hair length, dress codes, failure to promote, granting sick leave, building a new school or closing an old one, transportation of pupils, or the granting of pay increases. Depending upon the individual situation and the issue or issues involved, supporting community members may be encouraged to express views that assist in neutralizing the impact made by those entering into legal action against the school district. They may even be witnesses in the courtroom. Community opinion regarding the legal action may have more consequences for the administrator than the court decision itself.

Another aspect of litigation and school-community interaction has to do with carrying out court orders. For example, racial desegregation changes practices that have existed in some communities for more than a century. A major study of ten cities showed that most of them had no structure designed to encourage citizen participation in the planning process for desegregation (Willie and Greenblatt, 1981). The case studies indicated that the involvement of citizens may help to achieve school desegregation without conflict if proper planning takes place. The many forms this involvement can take are illustrated in the case studies of those cities in which citizen participation was used.

Legislature

The only manner in which one can legitimately influence a court decision is to present the better case during the period the court is in session. Presenting a better case is important for influencing a legislature, but the time periods are far different. Influence can be exerted in the office, over coffee, over lunch, at committee hearings, in lobbies between and during sessions, at fund-raising events, over the telephone, or back home in the yard of the legislator.

The whole matter of influencing legislation has received a great deal of attention among educators. Both researchers and practitioners have become interested in this issue. Researchers have emphasized the history of educators' involvement with political systems and have put forth models seeking to describe current types of involvement (see Iannaccone, 1967; Campbell and Mazzoni, 1976). Such studies have been largely descriptive and are attempts to classify events, organizations, and procedures. They have contributed substantially to understanding the politics of education.

This discussion takes the practitioner's point of view and emphasizes approaches used in dealing with the legislature. Certainly, the more important issues bring the strongest attempts to unify educators and supporting groups. Such supporting groups as PTA's, school board associations, and employee groups become involved in "cooperative lobbying" with educators. The more united these groups are in their views, the greater the chance for impact on proposed legislation. For example, the passage of Proposition 13 by the voters in California in June 1978 led to greatly expanded state financial support for education. To achieve this, California educational interest groups mobilized their resources. These heretofore diverse groups coalesced in a manner not seen since the 1950s (Kirst and Somers, 1980). Elsewhere, crisis situations see coalitions form and strengthen when the "common good" is threatened. These groups reach out in a variety of ways to seek support beyond their own groups to achieve citizen backing for their goals. Community members are enlisted and involved in the struggle to overcome the crisis. One bulletin to members in such a crisis situation made the following exhortation: "Now is the time for every senator to be inundated with telephone calls, telegrams, letters, and postcards urging action. . . ." (Buckeye Association of School Administrators, no. 1, 1981). In addition to this appeal, another strategist said: "We'll send people to the legislators at their homes. That's much better than demonstrations here at the capitol. After all, they are elected back home" (Hall, 1981).

These statements imply that local educators will marshal support from their school communities to bring pressure upon legislators. These local educators are sometimes in a position of gaining local citizen support for their own tax requests on the ballot and for assistance from some of the same people in influencing legislation. Complications do arise as legislative actions or contemplated actions impinge upon the local scene. One educator blamed the loss of his local tax levy on confusion brought about by the legislature over the effect of reappraisal of property values on tax bills and the proposed state budget figures that might have made some voters feel the levy was unnecessary.

In another instance, an educator said the defeat of the local levy threw school funding squarely back to the legislature. Seeing little possibility of voters supporting school levies in the future, he suggested that it was time for the legislature to come up with a new method of financing schools ("Mansfield Levy," 1981). In the interpretation of some observers, the local voters had sent a message to the legislature to do exactly that. Also implied was a request to place less reliance on the local property tax for education. It can be seen that local citizens as individuals and as groups have substantial potential in sending messages to legislatures.

Marshaling support from the school community involves two-way communication. Community members' concerns must somehow get into the "mix." Voting on local levies is only one way and probably not the best way. Direct communication at individual or group sessions designed for the purpose probably provides the best avenue.

In the private sector of our economy, certain corporations have great interest in governmental actions at both the state and national levels. A technique called "trickle-down lobbying" is practiced. Employees are asked, allegedly with certain forms of pressure, to write or call legislators. There have been reports that some companies are "brow-beating employees into lobbyists." Although some are happy to write or call in hopes of preserving their jobs, others may be forced to choose between their jobs and their political conscience. The introduction of legislation to protect the employee from this offense is being considered ("Banning," 1982).

In the public sector of which schools are a part, there is perhaps less likelihood that the pressures upon the employee would be so great. Legislatively granted job security provides some insulation. Yet, it is conceivable that some publicly employed persons are subject to such pressure, and the legislation prohibiting it could apply to public institutions. With regard to community members, it is difficult to picture any kind of coercion that educators might be able to apply to them. Citizen support is quite likely to be given willingly by parents and others with an interest in schools.

While a show of support from employee or citizen groups may be a most worthwhile contribution to a lobbying effort at certain crucial points, in the long haul it is necessary to employ persons to spend their time continuously in such activities. These lobbyists, who are sometimes referred to as legislative agents, certainly must communicate regularly with their constituencies and, in the case of a local district, must be in communication with citizen groups of various kinds. "Grassroots" support is a major power base for lobbying activity.

Employed lobbyists are a part of the organization of interest groups, corporations, and government agencies, in fact, any cluster of individuals whose welfare is influenced by legislation. They comprise a substantial group of people. In a recent count in one legislature of 132 members, there were over 1,400 legislative agents representing nearly 600 different organizations (Ohio Senate Clerk's Office, 1981). Laws generally require that lobbyists register their names and the organizations they represent.

A proactive role for educators with the legislature must include lobbyists if any impact is to be secured. Only the largest of school districts could afford to employ a full-time lobbyist. Generally, most school districts do not have even a part-time lobbyist. Statewide organizations made up of various education interest groups carry on the lobbying activity. These organizations may represent teachers, school employees, administrators, board members, PTA's, or even citizens' councils financed through contributions from foundations and individuals. Each organization may employ one or more lobbyists.

Those school districts that do employ a lobbyist have the potential to make certain gains. Other lobbyists, representing broadly based organizations, sometimes are not in tune with a specific school district's needs or status on a given issue. One incident might serve as an example. The state legislature was in the process of appropriating several million dollars to school districts to use in improving the education of disadvantaged youngsters. A graduated scale had been created whereby the per-pupil allotment increased for those districts having higher percentages of pupils receiving Aid to Dependent Children (ADC). The lobbyist for a school district knew that his district had a percentage of ADC pupils just below the cut-off percentage required for a higher bracket. By working with the legislators from his area, he was successful in getting an amendment that lowered the cut-off to a point above which the district would fall, yielding several thousand additional dollars of revenue to the district. He earned his salary that year.

Legislators from the local area are important people with whom to relate, even more so if such legislators hold key committee or house positions. Much of the time, however, a school district lobbyist may be engaged in working with those from statewide education interest groups. One individual from a school district indicated that "you have to lobby the lobbyist," meaning that getting your views into the thinking of these lobbyists is also very important. One additional problem of the part-time school district lobbyist should be mentioned. If the district is located some distance from the state capital, considerable time and money are spent in travel, and costs are increased by room and board in the capital city. Individuals with these responsibilities spend considerable time away from home and yet may be absent from the legislature or from the home office at crucial times. Statewide education interest group lobbyists generally live in the capital city and are continuously available.

With hundreds of lobbyists representing hundreds of groups descending upon a legislature, it becomes very necessary to employ the right person to represent a district or interest group. The list of requirements for being an effective lobbyist is long. Those who desire big challenges, a never-ending supply of things to be done, and almost continuous unreached goals should be quick to choose this vocation. Personal characteristics include an open and friendly personality, high energy level, verbal ability, neat appearance, intelligence, and integrity. Beyond such standard items, the lobbyist must espouse the cause of the group for whom he works. Having had some period of immersion in the mission of the group is most helpful in developing the sense of loyalty and advocacy needed. The lobbyist must also become very knowledgeable about the subject matter with which he deals. If taxation and school finance are issues, it is necessary to become thoroughly familiar in these areas. The lobbyist provides information to legislators, and it must be accurate and authoritative. Credibility is at stake, and confidence is lost when bad information comes to light.

According to one lobbyist, the best situation is when a legislator asks for information and gets it as fast as he can. Legislators vary as to their backgrounds and expertise. One said that he felt comfortable in agriculture and certain other areas, but he needed help with banking. This legislator most respects those lobbyists who gave him both sides of an issue: "I want to hear his side and I want him to tell me what the opponents of his view will say, as well as his counterarguments to their points of view" (Senator Ben Gaeth, 1981).

Another area about which the lobbyist must become knowledgeable is found with the legislators themselves. Assessments must continuously be made of the power positions of individual legislators, of their probable stances on various issues, of their likelihood of reelection, as well as of their personal backgrounds and communication links with others. It's quite a task just to recognize 130 people on sight, let alone know a great deal about each of them. It takes years to establish relationships of mutual confidence and trust. Without the building of respect, the lobbyist will not be effective. One aspect of mutual respect should be mentioned here. On occasion, a legislator may say to a lobbyist: "I'm a little short, how about a twenty?" This may be a request for a bribe or it may be a test of integrity. The lobbyist had better have a strategy worked out ahead of time rather than being caught by surprise. (See Exercise 7.3.)

In other aspects of the role of the lobbyist, it would be helpful to be blessed with eternal optimism. There will be defeats and these must be taken in stride. An optimistic approach is more likely to win support than the opposite tactic. It would be helpful if lobbyists were also blessed with excellent hearing. Many remarks in a crowded committee room are made as an aside and are not easily heard. Speakers often move away from their microphones at the moment when what they are saying is most crucial. Still another helpful attribute is the willingness to sit through much unrelated business before the legislation related to the issues of the lobbyist's interest group comes up for consideration.

Legislative hearings are notably sporadic. They seldom start at the appointed hour, they are subject to recess at a moment's notice, and if behind-the-scenes communication is necessary, the five-minute recess becomes a thirty-five-minute recess. Adjournment may come well ahead of or well after the appointed time. Being comfortable with a flexible schedule is a requirement. In addition, it would not be unusual for the lobbyist to attend a 9:30 A.M. hearing and a 7:30 P.M. hearing in the same day. Afterwards, there may be a fund-raising reception that lasts beyond midnight. One should attend, because it is a chance to talk on a one-to-one basis with many people. The ability to stand around and talk to people is needed at the reception, between hearings and sessions, and during recesses. It takes a great deal of physical stamina to stand during long periods. One former lobbyist said that he had grown tired of spending time with people he didn't enjoy and making small talk with them on various occasions. "You can be popular around here if you don't ask for money," said another lobbyist. Indeed, most lobbyists spend a substantial portion of their time and effort on money-related issues. Those who ask for money from public coffers sometimes have verbal barbs thrown at them. Withstanding the barbs by having a thorough knowledge of the need and a heartfelt advocacy for the interest group are essential elements.

Lastly, lobbyists establish a camaraderie among themselves and learn much from one another. This is true especially if the organizations they represent are compatible. There is a satisfaction in comparing perceptions with those whose goals are similar. There may even be some in comparing perceptions with those lobbyists whose goals are dissimilar.

All of this is to indicate the demanding role of the lobbyist. Choosing those who are to represent a district or organization in legislative halls is serious business. The success of that enterprise is dependent upon a wise and careful choice.

Beyond choosing competent lobbyists, it is the responsibility of the proactive administrator to carry on his own program of legislative influence both at the federal and state levels. Maintaining continuing contacts with senators, congressmen, and state legislators who serve the territory in which the school district is located is particularly important. Direct personal contacts by phone, over lunch, or in small group meetings provide a means of increasing awareness of school issues. Opportunity might be taken to have the legislator appear in the school community to participate in a panel or address a group. A legislator living in the community might well be a participant in a citizens' committee studying curricular matters or making a building survey. The administrator must take the initiative in getting to know the legislator and in creating a climate of acceptance and willingness to discuss issues. *For all practical purposes, as the administrator relates to the legislators serving his school community, he is a lobbyist.*

This does not mean the administrator has no direct contacts with legislators serving other geographical areas. There are opportunities to serve on statewide or even nationwide committees with legislators. Valuable contacts are made in this manner or by initiating direct personal communication, particularly with those who have important committee chairmanships or offices within the legislature. Testifying on proposed legislation provides another avenue of making contacts and expanding one's knowledge about people and issues.

Being alert to the resources found in the school community for assistance in influencing legislation can be of utmost importance. Almost every community has individuals who already have communication links to legislators. These may be personal or political, casual or formal. There are also individuals who can develop these links. The proactive administrator will develop communication networks within his school community so that these individuals will be kept informed about important issues and will give assistance when needed. Such networks may be formed on an individual or group basis. Situations vary, and the administrator will have to decide on the best manner of utilization of these resource people.

The final suggested avenue through which the administrator will work is via the full-time lobbyists employed by educational organizations. This has already been suggested in this chapter, and it must be emphasized that the administrator of a school district has an obligation to maintain this contact so that the lobbyist is sensitive to the needs of his district. The administrator should contribute to the policy decisions of the organization and be an influence on the actions of the lobbyists carrying out those policies. Perhaps combining with other districts having similar problems would be an effective manner of making contact with lobbyists. The admonition to "lobby the lobbyist" contains a great deal of wisdom.

The last act in the cycle for the proactive administrator is the expression of appreciation when a "battle" is won—appreciation to the lobbyist, and to the legislator. Generally, it is the lobbyist who asks his constituents to thank the legislator. One interest group wrote its members a reminder:

> A number of legislators who voted for increased taxes as well as increased funding for schools are getting alot of cold pricklies from taxpayers but few warm fuzzies from us tax spenders. Thanking them for their efforts today could help pave the way for greater understandings tomorrow. (Buckeye Association of School Administrators, no. 1, 1981)

One superintendent wrote to a legislator:

> This is a brief note to thank you for your recent vote for the budget bill. You sure kept us guessing!
> I know that raising taxes is never easy and, especially in much of your senatorial district, requires significant political courage. Thank you.

For our part, we will spend the money wisely and will not forget your support. (Caumartin, 1981)

The legislator responded that the encouraging letters from people in education had balanced out the hostility he had received from some other constituents (Senator Ben Gaeth, 1981).

Suppose the "battle" is lost? The same principle applies. Those legislators who supported schools need to receive support and gratitude. There will be another round in the struggle for resources.

SUMMARY

We have seen that the actions of legislatures and courts have a substantial impact upon the operation of schools. We have also noted that dealing with these influences involves a great deal of school-community interaction. This provides a grassroots base for the activities of those employed by school districts. The importance of quality legal counsel and quality lobbyists cannot be overemphasized. With these factors in place and with continued efforts of educators as advocates for children and quality education, courts and legislatures have better potential to assist education. We can't just let things happen, or just watch them happen; we must attempt to bring about what we want to happen. That is the meaning of a proactive and enlightened role.

Exercise 7.1
FINDING YOUR LEGISLATIVE I.Q.

Below are acts of Congress that have had substantial influence upon school district operations. Mark each with the appropriate letter:
A = Never heard of it.
B = Have heard of it.
C = Know about the subject matter of the act.
D = Know the content of the act.
E = Know the impact of the act upon schools.
  1. Agricultural Adjustment Act
  2. Civil Rights Act of 1964
  3. Dingle-Hatch Act
  4. Elementary and Secondary Education Act
  5. Education Consolidation and Improvement Act
  6. Education for All Handicapped Children Act
  7. Education Professions Development Act
  8. Educational Rights and Privacy Act
  9. National Defense Education Act
10. Smith-Hughes Act

Analysis. It is possible to determine group (your class) awareness of individual acts by averaging the scores for each. A group overall rating can be obtained by averaging the individual total scores.

Scoring. For each answer except 3, award points as follows:
A = 0, B = 4, C = 6, D = 8, E = 10. For 3, reverse the scale: A = 10, B = 8, C = 6, D = 4, E = 0. (Dingle-Hatch is incongruous; it was never in Congress.)

Interpretation of Total Score.
  80–100 Statesman
   60–80 Diplomat
   40–60 Precinct captain
   20–40 Ward heeler
    0–20 Demand a recount. Check provisions of P.L. 94-142.

Exercise 7.2
YOUR COURTING COEFFICIENT

Below are cases decided by the U.S. Supreme Court whose decisions had substantial influence upon school district operations. Mark each with the appropriate letter or letters:

A = Never heard of it.
B = Have heard of it.
C = Know about the subject matter of the case.
D = Know the content of the decision.
E = Know the impact of the decision upon schools.

1. *Bradley* v. *Milliken*
2. *Brown* v. *Board of Education*
3. *Engel* v. *Vitale*
4. *Goss* v. *Lopez*
5. *Lau* v. *Nichols*
6. *Perry* v. *Sinderman*
7. *Pickering* v. *Board of Education*
8. *Rodriguez* v. *San Antonio School District*
9. *Ruddy* v. *Gore*
10. *Tinker* v. *Des Moines School District*

Analysis. Same as Exercise 7.1.

Scoring (except for 9). A = 0, B = 4, C = 6, D = 8, E = 10. For 9 reverse the scale and check the *Gilbert* v. *Sullivan* decisions.

Interpretation.

80–100 Chief Justice
 60–80 Jurist
 40–60 Hearing officer
 20–40 Referee
  0–20 Take the Fifth Amendment.

Exercise 7.3
"DON'T WANT NO SHORT PEOPLE"[1]

For this exercise reread the discussion on page 000, and pretend that you are the district representative or lobbyist who receives this request from a legislator: "I'm a little short, how about twenty?"[2]

Which of the following preplanned responses is closest to the one you might use?
1. Sure, here's the twenty.
2. I'll make out a check for you right away.
3. No, I can't do that.
4. I never travel with extra cash.
5. Are you joking?
6. That would be awkward for both of us because I am about to ask for your assistance with some legislation and I wouldn't want it to seem as though I thought you were obligated because of the loan.
7. Is this some kind of a test?
8. I gave at the office.
9. I never lend money to anyone.
10. Other (please supply).

Analysis. After you have made your decision, compare it with those of others in your class. Make a frequency count and determine which answer or which kind of answer (if number 10's are most frequent) was selected most often.

Then, consider the reasoning behind your answer. Depending upon the answer, some possible reasons follow:
1. To pretend it didn't happen.
2. To be perceived as someone who would be willing to show his appreciation of the legislator's support in a material way.
3. Not to grant the request but to avoid showing obvious disapproval at being asked.
4. To establish my position (no emoluments to legislators) clearly, once and for all.
5. Other reasons (please supply).

---

[1]From the song referring to persons of diminutive physical rather than pecuniary status.
[2]This is an academic exercise not intended to indicate a lack of respect for the integrity of the vast majority of legislators.

SUGGESTED ACTIVITIES

1. Interview a superintendent and find out what legislation he/she is "watching." Find out also how the superintendent is obtaining information about the legislation and whether the superintendent attempted in any way to influence the outcome of the legislation.

2. Read the daily press report of the most recent U.S. Supreme Court decision concerning education. Consider how it will affect your district and your school. Discover how directions for compliance with such decisions are transmitted to educational administrators.

3. Try to find a copy of your state school code and analyze the legislated curriculum requirements. Predict what the next requirement is likely to be. If you can't find a code, ask where the body of laws is kept.

4. Ask an administrator to tell you about his/her most recent involvement with any phase of court proceedings. Get an estimate of the number of persons involved and the amount of time spent by each in preparation for and attendance at proceedings. Try to compute the cost in personnel dollars of the proceeding.

5. Find out who would most likely represent you if you were to be sued for negligence in connection with an injury to a student on the school grounds during a school day.

6. Observe a committee hearing of your state legislature. List the groups represented by those appearing before the committee. Determine if those who appear are registered legislative agents (lobbyists) or if they are citizens who have asked to testify on a bill. What characteristics of those appearing seemed to you to result in the most effective presentations?

7. Interview an education lobbyist, asking what he/she likes best about the job and what aspects are least appealing. Determine what techniques he/she feels are most successful in influencing legislation. Find out how the position taken by his/her organization on the issues is determined.

8. Secure newsletters or brochures from two education interest groups which seek to influence legislation. Compare their approaches to issues as well as the facts and arguments used to substantiate their points of view.

9. Observe a court session in which school matters are at issue. Note the types of control the judge exercises over the proceedings. Determine what kind of precedents the attorneys for each side use in their arguments. If witnesses are questioned, pay particular attention to lines of questioning designed to reach the conclusions the attorneys intend.

10. Choose two case studies in *Community Politics and Educational Change* (Willie and Greenblatt, 1981). Compare a case in which community involvement was used and one in which it was not. List reasons for and against using both approaches.

SUGGESTED READINGS

Center for Educational Policy and Management, Administrative Processes Committee. *The Impact of Legal-Administrative Processes on Local Schools*. Eugene: College of Education, University of Oregon, 1981.

Committee on Youth Education for Citizenship. "How State Mandates Affect Curriculum." *Educational Leadership* 37(6) (January 1980):334-36.

Iannaccone, Laurence. *Politics in Education*. New York: Center for Applied Research in Education, Inc., 1967.

Lehne, Richard. *The Quest for Justice: The Politics of School Finance Reform*. New York: Longman, 1978.

Levin, Betsy. *The Courts as Educational Policymakers and Their Impact on Federal Programs*. Santa Monica, Cal.: RAND Corporation, 1977.

Levin, Dan. "Trouble in Trenton: Why the State of New Jersey Took Control of a Local School System." *American School Board Journal* 167(8) (August 1980):24-28.

van Geel, Tyll. "Two Models of the Supreme Court in School Politics." In *The Politics of Education*, Yearbook, National Society for the Study of Education. Ed. Jay Scribner. Chicago: University of Chicago Press, 1977, pp. 124-63.

REFERENCES

Alexander, Kern. *School Law*. St. Paul, Minn.: West Publishing Co., 1980.

Bailey, Stephen K., and Mosher, Edith K. *ESEA: The Office of Education Administers a Law*. Syracuse, N.Y.: Syracuse University Press, 1968.

"Banning Trickle-Down Lobbying." *Common Cause* 8(2) (April 1982).

Board of Education v. *Walter*, 58 Ohio St. 2d 368 (1979).

Bolmeier, Edward C. *The School in the Legal Structure*. Cincinnati, Ohio: W. H. Anderson Co., 1973.

Brown, Linda. "Problems in Implementing Requirements for Title I ESEA Parent Advisory Councils." Paper presented at meeting of the American Education Research Association, Boston, Mass., April 11, 1980.

Buckeye Association of School Administrators (Westerville, Ohio). *Legislative Report*, no. 14, October 16, 1981.

_____ . *Legislative Report*, no. 17, November 6, 1981.

Campbell, Roald F. "The Folklore of Local School Control." *School Review* 75 (Spring 1959):1-15.

Campbell, Roald, and Mazzoni, Tim. *State Policy Making for Public Schools*. Berkeley: McCutchan, 1976.

Caumartin, Hugh T. Letter to Senator M. Ben Gaeth, November 25, 1981.

Citizen's Council for Ohio Schools (Columbus, Ohio). *School Finance Factsheet,* no. 19, Winter 1982.

"Essay: Have the Judges Done Too Much?" *Time* 113(4) (January 22, 1979).

"The First Work of These Times." *American Education* 1(4) (April 1965):13.

Gaeth, Senator M. Ben. Interview, December 2, 1981.

_____ . *Letter to Hugh T. Caumartin*, December 2, 1981.

Goss v. *Lopez*, 419 U.S. 565 (1975).

Hall, John. *Interview*, October 21, 1981.

Hartley et al. v. *Berlin-Milan Local School District et al.*, 69 Ohio St. 2d. 415 (1982).

Iannaccone, Laurence. *Politics in Education*. New York: Center for Applied Research in Education, Inc., 1967.

Kirst, Michael W., and Somers, Stephen A. *Collective Action Among California Educational Interest Groups: A Logical Response to Proposition 13*. Mimeograph, 1980. Published in *Education and Urban Society* 13(2) (February 1981):235-56.

Lehne, Richard. *The Quest for Justice: The Politics of School Finance Reform*. New York: Longman, 1978.

Lukac v. *Acocks*, 466 F. 2d 577 (1972).

"Mansfield Levy Defeat Dismays Head of Schools." *Mansfield News Journal*, November 4, 1981.

Mills v. *Board of Education*, 348 F. Supp. 866 (1972).

Ohio Legislative Service Commission, *Summary of Enactments, 113 General Assembly*. Columbus, Ohio, 1981.

Ohio Senate Clerk's Office. *List of Registered Legislative Agents*, August 25, 1981.

Pennsylvania Association for Retarded Children v. *Commonwealth* 343 F. Supp. 279 (1971).

Perry v. *Sinderman*, 408 U.S. 593 (1972).

Robinson v. *Cahill*, 303 A. 2d. 273 (1973).

Roth v. *Board of Regents*, 408 U.S. 564 (1972).

San Antonio Independent School District et al. v. *Rodriguez et al.*, 411 U.S. 1, 36 L. Ed. 2d. 16, 93 S. Ct. 1278 (1973).

Stewart v. *Margaretta Local Board of Education et al.*, Case No. E-81-35 (1981).

Tallman, Clifford. "A Message from the Superintendent." *Otsego Local Schools Newsletter*. (Tontogany, Ohio), September 1981.

U.S. Department of Health, Education, and Welfare. *Parental Involvement in Title I ESEA*. Washington, D.C.: U.S. Government Printing Office, 1972, page iii.

West Publishing Company. "Advertisement." *American School Board Journal* 169(5) (May 1982):49.

"What's New in ESEA Amendments." *American Education* 3(2) (February 1967):18.

Willie, Charles V., and Greenblatt, Susan L. *Community Politics and Educational Change— Ten School Systems Under Court Order*. New York: Longman, 1981.

Yudof, Mark G. "The New Deluder Act: A Title I Primer." *Inequality in Education*, no. 2, December 5, 1969. Cambridge, Mass.: Harvard Center for Law and Education.

Part II
Affecting School-Community Relations

8

NEEDS ASSESSMENT

Perfection of means and confusion of goals seem—in my opinion—to characterize
our age.

(Albert Einstein)

In this chapter we will consider the problem of determining the
educational needs for a given school population. We assume that this
is necessary no matter what the pattern of educational control—
centralized or decentralized—no matter who is "in charge"—
bureaucrats or the citizens. The manner by which educational needs
are determined and the use made of this information both fall within
the definition of community relations adopted in Chapter 1. Experience and a review of the literature suggest that the entire issue of
needs assessment has been too long neglected by educators.

BACKGROUND

Readers who wish to review the origins of the public school curriculum in America will find a plethora of comprehensive sources (my
own favorite is Edwards and Richey, 1963; see also Butts and Cremin,
1964; Butts, 1978). These will reveal that some things were brought to
colonial education from the Old World and that this inheritance was
augmented and modified through interaction with the needs of the
New World. Since then there have been vast changes in society (e.g.,
industrialization, compulsory education, expansion of knowledge,
social awareness) that have had some reflection in the school
curriculum. Pressure groups have added studies. The curriculum has

grown, but it has been an uneven, unplanned growth. And, except for periodic national studies, there has been little serious attempt to relate the curriculum to the needs of learners and society at a particular time. (See, e.g., Educational Policies Commission, 1938; Educational Policies Commission, 1954; American Association of School Administrators, 1966.)

In a previous chapter we noted the confusing structure for the governance of education in the United States. This would seem to be the same legal network that would enable us to find out how the needs of the people are translated into goals for educational systems. The Tenth Amendment to the Constitution explains the preeminent position of the states. A tradition of localism contradicts, in practice, the dominant position of the state, in theory. And all of this is in a state of change. Some needs are mandated by the federal government, some by state laws and regulations, and some by local districts.

Educators and citizens alike have inherited this mixed bag of objectives from the Old World and the New. They have also inherited the ungainly mixture of centralized and decentralized—national, state, and local—governing bodies. That is why we must attend to all three areas when we consider the task of assessing educational needs. Our real focus is on the local level but the inherited curriculum and governance structure requires that we be aware of the importance of the national and state levels as well. Before taking up needs assessment, however, we need to recognize other ambiguities, this time semantic.

THE SEMANTIC PROBLEM

There are several thorny issues connected with the determination of the educational needs of a community. Consider first the question of who shall determine the needs. Would there be one set of needs if they were determined by scholars who are experts in subject matter, another if determined by humanists, another by vocational guidance persons, another by economists, another by theologians, and so on? Could the lists of all these different people be combined in one master list? Who would be empowered to accept or reject the inventory of needs, to add to it, subtract from it?

How should needs be determined? Does the absence of some desirable skill or ability necessarily mark that skill or ability as a need?

Should the educational system be designed to serve the particular needs of a given community or do the needs of a larger community take precedence? Is there some way of determining a priority of needs so that schools can respond selectively to the more essential needs to the limit of their resources? And, most perplexing of all, what of the community that "needs" selfish, mean, or trivial things? Consider, for instance, the community that needs a winning football team or 100 percent admission to renowned colleges for its high school graduates and so omits or short-changes "lesser" needs, for example, guidance programs, special education, life-long recreation skills, and fine arts.

Some communities will "need" pupils to develop attitudes based on the unquestioned assumption that persons with similar social and economic (or ethnic, religious, or racial) characteristics are inherently and everywhere superior to those with different characteristics. It is true that such a "need" would be found in the hidden curriculum of latent purposes of schooling, but it would, nevertheless, be met. Are there good needs and bad needs?

All of the questions raised above, and others not mentioned, are valid issues that educators "need" to face when they assess the educational needs of a community. The process selected to make the assessment will automatically answer some of the questions. For example, if a group of content specialists were given the task of assessing needs, we would not need to be concerned about their having doubts about recreation and vocational skills. Being human, they would tend to see the needs of others, any others, through the selective screen of their own area of expertise. (I once worked with a very able psychologist on general curriculum issues for the public schools. His first recommendation was that the study of psychology should begin in the first grade! This example, of course, proves nothing. The psychologist might even be right. It merely illustrates the problem of objectivity in assessing the needs of others. How many of us would expect the mathematician or the reading expert to recommend that the study of psychology should begin in first grade?)

If the process selected to assess educational needs does not provide for philosophical and psychological legitimation of the needs determined, we may attempt to do the undesirable or the impossible, if not both. That is to say, just because something can be done does not mean that it should be done. Also, unfortunately, just because something should be done does not mean that it can be done. There remain problems of feasibility and order of desirability. And, although overlooked by some and deliberately denied by others, there is the issue of function, of specificity of purpose. In effect, not only can, but *should* schools attempt to meet all types of needs identified?

This, too, is a difficult decision. Traditionally, schools have taken on other tasks by a process best described as accretion, an adding on. The humanitarian argument is simplistic: if something important is not being done for children and children will suffer for the lack of it, the schools should attempt to do whatever needs doing. Politically and pragmatically this strategy has flaws. If schools begin meeting, however poorly and at whatever cost to other functions, the new need, the pressure or bargaining power of those seeking to meet the need in other ways is destroyed. Pragmatically, bypassed institutions, already weak, are further injured if schools assume their functions even if the institutions are defaulting. For example, if a settlement house is not providing a program of evening arts and crafts and a public park that has a field house does not permit evening recreational activities, would it be better to attempt to persuade them or enable them to offer the programs, which are really in their specialty area, or to offer the activities in the school?

This argument should in no way be interpreted as a defense of a three R's, 8:30–3:30 public school. The Mott version of the community school does deliberately seek to provide all of the types of activities mentioned and others within an extended school day (see Campbell, 1969; Gehret, 1973). There is evidence of a trend for schools to become the site of more community activities. (See, e.g., McMurrin, 1972.) Our point remains that schools cannot do everything. The concept of a consortium of youth-serving or community-serving agencies has much to commend it. A close working relationship among several public and private agencies—including those with broad decision-making powers—could do much toward making *someone, somewhere* more responsive to the needs of the community.

These kinds of important issues should not be overlooked. Their resolution may, however, be postponed until we have obtained some idea of the actual educational needs of a community. So, with all of the several semantic nuances in mind, we shall adopt a temporary, working definition of *community educational need* as: some educational objective identified by members of the community (as narrowly defined) and requested or demanded by them. To put it simply, a *need* will be posited when the community wants the school to do something new, or differently, or to stop doing something.

ASSESSING NATIONAL EDUCATIONAL NEEDS

We know that pressure groups attempt to inform Congress of their perceptions of educational needs and seek the passage of legislation to enable or require educators to help meet the needs concerned. We saw (and some of us enjoyed the benefits of) the response of Congress to needs of veterans of World War II. We saw (and *some* of us put the equipment to good use) the frantic response to our national need for science and mathematics arising from a Russian space satellite. The federal government, like some super school board, continues to respond to perceived educational needs. (Campbell et al., 1971, Ch. 10, provides a helpful conceptualization of the process of policy formation; see also Campbell and Layton, 1969.) Policy formation at the national level is now receiving careful attention from educators as well as political scientists. (See, e.g., Wirt and Kirst, 1982.)

Commissions, Committees, and Task Forces

The appointment and convening of national blue ribbon committees or task forces to prepare recommendations on education (as well as on other areas) has been a common practice in recent years (see President's Commission on National Goals, 1960, Ch. 3). Associations, educational and other, often convene their own commissions or panels with a mission similar to that of groups appointed by the government. Depending upon their sponsors, the recommendations of these unofficial commissions have some influence.

The American Association of School Administrators appointed such a commission (1966) and charged it "with responsibility for identifying and stating in clear and concise fashion major educational imperatives that must be at the forefront as curriculums are modified, instructional methods revised, and organizational patterns reshaped to meet the educational needs of this country in one of its most dynamic periods" (p. i). After two years of study, the commission published a report in which it identified and discussed nine "imperatives in education":

To make urban life rewarding and satisfying.
To prepare people for the world of work.
To discover and nurture creative talent.
To strengthen the moral fabric of society.
To deal constructively with psychological tensions.
To keep democracy working.
To make intelligent use of natural resources.
To make the best use of leisure time.
To work with other peoples of the world for human betterment. (ibid.)

Phi Delta Kappa, a fraternity of professional educators, formed its own Commission of Education, Manpower, and Economic Growth. The report, titled *Educational Requirements for the 1970's* (Elam and McLure, 1967), consisted of seven position papers by nationally known authorities in different areas. Of special interest is Chapter 6, "Educational Policy and National Goals," by Gerhard Colm.

In August 1981 Secretary of Education T. H. Bell established the National Commission on Excellence in Education charged with "making recommendations to the nation and to the secretary to promote excellence in public and private schools, colleges, and universities" (U.S. Department of Education, "Announcement," 1982). More specifically, the commission was directed to pay particular attention to these issues:

Assessing the quality of teaching and learning in our nation's public and private schools, colleges, and universities.
Comparing American schools and colleges with those of other advanced nations.
Studying the relationship between college admissions requirements and student success in high school.
Identifying exceptionally effective educational programs and searching for sources of their success.
Assessing the degree to which major social changes in the last quarter century have affected student achievement.
Holding hearings and receiving testimony on how to foster higher levels of quality in the nation's educational system.
Defining problems which must be faced and overcome if we are successfully to pursue the course of excellence in education. (Goldberg, January 27, 1982)

The commission initially gathered data at six hearings throughout the country. We consider this an attempt at needs assessment by open hearings, supplemented by written testimony, interpreted by an expert jury.

In the approaches mentioned above, official and unofficial groups of experts come together to make their own estimate of the needs of education and then formulate recommendations for the public and educators to consider. Sometimes the government-appointed commissions may take on a global type of representative basis (e.g., labor, farm, professional) but the basic approach remains one of assigning to experts or acknowledged leaders the task of making recommendations for education without consulting the citizens or referring to other than the most general statistical data (namely, census reports). The equivalent of this approach can be observed at state and local levels as well.

The Education Commission of the States sponsors the National Assessment of Educational Progress (NAEP), which reports periodically on its assessments of knowledge of different content areas at various age levels. The NAEP has studied science, writing, citizenship, reading, literature, and music. Almost 90,000 persons participated in the social studies survey reported recently in the first of a series "that will present survey findings on what Americans—age 9, 13, 17, and 26 to 35—have learned about human relations, geography, history and government and their attitudes about the concepts implicit in these subjects" (National Assessment of Educational Progress, 1973, p. 3). Exercises for the testing were based on objectives selected by educators, content specialists, and citizens from all sections of the country and "were administered to small groups of students and to individuals through interviews. Paper-and-pencil questions, discussions and actual tasks were included among the exercises" (ibid.).

The general findings reported in the National Assessment of Educational Progress *Newsletter* were that "Americans Lack Knowledge of Civil Rights." Although the objectives were derived from a three-part sample (of educators, content experts, and citizens), the assessment was based on a subject-matter oriented survey. It is possible to replicate these national surveys on regional, state, or local bases.

Polling has become ubiquitous at the national level. Friends and foes of the Nixon administration waited eagerly or apprehensively for the reflection of the latest Watergate revelations on the president's confidence-popularity rating. During another president's administration, commentators speculated that polls in Israel were influential in the Reagan proposals for peace after the withdrawal of the PLO from Lebanon.

These examples of polling concerning national and international issues help us to recognize an important effect of polls. Polls are not merely assessing knowledge, opinions, attitudes; they are also a potential source of influence. Here we ignore deliberately biased polls (e.g., should the superintendent be fired? how soon should the superintendent be fired?), which seek to persuade rather than to secure information. Any poll both by its process (the way it is done) and its product (the reported results) can become an influence in and of itself. To stay with the unhappy example of Watergate, it is quite likely that some congressmen and party figures began to add their voices to criticisms of the administration only when they considered that it was the right time, a consideration based on the way their constituents were reacting.

George Gallup polls a national representative sample annually about their opinions concerning educational issues. The results are published in the September issue of the *Phi Delta Kappan,* which, with the help of the Lilly Endowment, supports the poll. The purpose of the annual polls according to Gallup is:

> The *raison d'etre* of these annual surveys . . . is to help guide the decisions of educators. Progress is only possible when the people are properly informed and when they are ready, through their tax dollars, to bear the costs of progress. For these reasons, these surveys are directed chiefly toward appraising the state of public knowledge and ascertaining public attitudes toward present practices, readiness to accept new programs, and ideas for meeting educational costs. In the performance of this work, we, too, sincerely hope that we are making a contribution to the field of education. (1973, p. 1)

In the 1982 poll, Gallup stated that the poll dealt with issues of greatest concern to educators as well as to the public. New and continuing trend questions composed the study (1982, p. 38).

Some of the Gallup results are reported here to support arguments concerning public confidence in education begun in the Introduction, continued in Chapter 1, and developed in subsequent chapters, especially Chapter 11, which deals with public relations. Over the years, the public's rating of the schools stays about the same, as was shown in Table 1.1. However, there is a ray of hope and an important insight for improving the image of education to be found in Table 8.1. The ray of hope is that the public rates the public schools in their own local communities higher than they rate public schools throughout the nation. The important insight for educators is that, contrary to the old maxim, familiarity does not breed contempt but rather that, in the case of public schools, the more familiar citizens are with their schools, the better they like them. Hence, we maintain that involving people with schools is mutually beneficial. But more about this in Chapter 12.

In Chapter 3 we displayed Gallup data to show the growing concern of the public over teacher militancy. This is reinforced by the data displayed in Table 8.2, which reflect the agreement among all the groups in the survey on the use of arbitration to settle teacher strikes. Gallup's data also pointed out the apparent inconsistency in the public belief that education is the road to success (80 percent of the national sample thought schools were "extremely important" to future success) and their seeming unwillingness to provide the necessary financial resources (Gallup, 1982, p. 46).

A telling example of the dual role of polls as influencing as well as determining public opinion was provided by the 1982 survey. The Sunday following dissemination of the survey results, Albert Shanker, president of the American Federation of Teachers (AFT), devoted his weekly advertisement in the *New York Times* to an analysis of the results. Under the caption "Gallup: Public Places Education First," Shanker

Table 8.1

Grading Schools:
Local Versus National (percentages)

How about the public schools in the nation as a whole? What grade would you give the public schools nationally—A, B C, D, or Fail?

	A	B	C	D	Fail	Don't Know
Public schools in this community	8	29	33	14	5	11
Public schools in the nation	2	20	44	15	4	15

Source: Gallup, 1982, p. 39.

Table 8.2

Arbitration to Settle Teacher Strikes (percentages)

In case an agreement cannot be reached between a teacher union (or association) and the school board, would you favor or oppose a plan that would require the dispute to be settled by the decision of an arbitrator or a panel acceptable to both the union and school board?

	National Totals	No Children in School	Public School Parents	Nonpublic School Parents
Favor	79	76	84	90
Oppose	7	8	6	5
Don't know	14	16	10	5

Source: Gallup, 1982, p. 44.

used the data to support the agenda of the AFT. Only occasionally was it even necessary for him to add commentary to reinforce a point, as in responses to the question about where, if forced to, school systems should cut. Here Shanker would not risk readers missing the point so he added: "And while some commentators believe the public is hostile to teachers, it didn't show up on this question, where cutting teacher salaries was favored by 17 percent but opposed by 76 percent" (Shanker, 1982). Readers must decide for themselves whether they care to ascribe any motivation to Shanker's reporting of another response to the same question: "Only one proposal was supported by a majority: 'reduce the number of administrative personnel' (71 percent favorable, 22 percent unfavorable, 7 percent no opinion)" (ibid.; see also Gallup, 1982, p. 41). It is also noteworthy that in his extensive analysis of the poll, Shanker made no mention of the issue reported in our Table 8.2, Arbitration to Settle Teacher Strikes.

One other phenomenon is worthy of special notice at this point in our consideration of polls and needs assessments. Gallup asked in one question what parents liked best about schools and in another question what their eldest child liked best about schools. In both of these questions Gallup secured the parents' perceptions. Interestingly, the parents' responses of their own "likes" did differ in some respects from their perceptions of the "likes" of their eldest child. The issue for those concerned with needs assessment is to make a clear, early decision about whether students' perceptions of their own needs should be part of the data collected. Thanks to Sirotnik, we know "that parents and their children are *not* highly congruent in their attitudes on an assortment of issues pertaining to their schools" (1981, p. 16).

In reviewing a decade of polls, Gallup concludes that the public schools have lost favor with the public. To restore confidence in schools, he offers this conclusion of particular interest to readers of this text: "One way to make certain that the public school system continues to command the strong support of the vast majority of citizens is to involve more citizens in the schools and in the educational process" (1978, p. 4). We leave Gallup and attempts at national needs assessments, but since the Gallup poll is specifically designed and made available for use by local citizens or educators, we can share additional data when we consider local needs assessment.

REGIONAL NEEDS ASSESSMENT

Any of the practices mentioned above can be applied at a regional and state level as well. For this reason, we shall discuss only one study each at the regional and state levels. An interesting and informative survey of four geographic regions in the United States and one in Canada was completed by a group at the Midwest Center of the University of Chicago in 1960. They secured a sample from the New England states, the Deep South, the Midwest, the West Coast, and the prairie provinces of Canada. (The way in which the sample was selected is described in Downey, 1960, pp. 30-31.) The instrument used to gather data for the study was called The Task of Public Education (TPE) Opinionnaire.

People completing the TPE had to make decisions about the relative importance of sixteen tasks (four each drawn from intellectual, social, personal, and productive dimensions) described on cards:

A fund of information about many things.
Efficient use of the 3 R's—the basic tools for acquiring and communicating knowledge.
A continuing desire for knowledge—an enquiring mind.
A feeling for other people and the ability to live and work in harmony.
An understanding of government and a sense of civic responsibility.
Loyalty to America and the American way of life.

Knowledge of world affairs and the interrelationships among peoples.
A well-cared-for, well-developed body.
An emotionally stable person—prepared for life's realities.
A sense of right and wrong—a moral standard of behavior.
Enjoyment of cultural activities—the finer things of life.
Information and guidance for wise occupational choice.
Specialized training for placement in a specific job.
The homemaking and handyman skills related to family life.
Management of personal finances and wise buying habits.

The exact method of ranking is called a Q sort. This permits a statistical analysis to take advantage of properties of a normal distribution (Downey, 1960, pp. 28-33).

At the bottom of the TPE form were seven slots. The sixteen cards were placed in those slots after being sorted according to directions (only the directions for the final sorting of the cards are quoted).

Now, sort them further into seven piles—the one most important in the first pile, the *two* next important in the second pile, *three* next important in the third pile, *four* in the fourth, *three* in the fifth, *two* in the sixth, and the *one* least important in the seventh. When you have finished, your sort will look like this:

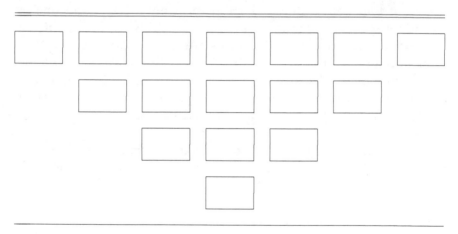

We are not interested in the findings of the task studies so much as in the methods used. However, it may be noted that there was considerable agreement about the task of the public school; geographic region appeared to be a determinant of educational viewpoint; occupation and amount of schooling were the best predictors of educational belief; age, race, and religion were less reliable predictors; community-type, income, sex, and proximity to school were not closely associated with educational viewpoint; and three different educational philosophies and three groups of respondents were discovered. These are responses to a set of needs derived by experts and presented to citizens for ranking. There may well have been important needs not included on any of the sixteen cards for either elementary or secondary schools. This study is of interest because of its scope and because elements have been adopted by subsequent students of educational needs.

A STATE NEEDS ASSESSMENT

The Ohio Department of Education completed a four-phase, fifteen-month, statewide "Search for Consensus." The result was to be: "Bicentennial goals for elementary and secondary education in Ohio, objectives for meeting those goals, and an accountability model" (Ohio Department of Education, 1973, p. 1). The entire process involving "more than 125,000 Ohioans, has included local, county, and regional meetings and a culminating statewide seminar" (Ohio Department of Education, 1973, p. 3).

To put the Ohio search for consensus in the overall perspective of community relations it is important to note that

the impetus for the April 28 Conference was Amended Substitute House Bill 475, in which the 109th General Assembly enacted a five-point accountability provision. The mandate required the Department to perform five functions and report its progress to the General Assembly by June 30, 1973. The five functions are:

1. Define the measurable objectives for which schools are to be held accountable.
2. Develop a process to determine the extent to which the objectives are met.
3. Identify the relevant factors relating to the teaching-learning process.
4. Develop uniform accounting methods.
5. Report findings to all interested persons.

Following the enactment of House Bill 475, the State Board of Education's Committee on Redesign and Improvement met and concluded that determination of the goals and objectives for which education should be held accountable . . . should come from the citizens of Ohio. Thus, the concept of "Search for Consensus" was initiated. (Ohio Department of Education, 1973, p. 6)

Readers will recall that our consideration of interest groups in a previous chapter suggested that states would soon be responding in some way to demands that schools become accountable.

Phase 1 of Ohio's search began at the local level where 605 of the 623 school districts in the state held "Local Citizens' Seminars." From these meetings 12,500 written recommendations were received. Two out of the ten concerns mentioned most often among the recommendations were about school-community relations—numbers 1 and 6:

> Communication between the school and community must be improved.
> The public should be kept informed about their schools through additional printed materials such as a school newsletter or the local newspaper. (Ohio Department of Education, 1973, p. 1)

Almost 56,000 citizens completed an eighty-eight-item questionnaire during phase 1. Results were processed and returned to local school districts for their use.

Phase 2 involved 20,000 persons meeting in eighty-eight County Citizen Assemblies during October 1972. These assemblies reviewed tentative goals that had been drawn from the local meetings in May and analyzed by the Ohio State University Evaluation Center.

During phase 3, twelve regional meetings were held. During February 1973, 4,000 persons met in the different regions of the state to express their opinions about the goals derived earlier and related issues.

Phase 4 was the concluding conference attended by 1,500 persons in the state capital on April 28, 1973. Participants were divided into forty-four small seminars directed by a chairman who was assisted by a resource person and a recorder. Twenty-three of the seminars considered accountability models; the other twenty-one took up the goals derived in earlier phases.

The information of most interest to our present concerns is shown in Table 8.3, which is based on data abstracted from the complete report of action taken on fifty different items (based on data in Ohio Department of Education, 1973, Appendix I, p. 19). The data speak for themselves. In all cases these participants give overwhelming endorsements to practices intended to increase communication and provide more opportunities for citizens to participate in school activities.

The problems of a statewide assessment such as this are apparent. The goals attended to are, of necessity, general. One wonders what happened to goals endorsed by a minority of participants during any

Table 8.3

**Vote by Percentage of Representatives
at State Conference on Goals for Education**

Issue	% Voting	
	Yes	No
Would you favor the inclusion of visitation and study of various community resources as part of the requirement that students be in school six hours per day?	95	5
Would you recommend that local school districts periodically hold citizen assemblies so that the public will have the opportunity to review goals and objectives for their schools?	98	2
Would you favor periodic (at least twice a year) reporting of student profiles to parents?	94	6
Would you favor the expanded use of suitable publications (on a monthly basis) between the school and persons without youngsters in school?	95	5
Would you favor greater cooperation between and among school and community officials over the use of facilities?	99	1
Would you favor the sharing of construction and operation costs for facilities such as libraries, swimming pools, etc.?	96	4
Would you favor use of the community school concept which provides that schools be open during the evening for educational and recreational use by the citizenry even if such services required additional local taxes?	94	6

Source: Ohio Department of Education, 1973, Appendix I, p. 19.

of the four phases. The very title, "Search for Consensus," makes it clear that objectives put forth by less than 50 percent (in most cases 75 percent) will be eliminated. Consensus, after all, implies not only majority but unanimous approval. Unanimous approval is not easily secured for any but the most general objectives at a statewide level.

The problem of representation needs to be addressed if the search is to signal a significant change in direction. It then becomes necessary to clarify the basis on which persons are empowered to speak for others.

Finally, what authority is vested in the recommendations of the 125,000 Ohioans? Clearly the recommendations are the result of much thought and effort. As such, they will have some influence. But, at what level? This brings us back to the first question raised about statewide needs assessment. If the decisions are being made at a local level, the recommendations of a statewide body are advisory at best. The Ohio effort is a sensible response to conditions of the day. Its significance will be determined by future actions of the Department of Education. For most purposes, the important area for assessing educational needs is the local community or school district.

ASSESSING COMMUNITY EDUCATIONAL NEEDS

Many of the same approaches used at state, regional, or national levels have been applied to the local community level as well. As we noted above, the Gallup poll is designed to permit this and the originators encourage the use of the poll items at any level. They do not permit the name "Gallup" to be used in reports of the surveys, but this is the only restriction placed on the use of the materials. The advantage, aside from work saved in designing materials, of using these materials is that they permit comparisons with the national sample, and specific types of respondents within the sample. The disadvantages are probably that the benefits of the process of involving persons in the design of the survey materials are lost and, of course, the nationwide approach may not be suitable to assess particular local concerns.

Gallup Polls

The national Gallup poll includes more than 100 questions. Gallup advises those selecting questions for local use to cut the number of questions used to those that can be answered in an interview of thirty minutes or less. They also advise limiting the number of "open" questions—those for which the respondent himself supplies the answer and does not select from among answers prepared in advance by the interviewer. A complete word-for-word script is provided to guide potential users (Elam, 1973, pp. 191-93).

Users of the Gallup poll materials are advised to consult the head of the sociology department or school of education at their nearest college to get help on drawing a sample population for their adaptation of the interview (p. 193). There is nothing wrong with this advice, but it will be a rare school administrator who does not either have a competent staff member or a continuing relationship with some kind of educational research center for this kind of help. The smallest districts have no sampling problem; they will interview the entire population.

Interviewers must be recruited.

Parent organizations, A.A.U.W., Jaycees, and other groups of concerned citizens are prime sources of volunteer interviewers. In recruiting try to obtain a large cross-section of citizens; this helps to prevent a bias in influencing responses to questions. Explain that the assignment will take about 10 hours of each person's time, including a training session. (p. 194)

One survey handled the problem of bias by selecting two interviewers from each of eight categories: professional, managerial, technical, sales and clerical, unskilled labor, unemployed, retired, and skilled labor (Project Kansas 76, 1972a, p. 3). More interviewers than the exact number needed should be recruited to make substitutes available.

Another survey group was able to adapt the poll to a mailed questionnaire response. This was followed up by telephone calls to those who did not respond. They drew their sample by requiring each principal to select a random sample of students and send the names and addresses of their parents to the project staff (30 students from each elementary school, 92 from the junior high, and 98 from the high school). Out of this sample of 430 parents, they received 158 responses (Project Kansas 76, 1972b, p. 3).

When the interview procedure is used, it will be necessary to furnish baby-sitting service during the training session. The training session is used to explain the importance of the survey and to emphasize the need for interviewers to be completely neutral. They should then be given a few procedural rules before role playing sample interviews—actually interviewing each other in pairs. The volunteers receive their assignments and materials at the close of the training session. The packet of materials for each interviewer using Gallup materials contains: an instruction sheet, identification button or card, questionnaires, hand-out cards, assignment sheets, maps. It is suggested that each volunteer take no more than five or six interviews, preferably on streets where he is not known (Elam, 1973, pp. 195-96).

The results of the polls should be processed so that all of the data can be reported in a few pages of tables. Responses to both open and closed questions are coded and punched on cards. The cards are counted and sorted and the report can then be prepared. To suggest the capability of this approach to those not yet familiar with the Gallup reports, we cite summaries of answers to two major open questions from the fifth annual poll. Table 8.4 shows the percentages of the national sample ($N=1,557$) who mention each item as a big problem of the public schools. The breakdown into subgroups shows the variance for each item and permits a more complete analysis of the results. Table 8.5 presents the findings elicited by the question: What is the main thing you like about the public school that your eldest child attends?

The data from the national sample speak for themselves. In general, they confirm our impressions of how the different subpublics would respond. Local communities using the same data have some basis for comparison. For example, in Wichita, Kansas, citizens responded similarly when questioned about what was particularly good about their public schools, but 53 percent chose not to answer that question! In regard to the question on problems, again responses were similar but the most frequent response for the Wichita sample was: "Teachers' lack of interest/ability." Elaborations of this response included criticisms of teaching methods, lack of a system to evaluate teachers, use of abusive language by teachers, and student-teacher relations. Obviously, the Wichita survey added to the findings of the national sample and revealed more local concerns (Project Kansas 76,

Table 8.4

Problems of Public Schools (percentages) [a]

What do you think are the biggest problems with which the *public* schools in this community must deal?

	National Totals	No Children in School	Public School Parents	Nonpublic School Parents
Lack of discipline	27	27	26	25
Lack of proper financial support	22	21	26	18
Use of drugs	20	20	20	19
Poor curriculum/ poor standards	11	13	11	12
Difficulty getting good teachers	10	9	11	8
Teachers' lack of interest	7	6	9	10

	National Totals	No Children in School	Public School Parents	Nonpublic School Parents
Integration/busing (combined)	6	7	5	10
Pupils' lack of interest/truancy	5	5	4	4
Parents' lack of interest	5	4	5	7
Large schools/over-crowding	4	5	4	2
Mismanagement of funds	3	3	3	6
Crime/vandalism	3	3	2	2
Drinking/alcoholism	3	3	3	2
Lack of respect for teachers/other students	2	2	2	3
Lack of needed teachers	2	2	2	1
Moral standards	2	2	1	7
Lack of proper facilities	2	1	3	—
Problems with administration	2	1	2	2
Too many schools/ declining enrollment	2	1	2	4
Transportation	1	1	1	2
School board policies	1	1	1	2
Communication problems	1	1	2	1
Teachers' strikes	1	1	1	—
Fighting	1	1	2	2
Non-English-speaking students	1	1	*	—
Government inter-ference	1	*	1	1
There are no problems	1	1	3	2
Miscellaneous	2	2	4	1
Don't know/no answer	11	14	3	6

[a]Figures add to more than 100% because of multiple answers.

*Less than one-half of 1%.

Source: Gallup, 1982, pp. 38-39.

Table 8.5

**What Parents Like Best About the Schools
Their Children Attend (percentages)[a]**

And what is the main thing that *you* like about it [the school he/she attends]?

	Public School Parents	Nonpublic School Parents
Quality of education	13	25
Teachers' interest	11	14
Curriculum	11	8
Children are learning	10	11
Qualified teachers	10	5
Faculty are nice	7	3
Location	7	5
Parents kept informed	4	7
Discipline	4	20
Teacher/child relationship	3	6
Students are motivated	3	4
Morals/values taught	1	10
Extracurricular activities	3	2
Emphasis on the basics	1	1
Classroom size	1	2
Miscellaneous	3	4
Don't know	10	8

[a]Figures add to more than 100% because of multiple answers.

Source: Gallup, 1982, p. 49. Reprinted with permission.

1972c, pp. 1-2). Project Kansas 76 used 215 volunteer interviewers for the survey.

Determining Goals

A program, "Educational Goals and Objectives," is sponsored and made available through Phi Delta Kappa. The entire program provides "for the involvement of members of the community, the professional staff and students in ranking educational goals in order of importance; determining how well schools' current programs meet ranked goals; and developing performance objectives to meet ranked goals" (Rose et al., 1971, p. 1).

The basic task to which carefully selected groups attend is to rate and rank order this list of eighteen goal statements:

To gain a general education.

To develop skills in reading, writing, speaking and listening.

To learn how to examine and use information.

To develop a desire for learning now and in the future.

To learn about and try to understand the changes that take place in the world.

To help students develop pride in their work and a feeling of self-worth.

To develop good character and self-respect.

To help students appreciate culture and beauty in their world.

To learn how to use leisure time.

To develop the ability to make job selections.

To learn to respect and get along with people with whom we work and live.

To learn how to be a good citizen.

To understand and practice democratic ideas and ideals.

To learn how to respect and get along with people who think, act and dress differently.

To practice and understand the ideas of health and safety.

To prepare students to enter the world of work.

To understand and practice the skills of family living.

To learn how to be a good manager of time, money, and property.

(Appendix, p. 12.)

Participants get a packet of materials that contains the goal statements on eighteen cards, a display board and forty-five red discs. The cards are placed on the display board in any manner. Discs are placed next to the cards to indicate the importance of the statement on each card, the most important statement getting five discs. Of course, the participant must soon reorder his priorities as he quickly runs out of discs.

After making his decisions, the participant enters the data on a form, leaves his display board in place and joins a small group that attempts to reach consensus on each goal statement. The group leader prepares a summary sheet of the group's ratings of the eighteen goals. These are collected and a master composite display board is made.

The next phase, using the same materials, is to get the perceptions of the community, staff, and students on how well goals are being met. The manner in which goals are being met is marked on a scale from 0 (not at all) to 200 (way too much).

The third phase consists of translating district needs into performance objectives. A district task force selects volunteer teachers to serve as a training cadre and an in-service training program on how to write performance objectives is arranged. The performance level objectives are set by building level or by districtwide program level according to the plan selected.

This is an overview of the plan. There are explicit directions for all aspects of the program in the materials packets and manual. Advantages and disadvantages of five ways of selecting the committee of participants are described and range from arbitrary selection by the superintendent to an unstructured technique of selection by which the superintendent believes "an open invitation should be extended to all citizens residing within the boundaries of the district to participate in the identification and ranking of the district's educational goal" (Rose et al., 1971, p. 7).

The advantages of these materials is, again, that the work of devising the instrument has been done and a careful procedure has been perfected. Moreover, the cost is modest. A major disadvantage is that the focus on eighteen predetermined goals almost insures that only those eighteen will receive careful consideration. The designers attempt to provide for the possible introduction of new goals but it is not reasonable to expect this to happen.[1] It is something like the probability of the write-in candidate winning an election. He starts at a real disadvantage. Then, there is a concern with all of the approaches we have discussed so far. The process of contributing to the creation of goals or the rank-ordering of goals can cause participants to believe that the results of the process *will be implemented.* And, ideally, implementation should follow the process. The constraints of time and resources may slow or block some promised goals. This kind of frustration could rebound and turn a supporter into a skeptic. Hence, care must be taken to point out obstacles and to involve the goal designers in the subsequent search for resources and legitimation by the entire community.

The entire Phi Delta Kappa Educational Planning Model was revised in 1978. Over one third of a million dollars of the materials have been sold (Bugher, 1982). (For information about the most recent version of the materials, contact Wilmer Bugher at Phi Delta Kappa headquarters.)

Examples of needs assessments are easily obtained. The Sylvania City Schools in Ohio prepared an interesting, thirty-five-question

---

[1]At the bottom of the instruction sheet in a footnote are these directions: "Those Committee members who have developed goals in addition to the original eighteen goals, must inform the program moderator at the beginning of the meeting for additional directions."

School Opinion Survey, which was sent to all 13,500 residences in the district with a return of 1,266 (9.37 percent). Data were gathered and compared according to school attendance areas. The district staff also completed the survey. Some items for the total sample are of particular interest to us and will help to understand the forthcoming issues of communication and public relations.

From which of the following sources do you gain the majority of your personal information regarding the operation of the schools?

A.	Students	$N = 433$	$\% = 35.76$
B.	Teachers	278	22.96
C.	Administrators	145	11.98
D.	Other school staff	66	5.46
E.	Parents	289	23.87

If you have a question about the schools, to whom do you generally direct your inquiry?

A.	A board member	94	8.36
B.	A principal	514	45.69
C.	A teacher or counselor	392	34.85
D.	The superintendent's office	99	8.80
E.	A parents' organization	26	2.32

(Hauman, 1982)

From their analysis of questions such as these, the Sylvania team inferred needs. Some suggestions that may be traced back to items such as those quoted are:

Organize a network of neighborhood information volunteers similar to precinct committee chairpersons. The simple task of these people would be to disseminate school information to the neighborhood and feed back information to the local principal.

Organize a permanent public relations committee of interested community leaders which the school system continually provides information and from which school officials periodically request feedback.

Consider the public relations image you project as a topic for a future in-service meeting with the proper noncertified staff. Items to be addressed might include effective telephone techniques, emergency preparedness, and the handling of an unexpected "visitor." (Hauman, 1982)

Daniel Stufflebeam, of the Evaluation Center at Western Michigan University has designed a checklist to use as "a flexible aid to planning and reviewing needs assessment studies" (Stufflebeam, 1977, p. 17).

There are three sections in this checklist, fifteen subsections, and sixty-three specific items. The sections and subsections are reproduced in Exhibit 8.1.

Exhibit 8.1

**Sections and Subsections of a Checklist
for Designing Needs Assessment Studies**[2]

A. Preparation
　1. Determine the *key elements* of the proposed needs assessment.
　2. Clarify the *reasons* for the study.
　3. Make an initial approximation of the client's and audiences' *information needs.*
　4. Secure and maintain *political viability.*
　5. Characterize the *subject(s)* of interest.
　6. Identify other *variables* of interest.
　7. Formulate a general *design* for the study.
　8. Develop a *management plan.*
　9. Summarize the *formal agreements* that will govern the needs assessment.
B. Implementation
　1. Acquire the needed *instrumentation.*
　2. Collect the *data.*
　3. *Analyze* and synthesize the obtained data.
　4. *Report* the findings.
C. Application
　1. Assess the *merit of the study.*
　2. *Apply* the conclusions and projections.

[2]Stufflebeam, 1977, Exhibit 8.

Commercial Materials

Other inexpensive materials are available from several sources. One publisher, Allyn & Bacon, provides alternate modes of data collection. A "School Goals Questionnaire" is designed to be completed at home and mailed to the school. One hundred and six different goals are briefly described. Citizens are asked to rate each from one to five with accompanying verbal designations:

1. Unimportant, irrelevant.
2. Marginal importance.
3. Average importance.
4. Moderate importance.
5. Most important.

The first paragraph of directions reads:

In order to do the good job of teaching you want done, our school has sent you this questionnaire. The questionnaire was developed to enable you to give your opinions on what should be taught in your community's schools. The school wants and needs your opinions. Please take the time to participate in the survey of parents and other members of the community by completing this questionnaire.

Another form, "Rating School Goals," from the same publisher uses a pack of cards with the same 106 goals, one on each card. Five rating mats are provided. The citizen-respondent sorts the cards out on the mats, which are coded from one to five exactly as the response blanks on the "School Goals Questionnaire." The directions require the respondent to put at least five cards in each pile. When the sorting is completed, there is a form, with the same information, which is used to record the rating of each goal. All materials—cards, rating mats, and the form—are to be returned to the principal or his representative.

The same comments made about the advantages and disadvantages of commercial materials apply to these as well. One wonders at using both the card sort and the rating in the second example. Perhaps it is to introduce an element of novelty or fun. It does seem to require the user to perform an extra operation.

In Ohio, the Battelle Center for Improved Education "has developed a needs assessment technique that school districts can use to determine their needs in a systematic way . . ." (n.d.). The Battelle materials are similar to the others already described. They feature a "needs profile," which presents a graphic illustration of the discrepancy between the extent to which the stated goal actually exists and the extent to which it should exist. They also compare the perceptions of groups of respondents—students, faculty, parents, community-at-large, administrators, and board members. A representative of the Battelle Center advises the local coordinator about how to administer the survey. The Center codes and analyzes the data and provides copies of the statistical report.

The National Study of School Evaluation is another commercial source of materials that can be used to survey educational needs. Among these are a "Parent Opinion Inventory," which provides for entries in response to open-ended probes as well as an array of fifty-three items to which respondents need only check the most appropriate of five Likert-type items (strongly agree, agree, no opinion, disagree, strongly disagree). Similar forms are available for students and teachers. They also have open-ended survey instruments (e.g., "Plans and Priorities" for elementary schools and "Major Educational Priorities" for middle schools) intended for use as part of an overall evaluation plan (1981) (National Study of School Evaluation, 5201 Leesburg Pike, Falls Church, Va. 22041).

A Research Approach

Eva Baker of the University of California at Los Angeles designed a study to get parents' responses to more specific goals and to involve students in the survey as well as teachers. For Baker, "needs assessment requires an appraisal of the operation of a system to determine what program goals should be established" (1972, p. 403). The objectives used in the study were drawn from the collection of the Instructional Objectives Exchange, a nonprofit agency. (See, e.g., *Measures of Self Concept,* n.d.) The study concerned fifteen mathematics objectives, although teachers received and rated forty-three objectives for research reasons. All groups rated the importance of each objective. Teachers estimated the level of performance for their class on each objective. Parents were asked if their child could now master the objective. Students predicted their own performance on the objectives and were subsequently tested to determine their actual performance level (Baker, 1972, pp. 410-11).

Baker's substantive findings do not concern us here except to note that seven of the fifteen objectives received high importance ratings and four of these were the lowest in terms of student achievement. What does concern us is the positive reaction from parents—84 percent thought the project was a good idea and 83 percent were willing to do the same kind of thing again.

In this study we can see the relationship of school-community relations to the process of needs assessment. Although this was not a major concern of the study, it seems fair to conclude that school-community relations were improved by the involvement. Such a conclusion could be supported by building a way of pre- and posttesting attitudes about the school into the design. This seems a bit contrived and almost self-fulfilling. In practice it would seem better to look for informal, unobtrusive measures of change in the parents' attitudes rather than to complicate the design of the study by including a formal assessment.

As far as needs assessment goes, this study suffers from the same disadvantage we have noted so often. When a collection of goals is presented to groups, we forgo the consideration of other goals. Certainly this comment is not a criticism of Baker's research. It is a reminder to school administrators not to assume that a valid needs assessment can be obtained by treating in some way (rate, rank order, change) the existing array of objectives. There is a problem for users of the Instructional Objectives Exchange here. They need to ask to what extent objectives set forth by others (no matter what others) can be transported and applied in their localities.

One Local Needs Assessment

A sixth-grade teacher in a Pittsburgh area school designed and supervised a needs assessment survey without using any of the materials described above. John Phillips reports that he attended a board of education meeting where "there was general agreement among the board members, administrators and the audience that [policies] should be geared to the expectations of the community. However, no one was able to say what those expectations were" ("Survey," 1972, p. 9). Mr. Phillips then secured unanimous approval from the board to conduct a survey.

"The plan required maximum community involvement beginning in the earliest stages" (ibid.). Cooperation was sought and secured from "key groups in the district," such as business associations, church organizations, PTA, and civic action groups. There was a representative of each group on the survey committee. Mr. Phillips, the only representative of the school system, served as an advisor and provided liaison with the schools.

A series of meetings of the survey committee was held to determine the questions to be asked, methods and timing of the survey. The first draft of the questionnaire was given a pilot administration with a small random sample of residents. The final draft included these sixteen questions:

What do you think of the educational program in grade schools, junior high and senior high? Would you rate it: excellent, good, satisfactory, poor, very poor, or don't know?

What type of job do you think the administration is doing at the school your child is now attending: excellent, good, satisfactory, poor, very poor, or don't know?

Do you believe the administrative staff to be: understaffed, overstaffed, or about right?

Do you believe that the teachers of the school system, on the whole, are well qualified?
Are fundamentals (reading, writing, spelling, etc.) adequately learned in the elementary schools?
Are fundamentals being learned adequately in the junior high schools?
Are fundamentals being learned adequately in the senior high schools?
Are you satisfied with the school system: very well satisfied, satisfied, dissatisfied, very much dissatisfied, or no opinion?
Do you believe that the school system has a problem with overcrowded school rooms?
Should the school system provide: Adult education after regular school hours? Adequate academic program for college preparation? Vocational program for noncollege preparation? Band and chorus? Kindergarten program? Inter-scholastic sports?
Do you consider your responsibility to the school system as a continuing one whether or not you have children in school?
If one or the other must be done, should taxes be increased or should school services be cut?
Do you believe teachers should be employed on a nine-month or a twelve-month contract?
How would you rate school-community relations in the school district: excellent, good, satisfactory, poor, very poor, or don't know?
What, if anything, do you think is wrong with the school system?
What are some things or areas you believe commendable about the school system? (Ibid.)

The revised questionnaires were mailed to a random sample of twenty-four hundred of the ten thousand families living in the district. The forms were coded to show which of the nine attendance areas they represented. Slightly more than half (1,275) of the questionnaires were returned. The interview approach was rejected because of the potential expense of hiring poll takers. "The use of the mails kept the cost of the survey at a level low enough to be attractive to all but a most frugal school board" (p. 10).

One of the findings of this survey was that the community desired to be more actively involved in school affairs. Over 20 percent of the respondents rated school-community relations "poor" or "very poor"; less than 10 percent rated them "excellent." In the open-ended question asking what is wrong with the school system some comments were:

Parents should have more to say about the curriculum.
You keep information away from the public.

Teachers should be more friendly and cooperative with parents.
Why doesn't the school make use of capable people from the community?
It should be made easier for people to find out what's going on.
It's about time somebody did this.
I appreciate this opportunity to express my views. (Ibid.)

Following the survey, a two-day workshop was held at each school for board members, faculty, and parents. Recommendations and provisions for further study resulted from these meetings. Phillips maintains that this type of survey can be easily replicated elsewhere.

This example of a low budget assessment should be reassuring to those who find even the modest fees of the professional materials and services to be prohibitive. It also has the added virtue of continued involvement at all stages and focus on particular local concerns. It is especially noteworthy that something happened as a result of the survey. We can quarrel with Phillips on minor issues (e.g., the wording of his questions, his decision not to try to recruit volunteers) but the extent of his project with little or no additional resources is impressive.

Charrettes

An approach with the intriguing name, *Charrette,* has been used to permit wide involvement of citizens in educational planning. One advantage of the approach is that people are brought in to consider a problem that is important to them but that is not in their area of specialization. This is done in the hope that such groups may come up with creative, feasible ideas that the experts, because of their disciplinary focus, would not consider.[3] The example we have selected, "Charrette 71," was an intensive effort to involve inner-city residents of Des Moines, Iowa, in planning for new schools. In education, the charrette procedure has generally been associated with a facilities planning task.

Before considering the use of the charrette concept, educators are advised to secure affirmative answers to all of the following questions:

---

[3]See Chase, 1970, "Anyone," 1971. Literally, a *charrette* is a two-wheeled cart. Charrettes were used by the Paris School of Architecture to collect the students' drawings at the end of the term — hence, its usage here emphasizes time constraints, frantic planning, deadlines, and creativity.

Are educational planners willing to "share their role" with community residents?
Is the school district interested in cooperating with other local agencies to "revita-
    lize the community"?
Are funds available to assure community participation in planning activities?
Will the school administration and board of education allow residents to
    "participate in the decision-making process"?
Is the school system willing to solve problems by "entering into meaningful dia-
    logue" with representatives of the community?
(Educational Facilities Charrette 1971, p. 4)

When these conditions were all met in Des Moines, a director was
appointed and a representative steering committee was created. Community residents, elected at open meetings, had a voting majority on
the steering committee. Eight additional committees, each chaired by
a resident, were organized to implement the charrette.

The charrette itself was a ten-day (evenings included) session, with
working lunch hours. Residents received twenty-five dollars per day
or their regular daily income (whichever was larger). High school
students received ten dollars a day. All twenty-seven steering
committee members participated, as did sixteen representatives from
each of four elementary school districts and nine representatives from
the community at large. Steering committee members selected the
other members from a pool of applicants. Each elementary district
sent two students, six adults between nineteen and thirty years of age,
five adults between thirty and sixty-five, and two adults over sixty-five.
Care was taken to reflect the racial composition of the school and to
represent both sexes as well as different viewpoints (Educational
Facilities Charrette, 1971, p. 7).

The activities of this particular charrette were organized around
four topics. Each topic area had a resource team that stayed in one
place as four different community groups were rotated through the
stations before selecting one area for special attention. The outcomes
of all of this concentrated attention and effort were portions of the
program and building specifications; preliminary proposals, which
were developed and presented to the community and decision makers
during the charrette; and an account of the formation of an interim
community advisory committee to carry on the work of the charrette.
The sponsors of the project did not expect several finished products.
In their estimation "the charrette has produced an assessment of
needs, an evaluation of current activities, and a series of value deci-

sions which form the basis and the beginning of activities for improving education and life in these communities" (Ibid.).

The charrette example reinforces important aspects of needs assessment surveys. The process of involvement is almost more important than the product—the list of needs. The work and considerable expense of the charrette ($54,700) seems, by implication, to have been justified by the process of creating trust and cooperation. Some of the subjective data cited suggest that this attitude may be right. For example:

Participants revealed a relatively high degree of suspicion at the beginning of the charrette. However, this distrust diminished toward the end of the charrette. Some continued skepticism is shown by 84 percent of the participants who believe that "the community will have to be a watchdog to be sure the charrette work does not go down the drain." (p. 22)

Despite the repeated assertions in regard to the charrette, and that all of the means of needs assessment noted that the widespread benefit of participation is a significant outcome in itself, there are dangers that need to be acknowledged. First, to rouse the public with high expectations may, as we have already warned, turn believers into cynics. Even more disastrous for the unwary, unwise educator, who seeks to manipulate a survey committee by letting it go through the motions of forming policy, is the danger of large-scale alienation, followed by opposition, followed by controversy.

A high-powered citywide committee of citizens was once brought together in the hope that its participation in the study of needs would make it, and its sponsoring organizations, boost a much-needed bond issue. Unfortunately, the committee was not empowered to take on any real activity. Because there was, in its perception at least, no real work for it to do, some of the school district's most staunch supporters drifted away over the months. Others talked of being used and of "bad faith." All of this was used by some real opponents of the public school administration who easily formed a coalition to take over the citizens' committee and use it to attack the school superintendent and raise serious questions about proposed projects. The lesson is simply that there must be a bona fide, clearly identified task for the needs assessment committee. The days of token involvement are no longer with us.

This caution in no way releases the school administrator from the obligation to continue to survey the needs and expectations of his community. Not to do so is to endanger the support of the school program. There is really no longer a need to press this point. Accountability is in the wings. Some states are mandating community needs assessment. (The Superintendent of Public Instruction in Illinois proposed "that each school district provide a state with a plan, assessing its own needs and how it proposes to meet them" ["Dr. Bakalis," 1972; see also Kearney et al., 1970].) The emphasis on data collection and the advantages of mechanical processing of information will be a boon to overworked school administrators. However, it is suggested that they, the educators, remain "in charge," for it is they who know the citizens and it is they who must do something about the findings, not Gallup, Roper, Phi Delta Kappa, or the educational research center.

SUMMARY

We have argued that the old needs for education, once unquestioned, have changed. Assessment and reassessment of educational needs are happening at national, regional, state, and local levels. It is as though the schools must reestablish their legitimacy. Commercial and locally designed materials and procedures are available. School administrators are advised to involve citizens in needs assessment and to ensure that appropriate response follows the stimulus of needs assessment.

Exercise 8.1
NEEDING IS ONE THING . . .

Conduct a needs assessment during two sessions of your class or before and after the break (if you don't have a break, you may "need" one).

First ask everyone to respond to this open-ended probe.

WHAT WE REALLY NEED TO IMPROVE THINGS FOR GRADUATE STUDENTS AT THIS INSTITUTION IS:[4]

Collect these responses and then organize them into categories to eliminate duplications. Drop items that are clearly facetious or only named by one person. Then list the remaining categories or items in alphabetical order on a sheet of paper, a transparency, or the chalkboard and ask the group to rank order this list in order of importance.

Analyze the list in terms of the possibility of securing some "needs." Consider the effects of the process on those whose preferred needs are dropped or given low average rankings. Ask what difference it would make if a need with a low average ranking was espoused by a single-interest group.

---

[4] If you are not working with a group of graduate students but are teaching, you could adapt this process to a class of your own students. There are obvious dangers inherent in this approach, and you need to consider these carefully.

SUGGESTED ACTIVITIES

1. Run a limited poll with a small convenient sample. Use just two open questions: What are the biggest problems and the particularly good aspects of public schools? Compare your findings with the nationwide results shown in Tables 8.4 and 8.5.
2. Find out when the last needs assessment was made in a school district. If recently, try to discover what impact it had; what use was made of the results. In your opinion, how might the results of that survey be different today? On what basis are you able to predict differences?
3. Make a small-scale needs assessment of your own, using any of the procedures described in the chapter.
4. Ask some teachers how they know what to teach. Continue to probe until you get past the answers of state laws, board rules, administrative directives, etc. Make a list of the ultimate justification for what educators are doing. Is it a formal statement of philosophy, tradition, a teachers' manual? How closely are the sources you discover related to some assessment of community needs?

SUGGESTED READINGS

Banach, William J. *Survey Feedback*. Arlington, Va.: National School Public Relations Association, 1980.

Brandt, Ron. "Overview." *Educational Leadership* 39(4) (January 1982):243. See also several theme articles in this issue.

Conway, James A.; Jennings, Robert E.; and Milstein, Mike M. *Understanding Communities*. Englewood Cliffs, N.J.: Prentice-Hall, 1974.

Elam, Stanley. *A Decade of Gallup Polls of Attitudes Toward Education, 1969-1978*. Bloomington, Ind.: Phi Delta Kappa, 1978.

English, Fenwick W., and Kaufman, Roger A. *Needs Assessment: A Focus for Curriculum Development*. Washington, D.C.: Association for Supervision and Curriculum Development, 1975.

Harris, Yeuell Y. *Community Information in Education: A Handbook of Standard Terminology and a Guide to Its Collection and Use*. Washington, D.C.: National Center for Education Statistics, 1979, Ch. 6.

Houston, W. Robert, et al. *Assessing School/Community Needs*. Omaha, Nebr.: Center for Urban Education, 1978.

Kaufman, Roger A., and English, Fenwick W. *Needs Assessment: A Guide to Improve School District Management*. Arlington, Va.: American Association of School Administrators, 1976.

Ohio Department of Education, Division of Planning and Evaluation. *Needs Assessment Guidelines*. Columbus, Ohio, n.d.

Ryan, Barbara. "Assess Your District's Needs: Here's How." *American School Board Journal* 168(11) (November 1981):35-36.

Smith, William D. "Polling Local Attitudes." *Phi Delta Kappan* 64(1) (September 1982):51.

REFERENCES

American Association of School Administrators. Commission on Imperatives in Education. *Imperatives in Education*. Washington, D.C., 1966.

"Anyone for a Charrette?" *Appalachian Advance* 5(3) (1971).

Baker, Eva L. "Parents, Teachers, and Students as Data Sources for the Selection of Instructional Goals." *American Educational Research Journal* 9(3) (Summer 1972):403-11.

Battelle Center for Improved Education. "Needs Assessment for Local School Districts." Brochure. Columbus, Ohio, n.d.

Bugher, Wilmer. Personal letter, September 21, 1982.

Butts, R. Freeman. *Public Education in the United States*. New York: Holt, Rinehart and Winston, 1978.

Butts, R. Freeman, and Cremin, Lawrence A. *A History of Education in American Culture*. New York: Holt, Rinehart and Winston, 1964.

Campbell, Clyde M. *Toward Perfection in Learning*. Midland, Mich.: Pendell, 1969.

Campbell, Roald F.; Bridges, Edwin M.; Corbally, John E.; Nystrand, Raphael O.; and Ramseyer, John. *Introduction to Educational Administration*. 4th ed. Boston: Allyn & Bacon, 1971.

Campbell, Roald F., and Layton, Donald H. *Policy Making for American Education*. Chicago: Midwest Administration Center, 1969.

Chase, W. W. "The Educational Facilities Charrette." *Educational Technology* 10 (June 1970):20-21.

Downey, Lawrence William. *The Task of Public Education*. Chicago: Midwest Administration Center, 1960.

"Dr. Bakalis and Quality." *Chicago Tribune,* December 5, 1972.

Educational Facilities Charrette. *Charrette 71: How a Community Planned Two New Inner-City Schools*. Des Moines, Iowa: Des Moines Public School System, 1971.

Educational Policies Commission. *The Purposes of Education in American Democracy*. Washington, D.C.: National Education Association, 1938.

_____ . *Education for All American Youth: A Further Look*. Washington, D.C.: National Education Association, 1954.

Edwards, Newton, and Richey, Herman. *The School in the American Social Order*. 2nd ed. Boston: Houghton Mifflin, 1963.

Elam, Stanley, ed. *A Decade of Gallup Polls of Attitudes Toward Education 1969-1978*. Bloomington, Ind.: Phi Delta Kappa, 1978.

_____ , ed. *The Gallup Polls of Attitudes Toward Education*. Bloomington, Ind.: Phi Delta Kappa, 1973.

Elam, Stanley, and McLure, William P., eds. *Educational Requirements for the 1970s*. New York: Praeger, 1967.

Gallup, George. "The First Five Years: Trends and Observations." In *The Gallup Polls of Attitudes Toward Education*. Ed. Stanley Elam. Bloomington, Ind.: Phi Delta Kappa, 1973, pp. 1-6.

_____ . "The First Ten Years: Trends and Observations." In *A Decade of Gallup Polls of Attitudes Toward Education*. Ed. Stanley Elam. Bloomington, Ind.: Phi Delta Kappa, 1978, pp. 1-6.

_____ . "The 14th Annual Gallup Poll of the Public's Attitudes Toward the Public Schools." *Phi Delta Kappan* 64(1) (September 1982):37-50.

Gehret, Kenneth G. *Getting the Most Out of Our Schools.* Boston: *Christian Science Monitor,* 1973.

Goldberg, Milton. "Executive Director's Report." National Commission on Excellence in Education, U.S. Department of Education, January 27, 1982.

_____ , executive director, National Commission on Excellence in Education, Letter, February 18, 1982, and enclosures concerning commission program and hearings.

Hauman, Thomas. "A Study of the School Opinion Survey—1981—Conducted for the Sylvania City School District." Unpublished study. Sylvania Schools, Ohio, 1982.

Kearney, C. Philip; Crowson, Robert L.; and Wilbur, Thomas P. "Improved Information for Education Decision-Making: The Michigan Assessment Program." Administrator's Notebook 18, no. 6 (February 1970).

Measures of Self Concept. Los Angeles: Instructional Objectives Exchange, n.d.

McMurrin, Lee R. "Alternatives for Now and for 2001." In *Opening the Schools.* Ed. Richard W. Saxe. Berkeley: McCutchan Publishing Corp., 1972, pp. 258-81.

National Assessment of Educational Progress. *Newsletter* 6(9) (December 1973):3.

National Study of School Evaluation. "Parent Opinion Inventory, Revised Edition." Commercial survey instrument form, Falls Church, Va., 1981.

Ohio Department of Education. *What 125,000 Ohioans Want from Their Schools.* Columbus, Ohio, 1973.

President's Commission on National Goals. *Goals for Americans.* Englewood Cliffs, N.J.: Prentice-Hall, 1960.

Project Kansas 76. *Educational Leadership Planning Survey for the Junction City Public Schools III Community Survey.* Topeka, Kans.: Kansas State Department of Education, 1972a.

_____ . *Educational Leadership Planning Survey for the Manhattan Public Schools III Community Survey.* Topeka, Kans.: Kansas State Department of Education, 1972b.

_____ . *Educational Leadership Planning Survey for the Wichita Public Schools III Community Survey.* Topeka, Kans.: Kansas State Department of Education, 1972c.

Public Opinion Center. "How the Public Opinion Center Serves the Community Interests of Dayton." Brochure. Dayton, Ohio, n.d.

Rose, Keith, et al. *Educational Goals and Objectives.* Chico, Ca.: Program Development Center of Northern California, Chico State College, 1971.

Shanker, Albert. "Gallup: Public Places Education First." *New York Times,* September 12, 1982.

Sirotnik, Kenneth A. *Parents and Their Children: A Study of Congruence on Attitudes About School, Technical Report No. 13.* Los Angeles: Graduate School of Education, University of California at Los Angeles, 1981.

Stufflebeam, Daniel L. "Working Paper on Needs Assessments in Evaluation." Paper presented at the AERA Evaluation Conference, September 23, 1977, San Francisco, Cal. Also available in a cassette tape, *Needs Assessment in Evaluation.* Washington, D.C.: American Educational Research Association, 1978.

"A Survey Can Increase School-Community Interaction." *Pennsylvania Education* 3(6) (July-August 1972):9-11.

U.S. Department of Education, National Commission on Excellence in Education. "Announcement: National Commission on Excellence Hearings." Washington, D.C., 1982.

Wirt, Frederick M., and Kirst, Michael W. *Schools in Conflict.* Berkeley: McCutchan Publishing Corp., 1982.

9

DETERMINING COMMUNITY
RESOURCES

Ask, and it shall be given you; seek and ye shall find; knock, and it shall be opened
unto you.

(Matthew 7:7)

In this chapter we shall maintain that local community resources
are largely unknown and seldom used to full advantage by educators.
Some ways of discovering or creating resources will be presented.
Finally, we shall discuss strategies to introduce new and unusual
resources into the school and its programs.

WHAT ARE RESOURCES?

This chapter is a logical companion to its predecessor on needs
assessment. Ideally, there should be a relationship between needs and
resources. It is, also, quite possible to combine the search for needs
and resources in the same survey. One reason for doing so has been
suggested. The requirement that the same group that inventories
needs should also determine resources prevents irresponsible
demands for programs so expensive that there is no hope of establishing them with available resources. The flaw in this logic is found in our
usage of *resources. Resources* will mean *people or materials situated in the
school community that can help the school accomplish its objectives.* When used
in this way, there is no implication that resources should be sufficient
to meet needs. The only important test is to determine whether the
resources are related to the needs identified.

Using *resources* in this restricted way also prevents us from using a systems approach to present data. The systems model would identify all resources (inputs) used by the school and process this information to compare it with the product (output), which would be certain changes in learners. This is an economic approach that is both more inclusive and narrower in scope than our usage of *resources*. It is more inclusive in that it is concerned with federal and state funds (resources) as well as commercial materials and professional personnel not indigenous to the community. It is more restrictive in that it would not make provision for learning places outside the school and for personal services performed by citizens without formal contractual arrangements. Put in simplest terms, *resources* are people, places, and things in the community that can help the school.

Some special schools and special programs within some schools organize their entire instruction programs about resources external to and not controlled by the school. (We discuss this type of arrangement in detail in Saxe, 1972; Saxe, 1973.) Well known examples of this use of external resources are the Parkway Program in Philadelphia and the Chicago Public High School for Metropolitan Studies: alternative schools within the public system. They are characterized by voluntary enrollment and unusual use of learning places outside schools and classrooms. However, to the extent that (because of their unique mission) they use citywide learning materials, people, and places, they are not examples of community resources according to our meaning. That is to say, the Chicago Public Library, the Art Institute, the Museum of Natural History, the Board of Trade, the Planetarium, the traffic court, and similar institutions used by Metro High in Chicago are only resources in a citywide sense. They certainly cannot be claimed by every one of the more than five hundred schools, even though some of them may be used briefly during the year by some group from every school. (For example, is there any school that does not send some class to the zoo, probably always in the same two months of the year?)

Moreover, such citywide opportunities as concerts, demonstrations, and lectures are, in a way, too conventional to be considered community resources. They are similar in style to the usual modes and materials of learning in the traditional school program. There is, of course, nothing wrong in using conventional resources to the utmost;

one would be foolish not to do so. However, our focus is on community relations and the particular ways of relating the needs of local schools to all kinds of resources in their communities. Hence, the long list of citywide cultural resources prepared and distributed by the central office, although a learning resource, is not for us a community resource.

All citizens who participate in school activities will not be viewed as community resources, although they may be, depending upon whether they are there to control or to participate. Members of a governing body, although certainly of great importance to the success of the program, will not be listed as resources. If, however, their involvement is sometimes primarily service and facilitative, they can become a resource. Perhaps the best way of making this kind of distinction is to emphasize the use of the resource to facilitate learning. The other types of involvement of citizens and parents are better considered in chapters on communication and citizen participation.

Whether the community resource is human or material, its use in preference to the usual instructional materials can be justified only if it is superior in accomplishing the objective. Unlike Sir Edmund Hillary, who climbed Mt. Everest, educators must design their activities to accomplish an objective. Because the community "is there" will not do. Sometimes the objective may be in the affective domain (e.g., enjoy a social experience with classmates), and we have no quarrel with this so long as the "field trip" or excursion by any other name meets the currently rigorous criterion of *efficiency* in terms of our conventional resources of time, energy, and expense. If the objectives are presented solely in terms of benefits to the community rather than to the students, the activity is probably inappropriate and should be relegated to the extracurriculum or suggested to another social agency.[1]

---

[1] This is a conservative position biased by the realization that there are trade-offs to be assessed for all alternative ways of accomplishing an objective, and the conventional, in-school approach is often more effective and efficient. We deliberately avoid the philosophical argument that if it is good for the community, it must also be good for the school. The mission of the educational institution is changing, and the emerging role may assign additional broad objectives such as we have seen in interaction–desegregation developments.

KINDS OF COMMUNITY RESOURCES

The professional literature for years has included articles describing the benefits of inviting community residents in to speak to a class or even to an entire school at an assembly. The foreign visitor or the parent of foreign extraction would be brought in to display artifacts and talk about customs and conditions in another country. Parents would come in and talk about their occupations. Businessmen would be persuaded to discuss the qualities that lead to success. Local celebrities and illustrious alumni of the school would receive a forum to talk about the influence of their schooling in their careers. This use of human resources is well known to all.

Even such prosaic procedures as those described seem to have an aura of innovation, of creativity, about them. Frequently, student teachers seeking to add motivation and a higher dimension of reality to their unit or module, call on a parent, relative, or friend in an occupation related to the subject to come in and meet the pupils. Such "innovation" is generally received with great enthusiasm by pupils and with benign tolerance by the cooperating teachers (i.e., the regular teachers with whom the student teachers are assigned for their field experience), who expect such enthusiastic overdoing by the neophyte. And, after all, it will impress the college supervisor who is responsible for entering a grade for the student-teaching experience.

A dreadful television program portrayed the loss of self-esteem suffered by a psychologist who competed in a "tell about your career" day with persons with more dramatic (to the fourth-grade pupils) occupations. Hopelessly overshadowed by a fireman complete with axe, the psychologist secured a second chance. This time, for "show and tell," he brought a set of Rorschach plates.

Another series dealt with a middle-aged foreign woman who, because of her constant presence in and around the high school, became a nuisance. The enterprising social studies teacher saved the woman's self-concept by bringing her to speak to his students. Their rapt attention was almost believable.

The point of mentioning these programs is not to analyze the weird concepts of education and educators presented by the entertainment media. That is a problem best addressed elsewhere. It is merely to note that such obvious exploitation of an interesting person or glamorous profession is so well established as to be represented in television situation comedies. And, paradoxically, even these awkward, self-conscious departures from normal practice are viewed as praiseworthy events to be recounted in monthly reports of principals or superintendents.

This type of resource is still available to educators and certainly should be sought wherever appropriate to the curriculum. We turn now to more recent examples of the use of human community resources. To set the tone for the new orientation toward community resources, we begin with a statement by Cunningham:

Central to the concept of responsible autonomy is the belief that school communities have substantial resources to use in solving their own problems. Problems are there; resources are there. The genius is the ability to release those resources and bring them to bear on the problems that citizens of the school community define as most significant for them. A responsibly autonomous school should develop a posture of reaching out for help and resources. The processes of building community-school strength are not well known. Nor have they been taught to teachers and other professionals. Most buildings will need assistance with these matters—intellectual help as well as fiscal resources will be required—but the basic raw material for improvement is in each neighborhood in the country. (1972, pp. 93-94)

Bringing the Community to the School

Although many community resources are by design two-way between school and community, it will be easier to discuss them if we force them into a dichotomy: either bring the community into the school or take the school out to the community. The first problem met here is the issue of whether it is proper for some teaching to be done by persons other than professionals with certificates. This controversy occurs primarily about the ways in which aides, paid or volunteer, may be used. Up to this time affiliates of both AFT and NEA have been adamant in restricting the use of all such personnel to nonteaching, supportive functions. There has been much progress, however, and schools no longer face the hard line of opposition to even the presence of persons without certificates in the school. Our own bias is that whoever can be most effective at accomplishing a given objective should be encouraged to do so in a program coordinated by the teacher and arranged by the school.

It is not fair to accuse teachers and their organizations of self-serving protectionism when they raise barriers to the expanding role of others in instructional capacities. Their concern about the best interests of their pupils is valid. We have pointed out that they have good reason to be concerned about letting other adults observe their teaching because of the possibility of unfavorable evaluation and loss of prestige resulting from a misunderstanding of what is good teaching. Moreover, and more importantly, teachers feel guilty when they share their instructional role with others. They have long been conditioned to believe that instruction is their responsibility.

We have evidence of the problem that some teachers have in changing their roles from presenters of information to facilitators of learning. The widespread use of self-instructional materials has caused teachers much concern about not teaching as much as they did formerly. We even have some accounts of misguided supervisors criticizing teachers of programs in which self-instructional materials are used for not providing dynamic leadership. Such supervisors, too, need to be helped to find a new role for themselves as well as learn how to support teachers in new roles.

If some teachers are to become coordinators of learning resources—both people and things—they will need much support. Something analogous to this quandary has for some time plagued the registered nurse. She, too, feels guilty being a coordinator and manager of people and records instead of the bedside ministering angel. After all, the nurse was motivated to seek that career because of a desire to care—personally—for the sick. Teachers, similarly, were motivated (theoretically, at least) to enter their careers because they liked children and wanted—personally—to help them learn. (Although we found many other reasons for preparing to become a teacher, they did not change the fact that personally imparting knowledge to learners was an important expectation for future teachers. See Saxe, 1969.)

We need to study the effect of this profound change on the role of teachers. (In a study of Teacher Corps team leaders we found that they were concerned that they were "getting away with something" during the times they were not actively involved in working directly with pupils. See Saxe and Ishler, 1971, esp. pp. 57-60.) If they are not only to permit but also to welcome the intervention of others in the teacher-pupil relationship, this must be a part of their expectation of the job and of their training programs as well.

Before considering some of the many programs involving the use of volunteers in schools, we need to alert educators to at least two somewhat unexpected sources of opposition. The paramount expected source of opposition is, of course, the school staff. (Hubley, 1972, deals with the proper orientation of the school staff to the use of volunteers.) The unexpected sources of opposition are community control advocates and women's rights organizations.

Advocates of community control have mixed opinions on volunteer assistance. There are those who think it a good initial tactic to get inside the school on any pretext to gather data detailing educational shortcomings to be used in subsequent open attacks on the board and administration. Others, probably the more confirmed opponents of the existing educational governance, fear that community residents will be in danger of being coopted by the school staff and lose their dedication to the cause of massive, violent reform. The importance of this information is that the administrator should expect some reluctance and skepticism when he begins negotiations to involve citizens in school-supportive services.

The other somewhat unexpected source of opposition, the women's rights organizations, specifically the National Organization for Women (NOW), does approve of volunteers participating in the decision-making processes of schools, but considers volunteer service to schools an exploitation (National Organization for Women, n.d.). Since the vast majority of volunteers are women, NOW sees the practice as sexist. It seems unlikely that this position would dissuade parents from seeking to improve the education of their own children. It does suggest, however, that caution be exercised about permitting volunteers to perform tasks usually assigned to paid aides, which could be seen as using the volunteers to deprive others of needed income. Further, the assignment of volunteers to dull routine, away from teachers and pupils, could be perceived as exploitation. Administrators need to ask and have a good answer to the question: "What's in it for the volunteer?"

Volunteers serve in a myriad of ways. A Gallup study commissioned by Independent Sector[2] estimated that the dollar value of volunteer time per year in the United States was $64.5 billion. They further estimated that about 31 percent of all Americans spend two or

---

[2] Independent Sector, the successor to the Coalition of National Voluntary Organizations and the National Council on Philanthropy, is at 1828 L St. N.W., Washington, D.C. 20036.

more hours a week on volunteer activity (Gallup, 1981). Although the definition of volunteer activity used in this study is quite broad, the conclusion that volunteerism is still practiced is inescapable.

There is a national organization that has materials available to help administrators and citizens interested in beginning a volunteer program. It is the National School Volunteer Program (NSVP), 300 North Washington St., Alexandria, Va. 22314. There are also twelve state-level affiliates; for example, Ohio's affiliate, the Ohio School Volunteer Program, Inc., was chartered on November 6, 1981 ("OSVP," 1981).

A 1982 study by NSVP and the School Management Study Group (SMSG) focused specifically on education. Their findings, based on a sample of 600 districts of which 40 percent responded, were that 79 percent of schools used volunteers. Volunteers were used more extensively in elementary schools than high schools (88 percent compared with 60 percent). Parents were most typical volunteers (33 percent), older persons next (24 percent), followed by students (21 percent), business employees (18 percent), and others (4 percent). NSVP estimates that 4,362,000 volunteers work with 40,228,000 students. At a rate of five dollars an hour, if volunteers served one hour per week, the estimated value of their service would be $218,000,000.

Some school districts have assigned professional staff to recruit volunteers and administer the program. In Oklahoma City's public schools, Marilyn Oden currently serves as School Volunteer Coordinator. The title of Gene Berry's job with Salt Lake City Schools is Coordinator of Volunteer and Public Communication. The NSVP/SMSG survey reported that 39 percent of the school districts had assigned responsibility for volunteer programs to an administrator. Administrators without previous experience working with volunteers would be well advised to look at several handbooks of the type prepared by school district personnel. The NSVP has an audiovisual program, *Partners for the '80s: Teachers and Volunteers Working Together,* that would help prepare teachers for planning and participating in a program.

A list of the ways in which a principal may participate in a volunteer program taken from one handbook (Baltimore County, Maryland) gives a general idea of the implications of volunteer programs for administrators. The list follows:

1. Foster a positive attitude among staff members toward a volunteer program.
2. Assess the need for teacher interest in a volunteer program for the local school.
3. Set goals for the volunteer program appropriate to the school's commitment to education.
4. Identify with staff specific needs in which volunteers can be of help.
5. Select a compatible, interested, and qualified volunteer coordinator.
6. Define the coordinator's task and role.
7. Help in the provision of workspace, materials, and supplies.
8. Establish the procedures for selection of volunteers.
9. Provide for the orientation of volunteers and participating teachers.
10. Inform the volunteers of school board policies, procedures, and regulations.
11. Provide for liaison between the local PTA or PTSA and the volunteer program in the school.
12. Evaluate the local school volunteer program.

(National Association of Secondary School Principals, 1981, p. 2)

One use of volunteers is somewhat similar to the old and continuing practice of inviting celebrities or professionals in to talk about their activities. In a more highly organized form, this is found in offerings of special courses or activities. In some innovative schools minicourses are offered several times throughout the school year, for short periods of time, about an hour a day.

The minicourses may be taught by a combination of staff and volunteers. For example, if one teacher happened to have certain extracurricular skills and interests, he might offer a course for interested pupils. The same would apply for volunteers. A good way of seeing how this plan works is to look at some of the interest groups available at one elementary school (Motley School, Minneapolis, April 2-13, 1973) during a period of two weeks.

> Music—jazz, melody bells.
> Communications—advanced playmaking, black poems, black images.
> Social studies—Israel.
> Science—magnetism, insects, plant responses, beginning photography.
> Art—nature drawing, pottery, beginning beadwork, needlepoint.
> Physical education—soccer, wrestling.

All of these courses were taught on a first-come-first-served basis with students checking seven preferences. The minicourses offered the next session would be different and not necessarily taught by the same volunteers and staff. Parents had to sign their approval of the choices made by pupils.

Other volunteer service arrangements to use the special talents of community residents for one time or a short term are easily arranged. Former nurses and librarians have needed skills. Some primary level teachers have capitalized on volunteers' abilities to cook or do handicrafts or carpentry. A volunteer working on this basis had some advice for educators.

Make sure the volunteer will come on the day planned and be prepared with all equipment and materials. Keep the projects simple enough so that children can complete them successfully. Make sure safety precautions have been made. Plan this type of activity no oftener than once a week to keep interest high. (Fireside, 1972, p. 57)

We have a wealth of information on this way of enriching the curriculum. For years now teacher education institutions have been advising students to make a file of such resource persons (see, e.g., Sommers, 1972, p. 62). In some areas a list of volunteer talent and resources available is compiled and coordinated by a professional, full-time director (Weinstein, 1972, p. 14). However, such services, though helpful, do not discover the rich source of support among persons in the local school community who cannot or will not claim to be expert at anything.

Senior citizens, as indicated by the NSVP data (24 percent of volunteers were older persons), are a good source of volunteer help. There was a federally funded Retired Senior Volunteer Program with regional offices in ten states that provided leadership for about 250,000 volunteers (National Association of Secondary School Principals, 1981, p. 3). There is reason to believe that the involvement of elderly volunteers is a mutual benefit. This was the subject of a doctoral dissertation by Eileen Bayer at Hofstra University—"The Effect of Male Senior Citizen Intervention upon the Readiness of Kindergarten Children." Bayer tested three premises: that preschool children, especially boys, would benefit from more regular contact with older male models at the primary school level; that retired men would be a good source of enrichment and excitement; and that contact between very old persons and very young children would be an important experience for both. The study was arranged so that three kindergarten classes in a school were taught with the help of retired men and three other classes in the same school were taught in the usual manner. "Generally speaking parents and teachers—as well as the children—were delighted with the results. Evaluation shows that the experiment has had a positive effect on the children's interest in and readiness for reading" (Hechinger, 1972). The principal of the school reported that he was confident that the men had helped the pupils respect the role of older people. The men were enthusiastic about the experience.

Educators adopting this approach to using volunteers are advised to provide training and support for the volunteers selected. If they are not helped by the regular staff, it is not reasonable to expect them to succeed merely because they want to help. Although the research procedure will not be necessary in most cases, the idea of having some kind of an evaluation of the volunteer experience is good.

Parents are often willing to perform school services on a definite schedule. They can staff libraries or media centers (Brady et al., 1973-74, p. 33). Years ago they took care of kindergarten registration and lunchroom supervision. In Toledo they help prevent disturbances at athletic events ("Parent Groups," 1973). Erma Bombeck devoted one of her delightful columns to her experiences as a volunteer on a field trip in "School Trip Rivals Normandy Invasion" (1973). The National Education Association has put together a multimedia kit to help train volunteers.[3] One of the booklets in this kit has a list of organizations that will be helpful to those establishing regular programs for volunteers (National Education Association, 1972, pp. 54-64).

Students are reliable and enthusiastic volunteers. There is a trend toward permitting high school students to help in the elementary schools. Sometimes the service is performed for high school credit (Thomasy, 1973). Sometimes high school students are brought in through Future Teacher Clubs, sometimes through classes called community service, field work, or volunteer service. Some specially funded projects train the high school students and provide instructional materials for them to use with the elementary school pupils ("Teen-Age Tutors," 1974).

There is no shortage of information on ways of using volunteers. As one source puts it: "The range of possibilities extends as far as the imagination is able, and regular staff willing to go" (Mott Institute for Community Development, 1973, p. 6).

---

[3]*Parents and Teachers Together: For the Benefit of Children,* N.E.A. Publications Section 26, 1201 Sixteenth St., N.W., Washington, D.C. 20036.

Taking the School into the Community

An interesting and important change occurs when we reorient our search for resources to the use of such resources outside the school rather than their introduction into the building. There is, first of all, the psychological shift from host to guest. There is also, and this is the antithesis of bureaucracy, a loss of control, of predictability. The concept of territory seems to be helpful in understanding the reluctance of schools to venture into "their" communities. (Frederick M. Thrasher discusses the importance of territory to youth gangs in *The Gang,* a sociological classic first published in 1927; see esp. Ch. 9. For a scholarly analysis of territory for all species, see Ardrey, 1966. For a brilliant application of the concept to education, see Sarason, 1971, Ch. 2 and p. 30.) In one's own territory there are many advantages, not the least of which is security. Roles and relationships are better understood on home ground. Children must develop a kind of schizophrenia in fortress schools—discussed by Wayson (1972)—to accommodate the different forms of behavior expected by the school and by the community. If the school and community are separated by a moat and drawbridge, real or figurative, educators need to be aware of the rules of the game being played in the other arena—the community game.

The concept of territory also helps one to understand the prevalence of the folk wisdom dictum that teachers should reside in their school districts. If teachers are members of the community, it can be reasoned, they will be more disposed to meeting the real needs of the community when such needs differ from the purposes of the school as an institution. Of course, there is an economic basis for the folk wisdom as well, as we learned from the study, *Small Town in Mass Society* (Vidich and Bensman, 1968).

The importance of understanding different territories is well represented by cliches in American speech. "Like a fish out of water" captures an important element of the concept. The refrain of the salesman in *The Music Man,* "But he doesn't know the territory," includes another nuance of the meaning of territory. These brief comments on territory are not intended to discourage educators from leaving their castles and journeying out into the community. They are intended to emphasize the need for orientation and support for the fish who are out of water and salesmen who don't know the territory and apply to traffic flowing both ways through the boundary (visible or invisible) of the school's territory.

The discussion has prepared us to appreciate the position of many educators that the school must find ways to cooperate with all elements of the community. This perspective is represented by Barry and Tye in their treatment of "External Relations" in *Running a School* (1973).

Research has clearly demonstrated that . . . the influences of home and environment play a crucial and often a predominant part in a child's education, and that the impact of the school will be effective only to the extent that the child is seen by the school, not only as a pupil, but as a member of a family, of a peer group, and of a community, including the community of the school. It follows that no single factor in this process of interaction can make its full contribution in isolation; all must be aware of and responsive to what the others are doing and are planning to achieve. For the threads which make up the fabric of a child's experience of learning and growing are very closely interlinked, and cannot easily be disentangled. So it is important that, for the sake of its children (and for many other cogent reasons) a school should be sensitively aware of, and involved with, the world outside its walls. (pp. 209-10)

A more radical approach to the use of community resources is taken by Colin and Mog Ball (1973), a pair of countrymen of Barry and Tye, who cite beautiful examples of school children performing essential and humane services for and with the community. For the Balls, there should be no boundary between school and community, and we can all profit from the examples of creative service they describe. But to some extent it seems as though the radical ideology detracts from the usefulness of their message. They violate one of their own precepts by taking a position that implies that educators are rock-headed conservatives and that virtue is all on the side of the young. They should know that this is not the way to secure the cooperation of the group attacked. Moreover, it seems as though, in their desire for freedom—for doing one's own thing—they place a most difficult burden on children and adolescents. "Young people must serve the community on their own terms. Then they are not 'serving the community' but doing what they can do or enjoy doing, in ways and places which make them a service for others" (p. 101). It is perhaps because of the Balls' unhappy assessment of educators in Britain that they see no leadership role for school people.

A better strategy, at least for communities and students in the United States, if not Great Britain, is that used in Partners' School in Denver, Colorado. One of the outcomes of the Partners' program would be improvements in the community, but the prior objective for students (all of whom have been referred for some problem) is to understand themselves and to improve their self-image. "Often self-centered and seeking immediate gratification, young people at this age must come to an understanding of their basic human drives, and also explore more complex needs such as the need for companionship and structure (authority, guidance, etc.) before they can be expected to work effectively with others" ("Meeting Community Needs," 1981, p. 3). This investment of time to prepare students in advance of their community service is, we think, essential.

In this country, there is a kind of ideological, missionary force at work that can inspire the revolutionary zeal suggested by the Balls. The concern for the environment and ecology has much to offer science educators and history, government, and civics teachers. This concern and others are apparent in the account of learning activities in a Missouri junior high school:

Teams of ninth-graders have collected water samples from a stream polluted by a paint manufacturing plant. They took the samples for analysis to the labs of the Metropolitan Sewer District, which found the water polluted. Charges were brought against the company. Several classmates wrote a brochure cautioning teens against shoplifting; the local crime prevention agency circulated the brochure throughout the community. Other students design surveys, prepare data sheets, staff polling booths in elections, attend community meetings in ecology, education, politics, government. Some work as teacher aides in Head Start and Day Care Centers, or assist in devising activities for the elderly. (*Resources for Youth,* 1973, p. 1)

Such action projects and internships of varying lengths of time are becoming more frequent for high school students. This is one approach to taking full advantage of community resources, and an important one. Irving Rosenstein, a professor of urban education, believes that "only when teachers and administrators begin to perceive the community as a learning resource for individuals rather than entire classes will they really be able to exploit the local community for meaningful educational experience" (1972, p. 129). We can agree with Rosenstein about the merits of learning from the community, not about it, by activities that involve students. We must disagree with the implication of his statement that students individually, rather than entire classes, must learn in this way. Doubtless both approaches—individual and group learning—as well as others have merit. In anticipation of a consideration of public relations in another chapter, we must also question the use of "exploit" in regard to community resources.

Janowitz supports the use of the community as a learning laboratory by means of community service or work:

For the bulk of youngsters in the slum school, the formal academic and vocational programs alone are not able to afford sufficient gratification to be an adequate basis for self-esteem and a moral order. If students have to remain under educational supervision until sixteen, school experiences must be fused with community and work experiences. (1969, p. 106)

Janowitz notes further that:

again and again, for reasons that are only dimly perceived, youngsters will find in an outside educational program involvement and satisfaction that they cannot develop in a school setting. Success in an outside academic program can, over time, dampen negative attitudes toward the school. The existence of educational field stations in the community [is as] indispensable as second-chance agencies ... thus the school system must take the initiative to insure that a variety of facilities are available in the community for the slum students to do their homework, pursue musical and cultural activities, and form associations based on these interests. (ibid., p. 107)

There seems to be widespread support in the literature for arranging for students to go back and forth from school to community to serve, to learn, and, sometimes, to earn. Teachers and new types of educational personnel also work "both sides of the street"— school and community. Teacher Corps has the distinction of being the first program of teacher education that mandated continuing involvement in poverty-level communities throughout the entire duration of the program. In our own research, we found that Teacher Corps team leaders reported that they were not effective in the community component of the program although they did rank it as being important (Saxe and Ishler, 1971, p. 2). Only 5 percent of the total group of team leaders responding to our query reported that they most enjoyed community work compared with 54 percent who reported that they most enjoyed supervision (p. 3).

As a result of our survey we suggested these objectives for training programs for team leaders:

1. Team leaders will prepare a comprehensive list of community agencies and write a brief description of the goals and functions of each.
2. Team leaders will select five agencies (from above list) and describe ten important activities in which the interns might participate.

3. Team leaders will personally visit five agencies in their respective communities and hold exploratory conferences with agency personnel regarding the objectives of the Teacher Corps program.
4. Team leaders will visit the homes of ten pupils and discuss how Teacher Corps is changing what the pupils do in school. (p. 41)

Corwin's extensive study of the Teacher Corps program supports our findings about the role conflict and other difficulties arising when teachers go into the community (1973, p. 147). Despite the difficulties encountered, Teacher Corps accomplished much in articulating school and community efforts. They must surely be a rich resource of suggestions, tactics, and knowledge about sensitive problems of school-community cooperation. The Corps finally died in 1982 but, hopefully, some scholars somewhere are even now sifting through documents to tease out concepts that will add to our understanding of the mysteries of education.

Business and Industry

A publication of the National Institute of Education (NIE), in commenting on several programs, recommended the use of local resources:

There may be material and personal resources available beyond what can be purchased. Within the school system, slack time on computers, perhaps at night, might be used to print out individualized home study materials, test results, and invitations to meetings for parents. And required teacher attendance at evening meetings could be used for individualized conference instead of open house.

Outside of the school system, local Chambers of Commerce or similar business organizations might be willing to help publicize programs involving parents. Since most graduates will probably work in the locality, the business community stands to gain much from programs that will improve student performance. Parents or parent organizations might also volunteer to help run the program in areas such as contacting other parents and providing support services and advice on parent interests. (Collins et al., 1981, p. 14)

The NIE suggestions identify the interest of business and industry and suggest this be kept in mind as a possible source of resources. This interest, of course, is widespread and well documented, especially in regard to vocational and career education.

Examples abound. Projects arranged with the help of the Cincinnati Chamber of Commerce include twenty-five partnerships linking companies to Cincinnati Schools ("Partners in Education," 1982, p. 3). In Zanesville, Ohio, data on projects using the private sector have been placed in a computerized "Project Bank" (p. 2).

Superintendent Ruth Love arranged extensive business-school links in Oakland, California, and later in Chicago. Seventy-three Chicago companies, social service organizations, and academic schools have teamed with individual schools in the "Adopt-a-School" program (*Education Summary*, 1982, p. 2). Among other cities with thriving "Adopt-a-School" programs are Los Angeles and Dallas ("Competition," 1979). Administrators must, of course, assure themselves and, later, their constituents and critics that they are assured that the commercial interests will not unfairly exploit the relationship with the schools. The word *unfairly* was inserted in the last sentence because there seems to us nothing improper with a business receiving commendation for civic contributions and even boasting about their activities in annual reports or press releases. It might even inspire other businesses to emulate the practice.

FINDING COMMUNITY RESOURCES

A routine survey of a school community is helpful to educators new to that community. There are many forms and formats to guide such surveys. (See, e.g., Elementary School Evaluative Criteria, *School and Community*, from National Study of School Evaluation, 5201 Leesburg Pike, Falls Church, Va. 22041.) At the risk of boring veteran teachers, it is probably worthwhile to review basic data about the community from time to time. Occasionally one meets teachers and sometimes even administrators who are not aware of other agencies that serve youth in the community. Moreover, there are times when it matters for a teacher to know whether a given address is in the Robert Taylor housing project or the Thomas Jefferson group.

To locate volunteer speakers, an Ohio school district placed a coupon in the monthly district newsletter. The coupon provided space for identifying information, profession or hobby, topics, and employer. Accompanying the coupon was an explanation:

The Washington local schools are attempting to enlist the help of talented parents and other persons willing to talk to school children on unique hobbies or professions. Topics may include special interests, handicrafts, travel experiences or subjects dealing with any profession such as dentistry, carpentry, auto mechanics, printing, etc.

Requests for speaking engagements will be made by the individual teacher. A list is being compiled through the Information Services Department. . . . ("Community Support," 1974, p. 3)

Another district offered several daytime "Renewal Classes for Adults." They, too, provided a coupon for several types of school involvement. The information was secured by the form reproduced below.

HOME–SCHOOL PARTNERSHIP PROGRAMS

I wish to become involved in the Newark schools. Please send me information about:

    The school district resource and talent bank.
    The community advisory program.
    The Golden Pass program for senior citizens.
    The tutorial program.
    Daytime renewal classes.
    The volunteer school aide programs.
    The music-action committees.
    The Booster clubs.
    The parent surveillance programs. (*Superintendent's Newsletter,* 1972, p. 3)

The Community Council serving the Fall Mountain Regional School District (Unit 60) in New Hampshire prepared a resource file on people and places that could support and strengthen the school program. Among many other subjects covered in the file were accounting, antique airplanes, crewel embroidery, Galapagos Islands, smokehouse, stained glass, and local town history (Parsons, 1982). It is more than likely that similar resource inventories exist in most communities. The inventory is obviously worthless without leadership and support in appropriate use of the learning resources.

Before beginning the search for community learning resources, educators would do well to begin by reading the *Yellow Pages of Learning Resources.* [4] Some of the learning resources identified in this publication will be present in any city. On people as resources, the *Yellow Pages* has this comment: "Everybody can be a teacher" (p. 2). On places as learning resources, the *Yellow Pages* offers this advice: "As well as being spaces for meeting and learning in, many places are themselves learning resources. Very often things can best be learned by experiencing them first hand. . . . Any place where special things happen or that possess unique characteristics . . . can be a rich learning resource."

---

[4] Group for Environmental Education, Inc., 1214 Arch St., Philadelphia, Pa. 19107. The book is also available from the National Association of Elementary School Principals, MIT Press, and Educational Facilities Laboratories.

There are other systematic ways of unearthing community resources. Quite often, however, their location and utilization depend upon the ingenuity of the educator in the situation. Despite the psychological benefits derived from using community resources, educators need to keep their basic purpose in mind. The enhancement of learning opportunities for children is the primary goal. Hence, if the educator has good reason to believe that a given objective can be more effectively accomplished outside the school (and the costs are comparable), that is what should be arranged. Conversely, if the classroom, or the library, or the science laboratory are better learning places, that is where learning should be arranged. As for resources and talent, they may turn up in the most expected places as well as in the most unexpected places.

The implications for administrators are, by now, obvious. They need to provide support and encouragement for teachers to bring community resources in and, when appropriate, to take their students out of the school sanctuary to other learning places. Administrators need also to encourage those in possession of community resources to make them available to the school. Since no one really knows how best to do this, it will be a challenge for the administrator.

SUMMARY

We accepted a broad definition of resources to mean people or materials in the school community that can help the school accomplish its objectives. Some resources can be brought from the community into the school. There are predictable, but not insurmountable, obstacles to having other persons in the school, especially if they serve in an instructional role of any kind. Sometimes learners must go out into the community. Leaving the school territory has problems, but the benefits are worth it. Using community resources builds community support at the same time as it helps accomplish other learning or service objectives. There are many ways of locating community resources. They should be used whenever they are the most effective (and feasible) way of meeting objectives of the school.

Exercise 9.1
RE SOURCES

Whether you are reading these pages as part of a course or independently, it has probably occurred to you that certain persons or materials could be most helpful in your efforts to reach a better understanding of school-community relations. Your assignment now is to assume that you have complete access to such persons or materials without regard to geography, cost, or other constraints. With this assumption in mind, make a list of all the resources you would assemble to add to your knowledge of school-community relations. You need not restrict your resources to the classroom; if a visit to Clark Kent at the Planet will help, assume that you can do this.

When your list of resources is complete, separate it into two columns. One column should contain those external resources that you propose to bring in to aid your study; the other should list those external resources to which you would journey to learn on-site.

Next, consolidate the individual lists, and make a master list for the entire class arranged in order of frequency of mention.

Discuss this process with your colleagues and your instructor. What criteria were directing your selection of resources? Would it be feasible actually to introduce any of the resources identified or journey to any of those noted as potential off-campus learning sites?

If you are teaching, try this same process with your students for any subject or lesson (ignoring for the time constraints of bussing, permission, schedule conflicts). Try to implement one or another of the less ambitious ideas to bring in a resource or go out to a resource. If possible, share your success stories with your colleagues.

SUGGESTED ACTIVITIES

1. Make a list of all community resources—people and things—brought into a school during a given time. Put the items in categories that describe their contribution.
2. List all the incidents of individual students going out of the school into the community to take advantage of community resources. Classify the items in any way that seems appropriate to you.
3. Find out if a list of external resources is available for a school. How recent is it? What kinds of resources does it include and exclude? On what basis is the list distributed (who has copies)?
4. Make your own list of community resources along the same lines as the *Yellow Pages of Learning Resources.*
5. Find out what school or district policy applies to:
   a. bringing resources into the school, and
   b. taking or sending students out into community learning places.
6. Make a survey of parents of one school class similar to the one taken by the Washington Township Schools. Analyze your results. If you are the teacher, include an item asking whether respondents would be willing to share their resource with other classes as well as your own.

SUGGESTED READINGS

Gonder, Peggy Odell. "Exchanging School and Community Resources." In *Communities and Their Schools.* Ed. Don Davies. New York: McGraw-Hill, 1981, pp. 297-330.

National Association of Secondary School Principals. "Volunteers in the Secondary School: A Valuable Resource." *Practitioner* 7(2) (January 1981); see entire issue.

National Commission on Resources for Youth. *Resources for Youth* 10(3) (Summer 1981). For a publication list, write the Commission at 36 W. 44th St., New York, N.Y. 10036.

Saxe, Richard W., ed. *Opening the Schools.* Berkeley: McCutchan Publishing Corp., 1972.

Walker, Ron. *Education for All People! A Grassroots Primer.* Boston: Institute for Responsive Education, 1980.

REFERENCES

Ardrey, Robert. *The Territorial Imperative.* New York: Atheneum, 1966.

Ball, Colin, and Ball, Mog. *Education for a Change: Community Action and the School.* Baltimore: Penguin Books, 1973.

Barry, C. H., and Tye, T. *Running a School.* New York: Schocken Books, 1973.

Bombeck, Erma. "School Trip Rivals Normandy Invasion." *Toledo Blade,* December 1973.

Brady, Charlotte, et al. "Parents Staff Center." *Ohio Elementary School Principal,* Winter 1973-1974, p. 33.

Collins, Carter H.; Moles, Oliver; and Cross, Mary. *The Home-School Connection: Selected Partnership Programs in Large Cities*. Washington, D.C.: U.S. Dept. of Education, National Institute of Education, September 1981.

"Community Participation Class." *Resources for Youth* 3(1) (October 1973):1.

"Community Support Asked for School Speakers' Program." *School Life* (Washington Local School, Toledo, Ohio) 4(3) (January 1974):3.

"The Competition for Volunteers." *Successful School Administration* 6(7) (May 21, 1979):223.

Corwin, Ronald G. *Reform and Organizational Survival: The Teacher Corps as an Instrument of Educational Change*. New York: Wiley, 1973.

Cunningham, Luvern L. "The Reform and Renewal of American Education." In *Futures Conference: New Directions in American Education*. Ed. Carroll F. Johnson and Joan Booth. Washington, D.C.: Proceedings of the Conference, 1972.

Education Summary, June 15, 1982.

Fireside, Byrna J. "Use a Parent's Special Talent." *Instructor* 82(1) (August-September 1972):57.

Gallup Organization. *Americans Volunteer 1981*. Princeton, 1981.

Group for Environmental Education, Inc. *Yellow Pages of Learning Resources*. Philadelphia, 1972.

Hechinger, Fred M. "Grandpa Goes to Kindergarten." *New York Times*, October 1972, p. 29.

Hubley, John. *School Volunteer Programs: How They Are Organized and Managed*. Worthington, Ohio: School Management Institute, 1972.

Janowitz, Morris. *Institution Building in Urban Education*. Chicago: University of Chicago Press, 1969.

"Meeting Community Needs." *Resources for Youth* 10(3) (Summer 1981):3.

Mott Institute for Community Development. *The Use of School Volunteers*. East Lansing: Michigan State University, 1973.

National Association of Secondary School Principals. "Volunteers in the Secondary School: A Valuable Resource." *Practitioner* 7(2) (January 1981).

National Education Association. *Parent Involvement: A Key to Better Schools*. Washington, D.C., 1972.

National Organization for Women. *Volunteerism: What It's All About*. Berkeley, n.d.

National School Volunteer Program/School Management Study Group. *Survey of Volunteers in Public Education*. Washington, D.C., 1982.

National Study of School Evaluation. *School and Community, Form B*. Leesburg Pike, Falls Church, Va., 1981. (This is a commercial, copyrighted survey instrument.)

"OSVP Receives Charter." *Ohio School Volunteer* 2(1) (November 1981):1.

"Parent Groups Praised for Athletic-Event Aid." *Toledo Blade*, December 18, 1973.

Parsons, Cynthia. "Looking at the Workings of a Council." *Christian Science Monitor*, June 28, 1982, pp. 16-17.

"Partners in Education." *Ohio School Volunteer* 2(2) (April 1982):3-4.

Rosenstein, Irving. "Using Community Resources." *Educational Leadership* 30(2) (November 1972):129.

Sarason, Seymour B. *The Culture of the School and the Problem of Change*. Boston: Allyn & Bacon, 1971.

Saxe, Richard W. "Motivation for Teaching." *Teachers College Record* 70(4) (January 1969):313-20.

_____ . *Opening the Schools*. Berkeley: McCutchan Publishing Corp., 1972.

_____ . "Can We Have Alternatives and Schools Too?" *National Elementary Principal* 52(6) (April 1973):102-04.

Saxe, Richard W., and Ishler, Richard E. *Final Report:Team Leadership Development Project*. U.S.O.E. Project No. 452272. Toledo, Ohio: University of Toledo, 1971.

Sommers, Kathryn. "Make a Resource Person File." *Instructor* 82(1) (August-September 1972):62.

Superintendent's Newsletter (Newark, Cal., Unified School District) 2(1) (August 1972):3.

"Teen-Age Tutors Go Back to School." *New York Times*, January 13, 1974, p. 74.

Thomasy, Bernadette. "Volunteer Work Is Education in Itself for High School Students." *Toledo Blade*, September 30, 1973.

Thrasher, Frederick M. *The Gang*. Chicago: University of Chicago Press, 1927.

Vidich, Arthur J., and Bensman, Joseph. *Small Town in Mass Society*. Rev. ed. Princeton: Princeton University Press, 1968.

Wayson, William. "Educating for Renewal in Urban Communities." *National Elementary Principal* 51(6) (April 1972):5-19.

Weinstein, Grace. "Tapping Community Talent." *Scholastic Teacher*, November 1972, p. 62.

10

TWO-WAY COMMUNICATION

Except ye utter by the tongue words easy to be understood, How shall it be known
what is spoken? for ye shall speak into the air.

(I Corinthians 14:9)

In this chapter we shall maintain that communication is of major
importance to school-community relations. We believe that there is
not sufficient communication, that it flows almost exclusively one
way, from school to home, and that much of the communication
is poorly designed. In short, what we have here is a failure in
communication.

Some of the problems of communication will be analyzed and
promising practices presented. Although the chapter is all about communication, it is most certainly not about all communication. Our
focus will be on communication between schools and communities.
The vast literature on communications as art and science cannot be
reviewed here. There are departments and even entire colleges given
over completely to the study of communication. Unfortunately, we
cannot simply refer educators to these resources—the colleges and
departments of communication—and move on to other concerns.
Because of the particular interpretation of community relations
adopted in Chapter 1, communications is the fundamental issue
underlying the entire concept of community relations. We have been
discussing communications indirectly in the chapters on needs assessment (Ch. 8) and community resources (Ch. 9). In these pages we
specifically and directly consider issues in school-community
communication.

It is especially difficult to distinguish between communications that are primarily community relations and those that are primarily public relations. Just as *public relations* can be considered a category of the more inclusive term *community relations,* its procedures can also be considered a subdivision of communication. Thus, communication is the main element in the process of school-community relations and the particular procedures of public relations are one aspect of this communication. The distinction is arbitrary to a large extent, but it does help to arrange the mass of data for study and discussion.

The purposes of school-community communications are many. Sumption and Engstrom (1966) list ten objectives, four of which are better considered under public relations. Those that deal with community relations are:

> To provide the people with information about their schools.
> To provide the school with information about the community.
> To develop a commonality of purpose, effort, and achievement.
> [To] keep . . . the people informed of new developments and trends in education.
> To develop, through a continuous exchange of information, an atmosphere of cooperation between the school and the other social institutions of the community.
> To secure an unofficial but frank evaluation of the program of the school in terms of educational needs as the community sees them. (pp. 105-07)

A more general statement, which emphasizes the importance of two-way communication, is provided by Marx and Milstead. They maintain that there are two broad goals for school-community communications: "(1) to make the community aware of the policies and practices of its schools and the reasons behind them, and (2) to determine the opinions and expectations of the community relative to education" (1970, p. 27).

In discussing communications, we continue to opt for a broad inclusive meaning that permits us to include almost everything that happens in the school and a great deal of what happens in the school community. Thus, we view all behavior as communication. Recognizing that this position, although indicative of the inclusive meaning of the term, "communicates" little of specific use to readers, we need to attempt some refinement. *Communication* will refer to transmitting and receiving information, attitudes, ideas. It matters greatly whether the message intended by the sender was the same one perceived by the receiver, but even if this is not the case, we shall maintain that something has been communicated. We shall even insist that buildings, physical arrangements, and things communicate something, even though there has been no deliberate attempt to formulate a message to be sent by these means. (A locked gate at the school playground on weekends communicates something to persons seeking to use that facility. A schoolhouse with the lights on at night communicates something else.)

There are many ways of discussing school-community communication. A common approach is to deal with person-to-person communication separately from mass media communication. Because of our assumption that two-way communication—originated by either school or home—is essential, we find it more reasonable to organize the information under the general headings of "school initiated" and "community initiated" communication. Communication of the public relations type will be discussed in the next chapter.

SCHOOL-INITIATED COMMUNICATION

According to Cronin and Hailer: "Community relations cannot be improved without frank recognition that the problems of the past few years are based partly on the failure of school people and parents to listen to each other. This failure is a reflection of communication problems within the system itself" (1973, p. 43). The same emphasis on communication appears in a report of an extensive survey of the Cincinnati public schools. The survey, arranged by the Midwest Administration Center of the University of Chicago, began the discussion of "School-Community Relationships" with this statement:

Effective communication is essential to a school system—particularly a relatively large one which is located in an urban area, like Cincinnati. The successful functioning of such a school system—even its mere operation—is dependent to a great extent upon the degree to which the myriad units involved in public education achieve understanding of one another. Communication is the primary means through which such understanding is sought. It is a process characterized by complexity and variability in terms of the persons and groups involved and particularly with reference to their respective values and understandings, the nature of the messages transmitted, and the means of conveyance utilized. The units involved may be institutions or individuals, directly or indirectly concerned with education, and internal or external to the formal structure: the messages transmitted may vary all the way from a student's response on a test to the public's refusal of a requested operating levy; the means of conveyance can include everything from walkouts to report cards, from television to apples for the teacher. (1968, p. 9-1)

Table 10.1

Ways Parents Learn About School
(*N* = 286)

Communication Channel	No. of Responses	%
My child tells me	272	95
Neighbor children tell me	57	20
Conversations with adult friends and neighbors	160	56
School newspaper	280	98
Classroom newsletters	104	36
Teacher notes or phone calls	129	45
Parent-teacher conferences	237	82
Report cards	196	68
Notes or calls to school	101	35
Personal visits to school	128	45
Classroom visits or observations	111	39
PTA meetings	151	53
Other	7	2

Source: Sloan, 1973, p. 39.

Statements such as those quoted above are found throughout the professional literature. Indeed, it seems as though the argument for improved school-community communication has been accepted. If this is the case, as it seems to be, it will be revealing to consider some of the more common communications practices used by schools.

In a study of communication between her school and its parent community, Sloan (1973) examined communication between school and home and vice versa. Table 10.1 summarizes the findings for the survey of communication between school and home. There were 286 forms returned out of a total of approximately 350 families with children attending the Edgewater Elementary School in Toledo—a response of over 80 percent. Parents were invited to check all the ways in which they learned about the school. The school newspaper and being told by one's own child were almost invariably checked, followed by parent-teacher conferences in third place.

Sloan also asked parents to indicate ways in which they *preferred* to learn about the school. Table 10.2 shows the difference, in rank order, of ways in which parents *are* informed about schools and the ways in which they *prefer* to be informed. Only the five most frequently checked preferred ways of learning are reported. Table 10.2 reveals general agreement between the preferred and actual ways of learning about schools. However, Sloan notes that the absence of items in the preferred list may be because these ways of communicating are not used at Edgewater and hence unknown to these parents. Items dropped out of the preferred list were report cards (fourth in actual rank) and conversations with friends and neighbors (fifth in actual rank).

Mellor and Hayden (1981), studying parents of students in a Catholic girls' secondary school near Melbourne, Australia, found a surprisingly similar set of responses. The preferred ways of learning about what happens in school for this study of 108 parents were, in rank order:

1. By weekly circular from the school
2. By attending parent/teacher evenings
3. From my daughter
4. By the school contacting me
5. By attending parent and friend meetings. (p. 63)

It seems as though the five most popular ways of learning about schools in the Toledo study and the Melbourne study include the same elements in almost the same order. The Australian study provided for a negative rating of ways of learning and the parents there indicated strong disagreement for learning about school happenings "from other parents" (ibid.).

Table 10.2

**Rank Order of Actual and Preferred Ways
of Learning About School**

Channel	Actual Rank	Preferred Rank	Difference
School newspaper	1	1	0
Parent-teacher conference	3	2	1
PTA	6	3	3
My child tells me	2	4	2
Teacher note or phone call	7	5	2

Source: Sloan, 1973, p. 40.

Table 10.3

Ways Parents Are Informed by Multiunit Schools
(*N* = 121)

Media	No. of Principals Reporting
Newsletters and bulletins	97
Teacher-parent conferences	28
PTO/PTA meetings	20
Newspaper	20
Group parent meetings	19
Radio	13
Special letter	12
Open house	11
Telephone	7
School visits/tours	6
Unit-parent sessions	6
Television	5
Community clubs	4
Room meetings	4
Quarterly reports	3
Parent handbook	2
Pot-luck supper/coffee groups	2
In-service education for parents	2
Parent Advisory Committee	2
Audiovisual presentations	1
No entry	4

Source: Saxe, 1974.

In our survey of multiunit school principals in Wisconsin, we asked principals to report how the school communicated to parents. The replies are shown in Table 10.3. Except for items in Table 10.1 not under the control of the school (e.g., my child tells me), the ways of communicating illustrated in Tables 10.3 and 10.1 are similar. The common media for communication between school and home seem to be newspapers or newsletters, conferences, notes, and phone calls. The Cincinnati survey mentioned above identified six major ways through which the public learns about schools: informal conversation, community meetings, personal communications from teachers and administrators, visits to schools, school publications, and the mass media (Midwest Administration Center, 1968, pp. 9-13).

Although informal conversation with children, friends, and neighbors is the most readily available source of information about schools, it is not noted for its accuracy. Some schools attempt to supplement and correct information conveyed by conversation. They may employ parent aides or orient school volunteers about school activities. School employees who live in the district often help supply needed information and stop the spread of misinformation. This explains, in part, the once widespread practice of requiring teachers and other school employees to make their homes in the school district. The Parent Partner program mentioned in the chapter on community resources is an example of a program that helps improve the informal school-community communication. There are many such programs. Unfortunately, the continued existence of too many of them seems to depend upon additional federal or state funds. Educators are ignoring an important means of communication if they do not make every attempt to keep all categories of employees—paid or volunteer—aware of school activities.

Citizens learn some things about schools from the regular progress reports. These, once called report cards, are prepared in as many different ways as there are school districts. We need not take up the psychological and philosophical questions of whether it is effective and proper to assess and report students' progress in one form or another. We should be concerned about whether grade progress reports communicate clearly whatever it is they are supposed to communicate. All of us who have survived even one change in reporting practices know that this—unambiguous communication—is not easily, never universally, achieved.

The problems that can accompany a change in reporting systems are well represented by the experience of the Dallas Independent School District. As reported in Time ("Dallas Monster," 1974), the new report cards "may well have completely eliminated any communication between home and school." An 8½-by-14-inch sheet was used for kindergarten through third grade reporting. A thirty-two-page manual was supplied to help parents interpret the numbers entered on the sheet by teachers. The manual was titled: *Terminal Behavioral Objectives for Continuous Progression Modules in Early Childhood Education.* A board member termed the procedure "a monster" and stated that "70 percent of the parents will never raise the lid on a cover with a title like that."

Inside the explanatory manual were terms familiar to most, but not all, educators: "seven to twenty-three specific skills in thirty-nine 'modules' under seven basic curriculum areas." To explain the technical language, examples were offered: "Skill number 5 in the basic concepts module in the communications curricular area, for example, is 'oral response on a concrete level using objects.'" That means, the manual explains helpfully, that a child can "identify a toy car by saying a word, phrase or sentence about it." Another writer was put to work writing a pamphlet to explain the manual that explains the report form. (For another treatment of this same issue, see Hechinger and Hechinger, 1974.)

We can sympathize with the educators in Texas as well as with the bewildered recipients of the new report forms. The school was, in this case, striving for a new level of clarity, of specificity. It proposed to replace an *A, B, C, D,* or *F* in four or five subjects with new lists of exact behavioral competence. This is a commendable effort. However, if the report of the school's efforts is accurate, it has seriously under-estimated the problems of communicating information coded in technical terms to persons not familiar with the new code and the developments that lead up to it. This is easy to do for those of us who live daily with the terms and observe the introduction of variations and new meanings.

At a recent school meeting there was a long discussion of the advantages of career education. The first question from the audience was, "What is distributive education?" This is a fair question but should have caused the educator-speakers some concern because they had been using the term throughout their entire presentation. We are always willing to define terms for persons who raise questions but there are many who will not raise a question. They would rather remain uninformed than go to the trouble of finding out what educators mean by words such as *multiunit, behavioral objective, SMSG, NDEA, Title I,* and the like. Moreover, for those who do ask for clarification, there is a psychological cost involved. They must interrupt the flow of discussion as well as signal their own lack of knowledge. (Neil Postman and Charles Weingartner have prepared a book for amateurs "who want to know what all the hollering is about": *The School Book,* 1973.) It would be best to save technical terms for the technical audience. When they must be used for others, such terms should be explained when they are first introduced.

Educators have long believed that report cards, even sophisticated "monsters" like the Dallas innovation, are inadequate. One way of supplementing objective information was to write brief, pithy comments descriptive of some attribute of the learner that the teacher thought to share with the parent. Sometimes these unsolicited comments were complimentary, sometimes severely critical of the child described. We extracted a list of such comments from the margins of one set of report cards from one second grade class in a predominantly middle-class town in Indiana. The comments are verbatim; pupils' names are changed.

The statements in Table 10.4 have been used in several classes of teachers preparing to become school administrators. Rarely do teachers find anything objectionable in the content, or the tone of the marginal comments. Most seem to feel that it is the work of a conscientious teacher who deserves credit for going beyond the bare minimum of information required on the grade report forms.

There is no doubt about the motivation of the teacher concerned. She was popular and considered a good teacher who maintained a pleasant, although firm, classroom environment. What educators should consider is the propriety of passing judgment on the overall worthiness of children (e.g., "a delightful child"), of directing of parents to engage in specific instructional tasks at home, and the kindness and compassion of "publishing" harsh judgments for the families and friends of pupils to read. I am told that there are still homes in which the child's report cards are placed in the family Bible for posterity. Siblings and cousins, if no one else, may pick up comments such as garrulous Debbie Matheny's or giddy Dickie Springer's. There is also a classic example of pedaguese that rivals the best of the Dallas confusions: "Cathy is doing satisfactory reading with her reading group, but the group is reading below the level at which they should be at the present time." One might hope that there are better ways of communicating such information if, indeed, it should be communicated at all.

Individual notes and calls from educators to parents are common ways for parents to learn about schools. Sometimes the most carefully worded notes are misinterpreted by parents. The notes can themselves become a source of resentment either because of a real or imagined insult to the parent. The notes may be mailed or sent home

Table 10.4

Report Card Notes

Robert Brown. Robert should practice reading at home. He needs to pay attention and leave others alone.

Bonnie Butler. A delightful child—high ability—a good student.

Marie Casebeer. Marie is moving at an average pace.

Sarah Carson. Encourage to do extra reading at home for practice. Also work on number combinations with her so she can gain speed in her answer.

Gregg Collet. Gregg still needs to pay attention and to get busy with his work. He is reminded about that each day. Encourage reading at home for extra practice.

David DeLong. David has shown improvement, but he needs a lot of extra help.

Sue DeReamer. Sue has improved. She must learn to concentrate. She needs a lot of opportunity to read in her spare time.

Gene Fontana. Gene is a capable child. His work has improved.

Beth Fulka. A very pleasant young lady to have in the room.

Jeffrey Glass. A good, cheerful student. He follows directions well.

Julie Godlewski. Julie is a very fine young lady and a delight to work with. She'll make a fine third grader.

Jon Hendricks. Jon should strive to become a more attentive listener.

Stephen Huber. If Stevie would improve his work habits, his school work would be much better. He has days when he concentrates on what he is doing and his work is much better.

Patricia Jarrat. Pat has improved some about her attitude towards doing arithmetic and other work. She had to be reminded for a while to turn in her arithmetic which was hardly started even.

Jack Johnsen. Jack is an underachiever. Has a greater potential than his daily work indicates.

Donald Jones. Don's independent work in reading has been very poor since our conference. If he does not show some improvement within the next few weeks, he will not be able to remain with his present reading group.

Cathy Kay. Cathy is doing satisfactory reading with her reading group, but the group is reading below the level at which they should be at the present time.

Janet Kussmaul. Janet has a good quiet manner. Her fluency in reading is improving.

Jeffrey Lange. Jeffrey could do better work if he would pay attention and leave others alone.

Lori Lorcas. Lori is doing poor work—doesn't complete assignments—talks and plays most of the day and is very inattentive. We need a conference.

Deborah Matheny. Debbie talks and wastes time. Could do better in independent work.

Chris Patterson. Chris is a very good worker and helper.

Jimmy Savia. Jimmy is extremely weak in all areas.

Michael Schroeder. An excellent, cooperative worker.

Bill Shucker. No data.

Richard Springer. Will not take things seriously—laughs at everything! Below average.

Pamela Tappen. Encourage Pam to do extra work, extra reading on her own for practice.

Brian Ulich. Brian's attitude seems to have improved just during the past few weeks. He is still very careless about his work. I think he is capable of doing good work when encouraged. I hope this improvement will continue next year.

Bonnie Varga. A delightful child. She enjoys everything.

Dale Van Alt. Encourage Dale to do extra reading for practice. Also help him with his numbers so that he can gain speed.

Nita Sue Warner. Nita Sue does very careless sloppy work which is seldom completed. Orally she does a very nice job which indicates her written work should be better. I think she is capable of doing good work.

Robin Williams. She is doing satisfactory work. She can do better, but needs time to gain self confidence. Lately she has seemed very nervous in class.

with children. Some of them will arrive promptly, some will not. In some schools there have been so many unfortunate incidents connected with notes from teachers to parents that none is permitted to be sent until the principal reads and initials the note. This system has obvious disadvantages, but it does suggest the need for some assistance from time to time.

Nearly all educators send notes or letters to parents. The great majority of these are about problems. They signal something amiss to the recipients. The practice of calling or writing parents to compliment them or their child is still rare enough to be reported as a kind of creative innovation in educational periodicals. A letter from the school is still only slightly more welcome than one from the Bureau of Internal Revenue. This can be easily changed if some in-service time can be set aside to help teachers with the substance and the form of friendly letters. A collection of "over 170 model letters that school administrators, teachers, counselors, and central office personnel can use" has been published. The authors claim that it contains "every kind of letter you will ever need, already written for you" (Larson and McGoldrick, 1970). We seriously doubt the latter claim but such a collection (whether the published collection or one plucked from files and borrowed from colleagues) may be useful to beginning educators. In many situations, we believe, there can be no substitute for an individualized communication prepared for the particular occasion. (See also Mamchak and Mamchak, 1982.)

Bulletins, announcements, reports, newsletters, and newspapers all tell citizens something about their schools. Sometimes the quality of the reproduction is marginal. Sometimes they communicate clearly. Just as with letters, there are collections of bulletins available for beginning educators. (See, e.g., Keith, Infelise, and Perazzo, 1965.) There are also excellent sources on the technical aspects of printed bulletins, newspapers, newsletters (e.g., Kindred, 1960). We shall consider these media in more detail when we examine public relations oriented communication in Chapter 11.

The mass media (newspapers, radio, television) serve as both community relations and public relations communicators. For years, schools resisted releasing comparative data that might present the schools in an unfavorable light. Finally, after much pressure, nearly all records and reports (excepting personal data about students and staff) are available. When requested data are not forthcoming or are provided in only the most general manner, citizens or pressure groups are likely to seek assistance from the courts.

When the Business and Professional People for the Public Interest and the Lakeview Citizens Council asked the Chicago Board of Education and the city treasurer for detailed information on school spending, they received only the board of education's annual financial report. They termed this incomprehensible and complained that:

For example, there is no way to determine how much money the board actually spent on any individual school for teachers' salaries, textbooks, lunchrooms, maintenance, or anything else. We also found items such as $10 million for professional and special services and $21 million for administration, with absolutely no breakdown or explanation of what these items are. (Lauerman, 1974)

The citizens' groups went to the Circuit Court, charging the board of education with failure to comply with the Illinois School Code. The requested data were then assembled.

The reluctance of educators to release some kinds of information is as understandable as it is futile. Of course, test scores will be misunderstood and will lead to absurd comparisons between districts and between schools within districts. The author of this chapter is fond of sharing his rise and fall from grace in Chicago schools. In one school his students "topped out" all of the tests then in use. The principal could bask in his "earned" status as an outstanding administrator. In another school the students "bottomed out" all of the tests. In this case the principal, a dismal failure, could find some solace in the fact that scores by schools were not then given to the press. Same principal, similar teachers, but different communities with different resources. So we have empathy for those who were reluctant to reveal vital statistics to the press. Problems will accompany full disclosure. Consider a recent headline: "Latest City High School Tests Yield Grim Scores" (Banas, 1982). In the article the scores for each school were listed by grade. But the issue of disclosure has been resolved politically and legally, and educators must attend to how to demonstrate their accountability. This creates another educational challenge. The public must be helped to understand and interpret the new bonanza of information that is their due. Further, since every day may be visitors' day, educators must be most vigilant in keeping their own house in order for the public in general and for parents in particular.

As we mentioned previously, the physical environment of the school communicates something to the community. The several locked doors may be an unhappy, but, we hope, temporary, symptom of social disorganization, but the absence of a clear designation of how one is able to secure entrance is an unnecessary irritant to the visitor who must sometimes walk entirely around a building before discovering the open door. The manner by which one is greeted by the teacher, security guard, or student at the open entrance is also a kind of communication (see Brownell, 1982).

When the visitor is required to register in the school office and secure a pass to his destination, more communication occurs. The appearance of the office itself and the demeanor of the school secretary can be either hostile or friendly. Some administrators take advantage of the opportunity to meet the visitor and perhaps escort him to his destination. Others have prepared materials discussing school activities. Some administrators seem not to notice the curt, sometimes rude, reception given to visitors by the secretary. This encounter is rich in its potential for communicating attitudes and ideas about the relationship of the school to the community.[1]

---

[1]An extreme example of the prompt creation of a hostile attitude is the way in which a receptionist answered the telephone at one institution. Her usual answer was "Yeah, whadaya want?" Surprisingly, fearsome dragons such as this are often associated with friendly, kindly adminis-

Before taking up the processes of incoming communication—from the community to the school—we consider one additional concern of educator-communicators. This can be best discussed under the heading: What does the community want to know about schools? The answer to this question is not, as we might predict, everything. Parents and others desire only partial information about the schools. One of the problems for educators, therefore, is the necessity to prepare different messages for different groups of receivers. (Parents differ from businessmen or retired persons in the information they need about bond issues. Some writers use the terms *publics* or *subpublics.*) Another problem is that of determining the more important communication concerns of citizens.

Before considering the desirability of concentrating on specific communication needs, it is important to note that the frequent complaint of most groups about schools is the lack of sufficient accurate, understandable information. The need to concentrate on the most important information—as perceived by the group with which the educator seeks to communicate—in no way relieves the educator from the responsibility of providing free and open communication about all educational matters. (We always assume that information about individuals is privileged and provided only to those with a valid claim, such as parents and counselors.) If one must err in communicating, he would be better to err in over-communicating rather than in under-communicating. Much information that is meant to be disseminated to entire faculties stops at the principal's desk. Much information meant to be disseminated to parents stops at the teacher's desk. This kind of block to communication is a problem of any organization with a hierarchical structure.

The reasons for this block vary. Often, administrators see information as power and seek to retain power by retaining information. Other administrators may act out of more benevolent motives, seeking not to bother teachers with information that they do not need. This denies teachers the opportunity to decide for themselves whether they need information or not. A common example of this error is the official report of the board of education. Many administrators never

---

trators. There is a possibility that they—the administrators—are unaware of the behavior of the receptionists. This in no way absolves them of responsibility for discourteous behavior. In effect, an administrator has no right to be uninformed of such practices performed under his authority. The use of pupils to answer the phone is also a practice that should be obsolete by now.

make these reports available for the faculty to read. The caveat to be rigorously observed in this regard is that information directed to an administrator as the designated head of a school or district must not be considered personal communication. Many communications of vital interest to teachers are lost because of the failure of the administrator to move them off his desk. Sometimes secretaries route communications addressed to principals or superintendents to the persons actually interested in the content. In this case, care must be taken not to deny the administrator access to the same information.

Teachers might fail to share information with parents for the same reasons of misguided benevolence (thinking they will not bother parents with superfluous information). It is also possible that teachers may be less than enthusiastic about disseminating information with which they are not in sympathy. This is a serious concern for communicators in hierarchically structured organizations. The policy board at the top may officially take a position that can, in effect, be negated by failure to communicate at lower levels. (For example, some parents may never receive the pro forma invitation to visit schools; others may not be requested to contribute to the community fund.)

It is good practice for educators to be certain that citizens receive information about issues that are of great importance to them. Failure to do this will seriously endanger school-community relations. The other extreme—saturating citizens with information about which they care little—although not as harmful, should also be avoided. For these reasons, educators will need to be aware of the concerns of the community.

Sloan investigated this question in her study. The results are shown in Table 10.5. Parents were asked to check the extent to which they wished to be involved in thirteen selected school activities. They were also encouraged to enter other activities in which they wished to participate.

Inspection of Table 10.5 supports the concept of complete and open communication. Most of the parents want to be informed about all of the activities listed. The more important conclusion is found in the center column on participation. Here the faculty at this one school could quickly get a good idea of the activities that require particular attention and more complete communication: "learning problems of my child," "dress code," and "discipline."

Table 10.5

**Type of Involvement Desired by Parents
in Selected School Activities**
($N = 286$)

Activity	Type of Involvement by %		
	To Be Informed	To Participate in Making Decisions	No Involvement of Any Kind
Purchase of major school items	64	8	20
Hours of the school day	67	14	6
Safety concerns	77	16	4
Field trips	83	11	4
What subjects are taught	73	14	7
Size of classes	62	15	8
Clothing children wear to school (dress code)	60	31	4
Homework	79	12	5
Pupil evaluation (report card)	80	11	3
New programs/changes	72	16	1
Discipline, policy, and procedures	69	27	3
Lunch program	62	16	11
Learning problems of my child	62	36	0.9
Other (only 14 replies)	4	0.3	0.3

Source: Sloan, 1973, p. 48.

Interestingly, an activity that would seem to be especially news-worthy—"purchase of major school items"—was the one in which the largest percentage of parents requested no involvement of any kind. That parents (in this study) were willing to trust educators with the technical aspects of education but showed concern about activities relating to their own child is a hopeful sign that someday we will find a resolution to problems of the relationship between school and community.

The contrasting attitudes can best be conveyed by citing the comments of two parents. One wrote: "I always wanted to know about anything concerning my children" (Sloan, 1973, p. 49). Another wrote: "I am not a teacher. Therefore I believe that I should leave teaching to those who are qualified. The size of classes and subjects taught should be left to educators. But, discipline problems and learning problems are business of both teachers and parents" (ibid.).

The data in Table 10.5 do not show the extent of parents' interest in a particular activity. Some may be intensely interested; others only moderately so. Moreover, even the percentage reporting that they wished no involvement at all in some activities can be deceptive. For example, the 11 percent reporting that they wished no involvement in the lunch program could reverse their position if the activity changed significantly. They may merely be satisfied with the way things are at the moment. All of these limitations aside, this survey did provide the faculty with information needed to plan a more effective program of school-home communication.

COMMUNITY-INITIATED COMMUNICATION

In previous chapters we examined the ways pressure groups and power structures communicate with the schools. In the chapter on bureaucracy and school organization, we noted some communication problems associated with large, bureaucratically structured institutions. In these pages we consider the typical communication channels available for messages between the community and the school.

The most visible of these channels—the PTA—has been discussed as an interest group. Nevertheless, it bears repeating that the PTA is commonly considered the most generally accessible channel to provide a dialogue between community and school. The discussion of the image of the PTA and its changing role need not be repeated here, but educators are advised to reexamine their relationships with the PTA. In most situations there is much room for improvement. The PTA may be unable to function in some situations. In others, it may be a communication medium to be developed and improved. Readers will recall that the legacy of the PTA of middle-class morality (Harper Valley PTA)[2] and puppet spokesman for the schools must be rejected before the organization can become effective in most urban areas.

Sloan asked the parents of one school to check the most effective

---

[2]When Jeannie C. Riley sings: "The day my momma socked it to the Harper Valley PTA," she is conveying a long-standing resentment felt by those who have been intimidated or alienated by the image of the PTA as a sanctimonious repository of middle-class Puritan values.

Table 10.6

**Home-School Communication Channels
Considered Very Effective by Parents**

Communication Channel	Number Rating Very Effective	Rank Order
Direct approach by phone or in person	227	2
Parent-teacher conferences	261	1
Periodically scheduled open forum	70	5
PTA	167	3
Representative parent council	35	6
Surveys done by the school	92	4
Other	5	

Source: Sloan, 1973, p. 43

Table 10.7

**Home-School Communication Channels
Considered Least Effective by Parents**

Communication Channel	Number Rating Least Effective	Rank Order
Direct approach by phone or in person	26	5
Parent-teacher conferences	11	6
Periodically scheduled open forum	128	2
PTA	64	4
Representative parent council	142	1
Surveys done by the school	112	3
Other	9	

Source: Sloan, 1973, p. 45.

way and the least effective way of communicating with the school. The results are shown in Tables 10.6 and 10.7. Since parent councils and open forums are unknown to the parents completing the survey, the results for these two channels are meaningless. The two tables do show a correlation between the effectiveness of the channel and the personalization of the communication. That is, one-to-one communication is better than one-to-group communication and oral communication in person is better than printed forms or surveys. Although it does not show in the tables, Sloan found that parents differentiated between channels used for general information about the school (indirect is acceptable) and specific information about their child (direct is desired).

In our study of multiunit schools in Wisconsin, we asked principals to list the ways in which parents communicated with the school. These data are reported in Table 10.8. The procedures listed are generally well known to educators. However, some of the items reported by only a few principals suggest that administrators may be willing to receive communication from parents at all sorts of functions perhaps because (although this is only conjecture) of the lack of easily available regular communication channels for some parents. Once again, the findings from the Melbourne study are similar (Mellor and Hayden, 1981, p. 64).

What are missing from the studies reported are data showing differences in how parents and schools should communicate in regard to different issues. Such information could be easily gathered by listing issues in one column and providing space for either entering or

Table 10.8

Procedures for Parent-Initiated Communication
(N = 121)

Procedure	No. of Principals Reporting
Phone calls	51
Individual conferences	26
Parent visits	26
Note/letter	25
PTA/PTO	24
Group decision meetings	21
Parent-teacher conferences and report card conferences	20
Questionnaires/surveys	14
·Curriculum advisory councils and policy committees	6
Teacher-parent coffees and luncheons	6
Unit discussion sessions	5
Small group meetings	4
Parent volunteers	4
Gossip grapevine	3
Local bars and social functions	1
Old fashioned school picnic	1
In-service seminars (includes parents)	1
No entry	23

Source: Reprinted from Richard W. Saxe, "Multiunit Schools and Their Communities," *Elementary School Journal* 74, no. 2 (November 1974): 103-11, by permission of The University of Chicago Press.

checking the preferred way of knowing in other columns. It is almost certain that this approach will show that the more personal (more important) the issue is, the greater will be the preference of person-to-person contact. Mellor and Hayden collected information about preferred *frequency* for discussion of issues but, of course, some issues (e.g., homework was the issue about which most parents wished weekly discussion) requiring frequent communication are not necessarily of greatest importance (1981, p. 62).

OBSTACLES TO PERSON-TO-PERSON COMMUNICATION

Admittedly, facilitating person-to-person communication presents a challenge to educators. If we accept this as the most appropriate way of communicating, it will eventually lead to the necessity for some of us to go to the community, to leave our own safe territory. This explains, according to Kromer of the National Center for Community Education, why about 80 percent of educators' deliberate attempts to communicate with the community results in emphasis on media efforts rather than person-to-person efforts (1977, p. 6). Although, obviously, he cannot support his position with research, Kromer believes that face-to-face communication may actually be a work saver as it builds increased trust and understanding in a crisis-free situation.

Obvious deterrents to face-to-face interaction, in addition to the alleged exorbitant cost in time, are the lack of skills for both parents and educators, tradition, and lack of mutual trust. Kromer lists four additional barriers:

1. They don't want us.
2. We already know them.
3. They can come to us.
4. We are hired to do the job because we are professionals and do not need advice from lay people. (1977, pp. 5, 6)

Readers can probably reconstruct the arguments for rejecting all of the four barriers. If more convincing data are needed to persuade educators of the fallacies in the apparent obstacles to person-to-person communication, it is easily possible to design action research to deal with the first three. Faced with empirical evidence that their ostensible reasons are not valid, educators may be able to move to other, real obstacles such as anxiety over lack of skill and apprehension over possibly revealing that we may not be perfect after all. The fourth reason is a self-serving myth. Schools and their communities are part of a coherent, related whole. Democratic ideology and practical politics both deny the validity *and the utility* of the autonomous expert position.

It may seem as though this chapter is unbalanced, with a long treatment of school-initiated communication and a rather perfunctory consideration of community-initiated communication. This impression reflects the reality in most situations. There is much more evidence of outgoing—from the school—communication than there is of incoming communication. The Midwest Administration Center's survey on Cincinnati supports this position:

Another generalization which needs emphasizing is that the school-community communication program in Cincinnati appears to be largely a one-way effort, in that the Division of School-Community Relations is devoting most of its resources to the dissemination of information, to the relative neglect of improved "feedback" techniques. While the Board has recently employed a consultant to reflect feelings of the Negro community to the school system, it is questionable whether such a part-time effort is a real solution to the need for more effective opinion analysis and "feedback." (1968, p. 9-53)

The use of school employees, paraprofessionals, and volunteers, as well as teachers, as communication agents has been noted. In this case communication flows both ways. Additional ways by which the community initiates communication will be noted when we take up the topic of public relations. Because the predominant emphasis of such procedures (e.g., open house, budget hearings, science fairs) is public relations, they will be considered under that heading.

We have cited an Australian study to support our own investigations of communication between schools and communities. We shall suggest a reading from a Canadian source. Now, we close with findings from a British study. In their study of communication, researchers in the Cambridge Accountability Project sought answers to three questions. They asked:

1. Do the communication documents result in greater parental understanding?
2. Do they improve relationships between home and school?
3. Do they result in improvement in pupils' learning?

The evidence on the first question was "very encouraging," especially when interpreted in conjunction with discussions and all of the other channels of communication. On the second question: "It was obvious that parents appreciated the school's efforts to keep them informed and involved. There is little doubt that good will toward the schools was increased . . ." (Gibson, 1982, p. 329). Further, Gibson reported that the good will was "because parents came to recognize that the image presented in the documents matched the realities of school life" (ibid.).

The third question (improve learning) is one that researchers usually say is impossible to answer. The Cambridge Project staff admit that they cannot supply unequivocal evidence. They do, however, report that teachers and parents in the project *believe* that the communication improves learning. Their final argument seems to have logical validity: "It seems very likely therefore that as parental support and encouragement *is* a major factor in pupils' achievement, and as parents much value being kept informed and involved by schools, then good parent-teacher communication of the type discussed in this chapter is a vital contributory element in children's learning" (p. 330).

SUMMARY

In this chapter we adopted a broad definition of communication to include the transmission and reception of information, attitudes, and ideas. Public relations is one type of communication. School-initiated communication was discussed in the light of the findings of three studies. One of the problems observed was the need to translate the technical terminology of education into something intelligible to citizens. Community-initiated communication was seen to be relatively neglected and new channels will need to be devised.

Exercise 10.1
NOTEWORTHY?

Situation. A note written in pencil on a sheet of arithmetic paper is placed on the teacher's desk by Lori Lucas when she enters at 10:00 A.M. instead of the customary time. The note reads as follows:

> Mr(s). (Teacher's Name),
> Lori is late because
> I overslept.
> Mrs. Lucas

The teacher asks your advice because the reason for Lori's lateness is not one of those considered valid as described in the school handbook and the rules of the board of education. Lori has not been late previously, and the teacher is unaware of anything unusual in the home situation. The teacher has identified several possible courses of action and asks which, if any, is most appropriate.

1. Accept the note and file it in Lori's folder as you would any excuse note.
2. Write Mrs. Lucas and explain that the lateness must be recorded as unexcused because of the district policy.
3. Discreetly inquire of Lori as to the reason for her lateness.
4. Call Mrs. Lucas and politely remind her of the valid reasons for lateness to see if one of them might cover the situation.
5. Ask the attendance officer to check it out.
6. Ask for an interview with Mrs. Lucas.
7. Do nothing until the next parent interview day, and then "discover" the note in Lori's folder and go over it with Mrs. Lucas.

Directions. The teacher has already ruled out 5 as overreaction. Which option seems most appropriate to you? Poll your graduate class and see which options are most popular. Also identify other possible courses of action.

Finally, try to identify what concepts of communication and/or community relations support your decision.

Exercise 10.2
APOCALYPSE NOW!

The following letter to parents was typed by the PTA secretary and distributed with the permission of the Jefferson (fictitious name) School. Some of the alarming incidents are true (the break in), some are false (drunks driven home), others are, at best, rumors. The letter is not edited. It was mimeographed.

Dear Parents:

The executive board of the Jefferson PTA held its regular monthly meeting on Tuesday, March 13. We would like to thank the concerned parent whose letter was read to us at that meeting. This letter, along with comments from members of the board, brought to light many problems that exist in our schools at this time. It is the purpose of this letter to bring these to your attention, and we hope you will discuss them with your children.

1. There have been repeated incidents of strangers driving around both schools trying to entice youngsters into their cars. Please stress the message to your child never to talk to strangers or go with anyone but to immediately "run home and tell your parents."

2. We have a very definite drinking problem in our community, not just teenagers, but also our grammer [sic] school children. On Saturday, March 10, Jefferson School was broken into and a "beer party" was held in the kindergarten room. One youngster was apprehended. It is also a known fact that students have come to school drunk and have had to be driven home by our principal.

3. There are continuing reports of vandalism. On the weekend of March 3–4, there were 35 windows broken at Jefferson. Youngsters have been harassing area residents who have come to school seeking our help because their property has been vandalized.

4. Children, as young as 5th graders, are continually seen in the alleys on their way to and from school smoking (who knows what!). It is planned that a special night meeting will be held to get community input on these very pressing matters. We *can* make this a better place to live and also a safer environment for our children.

We urge you to discuss these matters with your children. Please make them aware and be aware yourself that these problems do exist. If you or your children have any information concerning these problems, or if you have a suggestion on what can be done to help this situation, we ask that you contact any board member or our school principal.

We also ask that you acknowledge receipt of this letter and show your cooperation by signing and returning the bottom portion to the class teacher.

In the Interest of All Children,
THE JEFFERSON PTA BOARD

NAME _____

CHILD'S NAME _____ ROOM _____

Directions. Consider:

1. The effect of this communication on recipients.
2. The propriety of sending the PTA board communication home with students.
3. The effect of poorly reproduced, imperfectly punctuated documents on the image of the school and its faculty.
4. What you as the principal would have done when requested by the PTA board to disseminate the message.

Exercise 10.3
THE MESSAGE IS THE MESS

An actual attempted school-to-parents communication is reproduced below. It was signed by five teachers and sent home with pupils in a suburban school. After you have read it, consider these issues:

What was the intent of the communication?
Was this intent successful?
What error, if any, is involved in the list of class rules in a statement purporting to be a "Discipline Plan"?

What problems can you foresee in the seemingly logical progression of sanctions in the list of "Negative Choices"? Consider the "Positive Choices," especially 3. How could this communication be best accomplished? Finally, what are some possible unintended reactions by parent recipients of this message, and how would you as an administrator deal with such issues?

Dear Parent:

In order to guarantee your child, and all the students in our classrooms, the excellent learning climate they deserve, we are utilizing the following Discipline Plan. We believe that all our students can behave appropriately in the classroom. We will tolerate no student preventing us from teaching or any student from learning. Because your child's education is a cooperative effort between home and school, we want you to be aware of what the Discipline Plan involves.
  Our Class Rules:
  1. Follow directions the first time.
  2. Raise hand for question or comment.
  3. Stay in seat (feet on the floor).
  4. Quietly prepare to start work two minutes after change of subject.
  5. Bring all supplies to class: sharpened pencils, paper, supply box (with glue, crayons, and scissors), and books.

Establishing these class rules gives to your child the option of following or breaking them. Below is an outline of the consequences of both choices.

Negative Choices

1st consequence—loss of noon recess.

2nd consequence—loss of recess and 30-minute detention.

3rd consequence—loss of recess, 45-minute detention, and call to parents.

4th consequence—loss of recess, 60-minute detention, and parental conference.

5th consequence—all of the above, principal conference, and removal from classroom.

Positive Choices

1. We will let your child know immediately that he/she is behaving appropriately.
2. We will send regular notes to you to notify you of your child's appropriate behavior in the classroom.
3. The students of each classroom will work together to earn classwide special events. We keep track of "bonus points" by dropping marbles in a jar when one or more children are behaving appropriately. On reaching a target number of points, the entire class will participate in an activity such as those listed below. Our extra activity might be an art activity, gym period, extra recess, or a popcorn party.

Utilizing this plan, we can be in closer contact with you regarding your child's progress in the classroom. If you have any questions, please feel free to call or write to us at any time.

Sincerely yours,

Dear

I read and understood the Discipline Plan for your classroom.

_____
Parent/Guardian Signature

SUGGESTED ACTIVITIES

1. Collect all the routine forms currently in use at a school. Assess their legibility, clarity, and tone. Select the least effective of your collection and try to improve it as much as you can.
2. Go through all of the incoming communications from parents to the teacher for one class for one month. Put them in appropriate categories (e.g., excuses for absences, permission notes, requests for information).What can you say based on your examination of this correspondence?
3. Prepare a one-page letter to parents of your class telling them what you expect to accomplish in the next month (term, year, whatever). Try it out on your colleagues and revise it until you are confident that it is clear. Then try it on some friends who are not educators and get their impressions of the meaning of your letter.
4. Make a survey of citizens on one city block. Find out what concerns they have about the schools. Try to find the appropriate communication channel to supply the information needed. If one doesn't exist, invent it.
5. Attend meetings of the PTA, Mothers' Club, or equivalent organization. Compare actual attendance with potential attendance. Interview some parents to find out why they do not attend. Suggest procedures that could remove obstacles to attendance.
6. Go over the report card form in use in your school with a pupil and his parent. Compare their perceptions of what the entries mean with your own. Do the same with another teacher and an administrator.

SUGGESTED READINGS

Coursen, David. "Communicating." In *School Leadership: Handbook for Survival*. Eds. Stuart C. Smith, JoAnn Mazzarella, and Philip K. Piele. Eugene, Ore.: ERIC Clearinghouse on Educational Management, 1981, pp. 194-214.

Goldstein, William. "What Are the Signposts? How to Communicate with Simplicity, Clarity." *NASSP Bulletin* 66 (451) (February 1982): 53-59.

Harris, Roger. "Parent-Teacher Contacts: A Case Study." In *Linking Home and School*. 3rd ed. Ed. Maurice Craft, John Raynor, and Louis Cohen. London: Harper & Row, 1980, pp. 165-76.

Hepworth, Eugenia B. *Parents as Partners in Education: The School and Home Working Together*. St. Louis: C. V. Mosby Co., 1981, Ch. 4.

Kindred, Leslie W.; Bagin, Don; and Gallagher, Donald. *The School and Community Relations*. 3rd ed. Englewood Cliffs, N.J.: Prentice-Hall, 1984.

Lucas, B.G., and Lusthaus, C. S. "Parental Perceptions of School Communications." *Canadian Administrator* 17(2) (November 1977).

REFERENCES

Banas, Casey. "Latest City High School Tests Yield Grim Scores." *Chicago Tribune,* April 26, 1982.

Brownell, Samuel M. "Give Visitors a Good Impression." *Executive Educator* 4(4) (April 1982):37.

Cronin, Joseph M., and Hailer, Richard M. *Organizing an Urban School System for Diversity.* Lexington, Mass.: Lexington Books, 1973.

"The Dallas Monster." *Time,* February 18, 1974, p. 59.

Gibson, R. "Teacher-Parent Communication." In *Calling Education to Account.* Ed. Robert McCormick. London: Heinemann Educational Books, 1982, pp. 319-30.

Hechinger, Grace, and Hechinger, Fred M. "Remember When They Gave A's and D's?" *New York Times Magazine,* May 5, 1974, pp. 84-92.

Keith, Lowell; Infelise, Robert S.; and Perazzo, George J. *Guide for Elementary School Administration.* Belmont, Cal.: Wadsworth, 1965.

Kindred, Leslie W. *How to Tell the School Story.* Englewood Cliffs, N.J.: Prentice-Hall, 1960.

Kromer, William F. "Communicating with Community." Paper presented at the 31st Annual National Conference of Professors of Educational Administration, Eugene, Ore., August 1977.

Larson, Knute, and McGoldrick, James H. *Handbook of School Letters.* West Nyack, N.Y.: Parker, 1970.

Lauerman, Connie. "Schools Sued; Asked Cost Data." *Chicago Tribune,* January 12, 1974.

Mamchak, P. Susan, and Mamchak, Steven R. *Encyclopedia of School Letters.* West Nyack, N.Y.: Parker, 1982.

Marx, Dionne J., and Milstead, Robin J. "A Better School/Community Dialogue." *Battelle Research Outlook* 2(2) (1970):27.

Mellor, Warren L., and Hayden, Martin P. "Issues and Channels in Communications Between a School and Its Parental Environment." *Journal of Educational Administration* 19(1) (Winter 1981):55-67.

Midwest Administration Center. *Supplementary Paper, Cincinnati Survey.* Cincinnati, Ohio: Cincinnatians United for Good Schools, 1968.

Postman, Neil, and Weingartner, Charles. *The School Book.* New York: Delacorte Press, 1973.

Saxe, Richard W. "Multiunit Schools and Their Communities." *Elementary School Journal* 75(2) (November 1974):103-11.

Sloan, Bonnie. "School-Home Communications." Educational Specialist Degree Thesis. University of Toledo, 1973.

Sumption, Merle R., and Engstrom, Yvonne. *School-Community Relations.* New York: McGraw-Hill, 1966.

11

PUBLIC RELATIONS

Neither do men light a candle, and put it under a bushel, but on a candlestick; and it giveth light unto all that are in the house. Let your light so shine before men, that they may see your good works.

(Matthew 4:14)

In this chapter we consider some public relations activities of schools. Our focus is on the local school and typical educators rather than on specialists in public relations. We shall advocate both an increase in the number and an improvement in the quality of public relations activities.

Another compelling reason for attention to public relations at this time is the widespread evidence of a weakening in the public's trust in the schools. We need not report the evidence of this educational malaise here. It is so prevalent that a recent text on school public relations is "addressed to principals, superintendents, public relations personnel, and school board members in . . . communities where open warfare has broken out between the education community and the public it is supposed to serve" (Hilldrup, 1982, p. ix).

Professional associations have clearly identified the crisis as one of confidence. The National Academy of School Executives offered a seminar in April 1982 titled "Bolstering Public Confidence in Your Educational Program" (American Association of School Administrators, 1982). The topics were:

Understanding the sources of public discontent.
Techniques to demonstrate district responsiveness to critics' concerns.
Educational accountability: Techniques to demonstrate student competency.
High visibility programs: more than frills—a matter of pride.
Working with the press to achieve accurate reporting.
Districtwide information dissemination.
Building-level community relations techniques.
The importance of projecting a positive districtwide image.

Phi Delta Kappa offered "Leadership Institutes on Restoring Confidence in Public Education" (Phi Delta Kappa, 1982). The American Association of School Administrators affirmed a continuing resolution as follows:

Public Confidence in the Schools
AASA believes that declining enrollments, shifting populations and changing financial patterns raise new issues relative to public support.

AASA shall establish as a major priority improvement in communications with the general public.

AASA, working in close cooperation with local, state and national organizations, shall initiate and vigorously support efforts to maintain public confidence in the schools. (1981, p. 28)

The National Education Association responded appropriately (see Figure 11.1) as did its affiliates; so too did the American Federation of Teachers and its affiliates. And so it went throughout the educational establishment. There was consensus that there was a lack of confidence by the public in educational institutions. There was almost as much agreement in the appropriate initial response: make better use of public relations practices to tell education's story in a manner that would regain the confidence of the public.

Figure 11.1
NEA Bumper Sticker

As evidence of the recognition of the new, crucial role of public relations note that the American Association of School Administrators distributed a course outline to educational administration professors in the *AASA Professor* ("NSPRA," 1982). The syllabus was prepared by the National School Public Relations Association (NSPRA) for three-credit-hour courses in School Public Relations. A twelve-page bibliography and a list of available NSPRA resources were also prepared.[1] The suggested course activities may be helpful to readers especially interested in public relations aspects of school-community relations. They also reveal the artificiality of boundaries between public relations and community relations; for just as our emphasis on community relations requires attention to public relations, so also does the NSPRA emphasis on public relations require attention to the complete area of community relations. The activities suggested for the NSPRA course in School Public Relations follow.

NSPRA Course Activities

1. Develop a school public relations (PR) program for a rural, suburban, or metropolitan school district. Begin by drafting a policy and conclude with a way of evaluating its programmatic effectiveness.
2. Design a questionnaire for a school survey that may be conducted by mail, telephone, or personal interview.
3. Structure and lead a panel or forum in discussion about a particular school issue.
4. Prepare a news release on a school event for the local newspaper, radio station(s), or television station(s).
5. Write and submit for publication an article that focuses on some aspect of school PR.
6. Prepare an oral or written report that interprets clearly and positively the student test scores of a typical school district.
7. Write a case study which, when resolved, illustrates the effective application of a communication principle or strategy.
8. Prepare a brochure for a building or budget campaign.
9. Set up a charter for a community advisory committee or council.
10. Choose a community and analyze it in terms of its power structure.
11. Develop an in-service program to communicate to administrators and staff their respective roles in a school PR program and present it to the class.
12. Prepare a thirty-second school public service announcement for a local radio or television station.

---

[1]For information about the availability of these materials, contact Dr. John Wherry, Executive Director, National School Public Relations Association, 1801 N. Moore St., Arlington, Va. 22209.

13. Design a research-based evaluation instrument to determine the effectiveness of a school PR program and use it to assess one area of an actual program.
14. Prepare a job description for the recruitment of a school PR specialist.
15. Prepare a slide presentation for a building campaign.
16. Develop a marketing plan to encourage enrollment in adult classes for a school's publics, tailoring appeal to specific audiences.
17. Write a scenario depicting the role of the school PR specialist in the twenty-first century. Describe media, methods, mode of school, and nature of community.
18. Outline a PR campaign to improve staff morale.
19. Outline a finance election campaign to gain community support for a school tax rate increase.
20. Prepare a ten-minute speech on "Facts About Your School" designed for presentation to a civic organization and deliver to the class.
("NSPRA," 1982, pp. 11-12)

Readers may wish to complete one or more of the recommended course activities. They serve as an orientation to this chapter. They represent learning activities of a typical course in school public relations.

In the first chapter we adopted a meaning for public relations that restricted it to efforts by the schools to inform and influence the community and bring about cooperation and support. There is no impropriety associated with public relations. On the contrary, public relations practices are necessary to respond to the public's right to complete information about its schools.

Professional public relations personnel are commonly assigned to the school district central office. They prepare publications and press releases. They maintain liaison with representatives of all communication media. They can compose, edit, crop pictures, arrange multimedia presentations. They are able to advise and assist school administrators and should be consulted early and often. There is a wealth of information on the techniques of public relations for professional public relations personnel. (See, e.g., "School," 1971; and National School Public Relations Association's "Educational Public Relations Standards for Programs for Professionals," n.d.)

Having taken note of the availability of expert help, we turn our attention to the amateurs. When it comes to public relations, all educators serve as more or less talented amateurs. Hence, most public relations practices in education are conducted by amateurs.

Among resources to help amateurs are two quite different

textbooks. Frank Mayer's *Public Relations for School Personnel* (1974) is comprehensive and dispassionate. The chapters and appendices provide the skeletal framework for a planned public relations program. Hilldrup's *Improving School Public Relations* (1982) is a provocative polemic in which the writer's philosophy is clearly evident. When one shares Hilldrup's values, and most administrators will, he is delightful reading. Perhaps there is a concept of public relations to be found in a comparison of the two approaches. We leave this question to readers and begin our survey of school public relations with the press.

The Press

The educator who is also the amateur public relations officer must deal with the professional press. This will continue to be necessary no matter what governance bodies are operative or what organizational patterns are adopted. Perhaps another personal recollection may be allowed to emphasize an important point in this relationship between the amateur (the educator) and the professional (the reporter or photographer).

In my early years as a teacher one of my additional duties was serving as sponsor of the school safety patrol. Early in the year one of my patrol boys, Eddie Morlan, was credited with saving the life of a kindergarten pupil by snatching her from in front of an approaching car at some risk to himself. A school assembly was arranged to honor Eddie and present him with an award from the Motor Club, which then served as a patron to all safety patrols.

The newspapers covered this event. They took several pictures. At the end of the program, one photographer asked Eddie to pose standing on a table with his award with all of the other pupils crowded around pointing at him with fully extended arms. This seemed absurd to me at that time (it does even now) and I told the photographer what I thought of his idea. He looked at me a moment and then remarked, in a pained manner, "Do I tell you how to teach school?"

The absurd picture was the one that appeared on the back page of the paper. The photographer knew his business, or at least he knew what his editor wanted, and that may amount to the same thing. As a slow learning amateur (I especially disliked the predictable shot of the children bursting out of the doors on the last day of school), I have questioned other media professionals over the years with predictable results. They know their craft.

Not everything will be deemed newsworthy by the representatives of the press. Bowers and Law (1982) studied the coverage of educational news by four Virginia papers for a four-month period. During this time there was a total of 392 articles. Articles were sorted into ten categories. The distribution of articles is shown in Table 11.1.

Table 11.1

**Educational News Coverage in Four Newspapers
by Category**

Category		% of Coverage
Finance		35.2
Local budgets	15.4	
Capital improvements	8.4	
Federal aid	3.8	
State aid	2.8	
Miscellaneous financial	4.8	
Curriculum		15.3
Bilingual education bill	3.6	
Sex education	2.8	
Textbook censorship	2.8	
Religion	2.6	
Vocational education	1.5	
Miscellaneous curriculum	2.0	
Litigation		7.7
Testing		6.9
Competency tests	3.8	
Standardized test results	3.1	
Integration		6.6
Busing	4.8	
Racism	1.8	
Special education		6.4
Teacher education		5.6
Certification	3.1	
Course work for teachers	2.6	
Superintendency		4.3[a]
Health and safety		2.8
Miscellaneous		9.2

Source: This table was prepared based on data in Bowers and Law (1982). Permission to use was granted in a personal letter (Bowers, May 5, 1982).

[a]Bowers and Law (1982) believe this to be an unusual amount of attention given to a superintendent who was forced to resign.

Readers can make their own interpretation of the table. A summary of the study appeared in the *Executive Educator* (1982). Obviously, finance dominates the educational news for the time being. It would be enlightening to replicate the Bowers and Law study in other areas. Unfortunately, they do not describe their procedures. Possibly they measured column inches of coverage and drew percentages based on the total inches of coverages. They may also have based their analysis on numbers of articles regardless of length. Either of these approaches fail to take account of placement, that is, front page or neighborhood supplement. Another approach to discovering what will be picked up by the press would be to consider all the attempts to secure publication by the school district and to analyze types rejected and types accepted.

Attitudes concerning the preferences and peculiarities of the press vary from the position that "Good News Is No News to Education Reporters" (Micklos, 1982) to more hopeful positions that all of the key elements of media are present in schools and thus schools are, in that respect, "good news" (Tilden, 1980, p. 4). Jack Bernstein takes the first position and advises us to "understand that bad news is good news to editors; they know that bad news is more avidly read than good news" (1982). His advice is to be forthright in responding to questions, tell your plans to remedy the situation, and get the bad news out of the way before it becomes a continuing story.

Advice on how to relate to the press abounds. Van Dusen (1982) offers advice to reporters as well as to school officials. Kennedy (1982) gives the reporters' side. Krajewski, a superintendent, gives his advice in the unique form of an interview with his reporter-daughter (1980). The Council for Basic Education devoted an occasional paper to *The Schools and the Press* (1974). The National Association of Elementary School Principals sent their entire membership a special publication titled "Working With—Not Against—the Media" (1982).

The Secondary School Principals Association established a continuing publication as part of their *Newsletter* with the revealing title "Building Public Confidence." One issue of this publication was "Working with Media Develops Good News" (1981). Several guidelines for working with the press were set down in this issue. We share the first five of these guidelines.

1. Get to know the reporters and editors covering your school. If you don't have a speaking relationship with them, pick up the phone and introduce yourself. Let them know that you would be happy to discuss educational issues with them.
2. Always be honest with reporters. Sometimes it's easy to respond to a question with a half-truth, but that could kill your credibility for years to come. In the long run, you will get a greater amount of positive coverage if you build a relationship of honesty with reporters even if that means a negative story now and then.
3. Suggest a list of story ideas from your school. Reporters generally have too much geography to cover to know the latest developments everywhere in their assignment area. A good focus is instructional activities. Do you have a project that is new, that uses unusual equipment, that involves the community, that adopts a new approach to teaching a traditional subject? All are story possibilities. You might brainstorm some story ideas with your staff and then suggest them to the reporters.
4. Don't be disappointed if all your ideas are not used. Remember, you are competing with many other institutions and individuals in your community. Keep trying. And there's nothing wrong with asking reporters what type of information would most interest them.
5. Keep your head about errors. If there is a mistake in a story, don't phone the reporter's boss and make a federal case out of it. The error may not even have negated the thrust of the story. A calm, low-key phone call to the reporter is appropriate to ensure that the mistake won't happen again.
(Reprinted with permission from the National Association of Secondary School Principals, *NASSP Newsletter,* February 1981)

The same issue of the *Newsletter* told readers how to prepare a news release. The usual but nonetheless important advice of including the "five W's and the H in the first paragraph" was offered—who, what, when, where, why, and how (p. 6).

Another lesson neophyte administrators should try to learn vicariously is that reporters are always on duty. Casual remarks made en route to a scheduled event may turn out to be more prominent in the report than the formal event. The simple lesson for educators who are relating to the press is this: if you do not want to see something in print, do not tell the reporter about it.

Some advice often given by veteran administrators to beginners is likely to lead to embarrassment for the educator and to a strained relationship with the third estate. I was often advised to insist on seeing all news reports in print before permitting them to be published. I can assure readers that this is a futile request. The press does not and will not operate in this way. Not only that, they will probably be offended by the request. Presumably such advice is offered by persons who feel that they have been misquoted, but have not attempted to apply the remedy they suggest to prevent this in the future.

Problems of press relations can be kept to a minimum if educators can acknowledge the freedom of the press. It is not that educators seek to censor news or even to deny access to the news. The trouble is that some of us do not admit that the press has the status of a basic institution in American democracy. When educators internalize the attitude that the press is present as a basic right and not on sufferance or with the permission of educators, the relationship should improve. When approached from this perspective, few reporters will not give careful attention to the suggestions of the amateur public relations educator.

If the press does not choose to use school press releases, it is the concern of the professional public relations person. It is not grounds to favor friendly papers and ignore others. Finally, the press is entitled to all the news, good and bad, and entitled to receive it promptly. Important events (sometimes called hot news) cannot wait for a carefully composed press release. It is good practice to let the school public relations person know when you have been interviewed by a reporter.

ROUTINE PUBLIC RELATIONS EVENTS

We turn from the press—where educators are the amateurs dealing with a professional press—to other public relations activities where educators are the experts. Some of the examples will ostensibly exist for purposes other than public relations. We maintain, however, that their public relations impact is as great or greater than the impact of the officially acknowledged purpose. If readers cannot recall this argument from previous chapters, it may be suggested by one example— sports. The ostensible purposes are physical education and the inculcation of attitudes of sportsmanship and fair play. The public relations function is to win support for the school, preferably by fielding a team that wins more games than it loses. A related public relations function is entertainment. There are more Machiavellian purposes to be served in some cases (e.g., diversion of attention or prevention of boredom and vandalism), but we need not be concerned with them.

Advice on routine public relations programs and events is available

from all of the professional organizations in addition to comprehensive texts such as Unruh and Willier (1974) and Kindred et al.
(1984). The American Association of School Administrators has
published *PR for School Board Members* (Bagin et al., 1976). The National
Association of Secondary School Principals published *Building
Confidence in Education* (Armistead, 1982). The National School Public
Relations Association provides *Building-Level PR Programs* (Magmer,
1980) and *PR Programs for Small, Suburban, and Large Districts* (Bachman
et al., 1980) as well as a host of other aids. And, of course, the
periodical literature regularly features articles about successful
practices in school public relations (e.g., Anthony, 1981; Lindsay,
1982; Trump, 1982). We begin our consideration of routine public
relations events with the most common, most routine parent
conference.

Parent-Teacher Conferences

A routine practice with great potential for enhancing or diminishing public relations is the regular parent-teacher conference. The time
at which these conferences are scheduled can convey consideration or
disdain for parents, especially working parents. The physical setting is
important. Teachers everywhere now know better than to expect
parents to occupy pupils' desks, but they do not all know that the
content of a parent-teacher conference is confidential. One can still
see lines of parents waiting their turn for a conference within hearing
distance of the conference in progress.

There are many opportunities to convey supportive or hostile attitudes throughout the conference. We can assume that teachers do not
wish to convey a negative attitude. We also assume that parents wish to
appear at their very best. Yet so often these conferences, instead of
improving communication, create new obstacles. The reasons for this
lack of complete satisfaction with the conference are not mysterious.
The situation is threatening to both parties. Parents are summoned to
hear someone else evaluate their children. Of course, they need an
objective appraisal, but it is folly to expect normal parents to be able to
be really objective about their own children. This is a most sensitive
task. We have already alluded to the reasons that teachers are appre-
hensive about the contact. Their tenuous role as expert is in jeopardy
before a partial judge.

We cannot deal with the expected defensiveness and anxiety of parents except through the actions of the teacher. Unfortunately, this extremely difficult and demanding task is virtually ignored in most teacher preparation programs. All administrators would be well advised to examine the assistance they offer teachers in preparing for conferences. Possibly in-service education will be in order. Role-playing and videotaping will reveal problems. Human relations and communications training may be indicated. Administrators and teachers' bargaining agents will need to acknowledge the wisdom of arranging some conferences before or after the usual school hours. A good set of suggestions for conferences is found in Unruh and Willier (1974, pp. 15-16).

Salt Lake City Schools provide each home with a set of guidelines (Thomas, 1982). We mention this practice and display the guidelines in Exhibit 11.1 at this point because of the possible influence of the guidelines in stimulating parent-initiated conferences and/or setting a tone for the initial routine parent-teacher conferences. A possible variation of the Salt Lake City form might be to add places for signatures of the principal, teacher, and parents. Another modification in wording would make it appropriate for the student also to sign the document. Of course this changes the emphasis from guidelines to a contract.

Bulletins and Newsletters

Most elementary schools and many high schools produce regular information bulletins for parents. Typically these announce the dates of meetings and holidays for special events, charity collections, and the like. Now that there has been a technological breakthrough from the hand-cranked duplicator machines, quality has improved greatly. Nevertheless, illegibility is still a frequent public relations error associated with publications produced by schools. The more difficult problem is the distribution system. Small children may lose the bulletins or forget about them for days or weeks. Ask any bus driver to tell you what high school students are likely to do with bulletins.

Despite the problems associated with bulletins for parents or newsletters as communication media, they are likely to continue to be among the most frequently employed by local schools. Educators preparing newsletters or similar publications may wish to begin by consulting their district public relations specialist, who can prevent common errors and give sound technical assistance.

Exhibit 11.1

Guidelines

GUIDELINES FOR PARENTS

Good education is the result of cooperative efforts from educators, students, parents and boards of education. The Salt Lake City Board of Education is committed to providing the best possible education through qualified and excellent teaching staffs, and fine educational facilities and equipment. Educators in the district are equally committed to offering your child opportunities to learn in supportive, humanistic classroom settings.

The other part of the team, you and your child, can work in cooperation with the schools so your child can achieve competencies in the skills needed for functioning in our community, state and the world.

You can help your child in many ways to make school time more valuable and important. You can encourage or praise . . .

- regular attendance
- arriving on time
- consistent homework
- quiet time without television or other interruptions when studying
- good school behavior
- appropriate rest hours and good nutrition

You can show an interest in . . .

- educational activities in the community
- school activities
- your child's teacher and other school staff members
- school community council, PTA or other community support groups

If you want more specific ideas on ways to help your child or to become better acquainted with your child's school work, talk to the teacher and the principal at your school. They will be glad to work with you on your special desires and needs. Your school board members will also be happy to talk with you.

_____   _____
President, Board of Education   Superintendent of Schools

Place these guidelines somewhere in your home where you and your child can see them easily.

_____

(Courtesy Don Thomas, Superintendent, Salt Lake City Schools)

One of the common errors is omitting the name of the school or other information that would identify the source of the information. This is easy to understand since most often the newsletter is carried home by the student. The person preparing the newsletter could easily assume that anyone receiving the publication from a student would know that it originated at the school.

Another common mistake in distributing bulletins and newsletters is to overlook some members of the faculty and staff when the publication is sent out. This is more likely to happen when only part of the school is directly concerned with the information. A moment's thought can provide any number of reasons why everyone should receive the information. For example, a primary grade teacher needs to know if the older student who usually picks up one of her pupils is going to be busy elsewhere—on a field trip or at a special program.

Administrators in other offices and other schools should be on the distribution list for all bulletins and newsletters. This permits them to make appropriate adjustments. For example, in my first principalship, our elementary school was only a few blocks from the high school. Occasionally this high school would have early dismissal for parent interview day or some special event. The first time that this occurred high school students on their way home came through our elementary school playground like a herd of wild horses, knocking the smaller children down in the sheer exuberance of unexpected freedom. After attending to an alarming number of bruises and contusions, I persuaded a friend at the high school to inform me of future early dismissals. It is much less time consuming (and in this case less painful) to have advance knowledge and time to make necessary adjustments.

Many of us in education do not believe that proofreading is necessary. It is easy to make a collection of funny and not-so-funny typographical errors to establish the need for careful proofing of bulletins and newsletters. With all the care in the world, some mistakes will end up in print. Without care, the result may well prove embarrassing and cause additional work for those who must clarify misunderstandings. And it is atrocious public relations!

The tone of the newsletter or bulletin is crucial. I have some in my collection that seem to have been prepared by retired servicemen— To, From, Re. Others seem to be friendly and informative. Even the salutation requires careful consideration. Many are addressed to

"Dear Parents" and this is probably as good as any for most purposes. A perfectionist might well raise a question, "whose parents?" but it is reasonable to use the term when the bulletin is meant specifically for parents and guardians of students and no one else. When a bulletin is intended for the entire community, another salutation seems in order. One school district uses "Friends of the Schools."

It should not be necessary to issue prohibitions or make criticisms in mass distributions such as newsletters or bulletins. Unfortunately some administrators believe it is necessary to include warnings needed only by a few in the broadside announcement. "It is expected that all attending the dance will conduct themselves like ladies and gentlemen." "Failure to comply with standards of conduct in the lunchroom will result in loss of the privilege of eating lunch at school." Such information is quite appropriate and parents and students alike have every right to be forewarned of the consequences of violations of the rules. The objection we raise here is only to the inclusion of such reservations in public relations communications. It is as though an acquaintance added a postscript to an invitation to a party: "Please note that I reserve the right to throw you out if you act improperly."

Bulletin Boards

The bulletin board should be kept current whether its purpose is primarily public relations, administrative, or instructional. The display of students' work, if properly acknowledged, can be a source of appreciation and support. Many schools are favored by a plethora of bulletin boards. These can and should be used and changed frequently. The administrator may have to exert personal leadership in orienting teachers to the use of such display areas. Many teachers mistakenly believe that bulletin boards are only showcases for superior products. Consequently, they devote undue time and effort to putting up the display when it is their turn, and look on the boards as more curse than blessing. The point that I think many administrators miss is that teachers will create their own overload of anxiety about the bulletin boards. Unless the administrator eventually counteracts the impression, they will perceive both the administrator and their colleagues as holding exalted expectations for the bulletin boards.

Everything we have said about bulletin boards can be applied to exhibits at the central office. If the duty is rotated among art teachers on a monthly basis, the excitement and diversion of energy can be as great as putting on a public exhibition. The purposes of the displays must be clearly identified and teachers must be kept from over-extending themselves because they misunderstand what is expected of them.

Telephones

For years the telephones of Chicago schools were unlisted. It was frequently stated that at least one more secretary would be needed in each school merely to attend to incoming calls. Now the telephones are listed and the dire predictions have failed to materialize. This incident is typical of a continuing problem in public relations. Whenever a request for more data or improved service is made, the protective instincts of administrators seem to take over. The request is too often met with untested reasons why it cannot be honored. For improved public relations, however, it would be better to respond with data rather than opinions. The listing of telephones could have been tested on a small scale forty years before social pressure forced the listing from a reluctant bureaucracy.

The telephone, now listed, needs to be answered and personnel need to be taught the procedures to be followed. The busy-executive-one-upmanship ploy of not getting on the telephone until the designated person is on the line seems presumptuous for public employees. It seems pompous for anyone and should be avoided if at all possible.

If a caller leaves a message, his call should be returned the same day. This is essential if the caller is not to receive the impression that he is being avoided or ignored. As we noted in Chapter 10, the practice of having students answer the phone is not a good practice.

Special Events

The public relations purposes of sports and some other activities are fairly evident. Commencement and graduation ceremonies give the schools an opportunity to win friends. Music performances entertain and persuade. Assemblies and programs have long been a part of the educational scene, a way of placing some small part of the school life on display. That the elements seen as appropriate for display are somewhat atypical and represent special areas of the curriculum is traditional. Forensics are the least popular of these programs and even these are designed to be more exciting and competitive than regular school lessons. That hardy perennial, the spelling bee, never was really a teaching device, but it survives as a highly questionable public relations practice.

Some really silly practices have been associated with school public relations attempts—even sillier than the bad old spelling bee. Consider the kindergarten graduation complete with cap and gown and Bachelor of Rhymes degree. That is really silly!

Science Fairs

Science fairs are still with us. It is to be hoped that they may some day join the spelling bee as quaint relics of a misguided past. Only the most naive educator believes that a project made by students has a chance of winning—if winning matters and, if one goes to competitive exhibits, it matters. Coaching by parents and teachers is endemic and projects constructed by parents are often poorly explained by their student demonstrators. Private resources, of material or advice, beyond those of the school are usually associated with winning exhibits. It is not fashionable to complain as yet about science fairs, but, when the dam breaks, we can expect to hear cries of resentment from teachers assigned to sit with students and exhibits during the contest while other unhappy teachers cover their classes—somehow. Surely, if an administrator with any professional autonomy wished to increase public understanding and support for science education, he could think of a better way. It is hard to think of a worse way. As administrators it may be your misfortune to be required by a benighted superior to carry out an inappropriate public relations activity. Your task in such a situation is one of limiting the damage and exploiting the more defensible aspects of the activity. A subsequent critique could lay the groundwork for modifications next time around. Begin by stating clearly the objectives that were to be accomplished by the activity.

Open Forums, Budget Hearings, and So On

It has become common to schedule occasional open meetings to permit citizens to express their opinions on educational issues and finances. To the extent that this is valid (that what the citizens have to say can make a difference), these meetings will be considered under the heading of citizen participation. Unfortunately many meetings are merely for public relations purposes, so that the board or superintendent can attest to widespread community input and even participatory democracy.

There is nothing objectionable in a public relations function designed to persuade the public that the professionals have done their jobs well. However, to pretend that such meetings are more than they are borders on deceit. It is easy to expose the ersatz community-participation meetings. Educators are not urged to give up the meetings, which can serve a useful purpose. They are asked to describe them honestly and not to pretend that they provide opportunities for decision making when they are merely giving information. There is a place for both kinds of meetings, but there is a real difference between the two that is often blurred by dishonest rhetoric. (It would be cruel to single out one example of this practice. It is ubiquitous. Visit one of the participation meetings and compare the actual event with the description provided beforehand.)

Open House

The periodic open house is the most readily accessible, legitimate means of building a good public relations image. The first task in planning this kind of special event is to make an explicit list of the objectives to be achieved. These should be placed in an order of importance, lest the accomplishment of a minor objective lessen the attainment of other more important objectives. For example, the objective of securing maximum adult participation could be ensured by bringing in a celebrity who has no connection with education. This could hurt the accomplishment of other objectives such as informing parents of an educational innovation or enabling parents to meet and interact with all teachers who work with their children.

Despite the concern about letting other issues detract from educational objectives, a wide spectrum of interests must be considered in planning the open house. It is good practice to schedule the time so that it does not compete with other events important to many members of the groups you hope to involve.

It is deflating to the egos of educators but realistic to avoid, if possible, competition with favorite television programs. In the early days of television, principals knew better than to schedule their open houses on Wednesday evening opposite the Wednesday night fights if they wished to have maximum representation of male participants.

Avoiding this conflict is a reasonable precaution. Going to the other extreme of inviting fighters or ball players (or whatever the current object of interest may be) to be featured speakers is shortsighted in view of the hierarchy of objectives to be accomplished by the event.

The actual program of the open house will vary according to the objectives set down. It is common to have parents exposed to the entire staff and curriculum by arranging for them to walk through an abbreviated version of the actual schedule followed by their children. Another common format is the large general meeting with a speaker or a panel of speakers either preceded or followed by visits to individual classrooms, ending with "coffee and" in the cafeteria or gymnasium.

One of the most difficult aspects of combining a large group meeting and classroom tour is the accessibility of teachers. All parents need to be recognized for at least a few minutes by the teacher and there just is not enough time for this. To complicate matters, some of the more outgoing parents may monopolize large segments of the time available at the expense of less aggressive persons who will be hurt and offended if the final bell rings before they have had their opportunity to chat with the teacher.

As if this were not enough of a problem for teachers, there is the matter of what is discussed. As we pointed out previously, information about the conduct and achievement of students is confidential. To reveal such information to others waiting impatiently for their turn with the teacher is unethical and may well meet the legal conditions of slander. If the physical setting is such that confidentiality is impossible, how, then, is the teacher to meet parents' expectations for the answers to the usual queries: "How is Mary doing?" or "Is Johnny behaving himself?" Obviously, the objective of providing an assessment of the student's progress cannot be met in this type of event. Nevertheless, many educators continue attempting the impossible.

One tactic intended to encourage more adults to participate is to provide some kind of attendance register. There may be a guest book in each room or one master register at the main entrance where parents "sign up" for all the rooms that are entitled to credit for their presence. Perhaps parents will be asked to write their names on the chalkboard so that students can see the list the next morning. Some teachers place packets of papers at each student's desk to be taken home or initialed by the parent. The variety of practices is unlimited.

Administrators and teachers too will want some kind of record of attendance at the open house. The practice of a symbolic or real reward to the winning class requires careful consideration. Clearly the inducement of a reward is extrinsic to most purposes of attending the open house. It is unfair to make any assumptions about those who do not or cannot attend. In some cases the rewarding of some can result in the unintentional punishing of others. Consider the competition for an ice-cream treat for all students in the room with the most parents represented at open house. Recently, when this happened in a middle-class suburb, the turn-out of parents (admittedly unrelated to the ice-cream prize) was outstanding. Of two fifth-grade rooms, one was represented 100 percent by parents, the other was lacking only one parent. The guilt of being recognized as the student who had personally (by his unfortunate choice of parents) cost his entire class a treat was not easily borne by the one boy. We need to collect our attendance data in less competitive ways.

DISCUSSION

Both routine and special events should be designed with a view to providing public information in a manner most likely to justify public approval and support. This recommendation is so obvious that it seems trite even to state it. Perhaps that has something to do with the perplexing realities of school-community relations, which often seem to ignore this principle. Educators may neglect the observance of the principle because it is taken for granted. That is, schools often provide information in ways that can confuse and alienate the public. This is one violation of good practice that is associated with an overly rigid bureaucratic orientation to the community. This type of error conveys the implication that "lay people" should refrain from meddling in professional business and do only what they are directed to do. The consequences of this syndrome were delineated in Chapter 2 on bureaucracy and school organization.

There is another class of error which is at the opposite pole of the bureaucratic hostility syndrome. This is the hard-sell, manipulative approach that places emphasis on impressing the public by any means that work without undue reliance on the facts. The assumption seems to be that if our public relations tactics are clever, the public will believe in us, and it is essential that they believe in us for their own good. This huckster approach to public relations can be associated with good sound educational programs as well as with chaotic, ill-conceived disasters.

Perhaps a discussion of some public relations practices may clarify errors of the second type. An article in the *Toledo Blade* was headed: "Sultry, Sexy Voice Coos Facts of School Construction Plans" (1973). School officials were seeking support of a $6 million bond issue needed to start a vocational education program, build a middle school, and construct ad litions to the high school. The article began as follows:

Come a little closer while I tell you about some v-e-r-y appealing figures," a sultry sexy voice coos, accompanied by the figure of a seductive, scantily clad woman. "Sorry, no skinny dipping," Cleopatra says about a proposed swimming pool for _____ High School.
In _____ school district, Cleopatra is everywhere—in slide shows, posters, signs— extolling the virtues of the district's proposed expansions.

Aside from the possible reactions from women's liberation groups (the teacher who prepared the materials thinks that "it's a compliment to use her [Cleopatra] to tell the story as opposed to Mark Antony"), the campaign seems inappropriate in many ways to represent a school building project. For one thing, the seductive approach of Cleopatra is irrelevant and dishonest in that the Empress of the Nile has nothing whatever to do with the project. As far as an educational project goes, there are certainly more appealing and honest approaches inherent in vocational education and the new school. The adjective "appealing" above may be a poor choice, but for educational purposes it can be maintained that enabling a potential dropout to gain self-respect and an occupation is, in its way, more "appealing" than the cute sex symbol. It is at least honest and related to the project.

Moreover, the campaign suffers from an excess of cuteness—"no skinny dipping!" Here the use of public relations tactics has come into what may be a confusion of means and ends. If my analysis is correct, the means are tasteless and dishonest. The fact that a noble end is at stake does not justify deceptive means. We shall never know the effect of this particular campaign. The issue may pass in spite of the approach rather than because of it. If it passes because of the slick campaign, the district may have sold the public something it does not want and will not support.

Other tried and true public relations practices are so patently absurd that one can only conclude that their continued existence is a tribute to tradition and a rejection of creative thinking. Consider the fund-raising gimmick of "Duck the Principal" or teacher or superintendent. In this carnival event, students buy baseballs to throw at a target that dumps the celebrity into a tank of water. Buying turns at throwing pies is a variation on this theme. The reasoning is that the event shows that the authority figure is a good sport at the same time as it provides an opportunity to raise funds by capitalizing on the student's hostility toward the good sport. This type of event seems ill-conceived and more likely to perpetuate disdain rather than increase respect for authority. Doubtless it would have vanished long ago if it were not for the implication that one is not a good sport if he or she does not accept the challenge. There are thousands of ways to use the talents of leaders. This type of activity is one of the least effective imaginable.

Making authority figures appear in the role of victim is related to another common tradition of casting them in the role of clowns for public relations or fund-raising purposes. The athletic contest between student and faculty (volleyball, basketball, baseball) is, if free from pressure to participate, a more harmless version of this. Typically the faculty presents itself in outlandish costume and may or may not participate seriously. The need for promoters of these comic events is to respect the human dignity of the participants, students as well as adults. Failure to do so is to use bad means to accomplish a good end. This will not be effective public relations in the long run.

The specific examples used above may seem extreme. I hope they do. Their use is intended to demonstrate excesses of the improper application of public relations practices that are not appropriate to the purposes to be served. Disdaining all efforts to court public favor is an extreme error of one type. Making the cultivation of public support an end in itself is another kind of error.

SUMMARY

We have seen the need for more open, better-designed public relations programs. We have not observed appropriate responses by educators. Much remains to be learned, to be done, before we even begin to meet the new demands of the public for clear, valid information and an open attitude that will regain their trust in education. None of this, we have maintained, will amount to anything but a sham if the substance of our actions—the teaching/learning functions—is not well done. The challenge is to work on the basic instructional mission at the same time as we deal with the ever-present, but newly important, task of public relations—all this with diminishing resources.

Despite the real or imagined shortcomings of public relations efforts, we maintain that they are now needed more than ever before. Because of the apparent lack of confidence in institutions everywhere, it is necessary that education, as well as the other institutions, find ways to inform the public. The identification and reaffirmation of purpose jointly by the educator and the citizen, the school and the community, can best be achieved at local levels. Whatever we call this—and it is certainly more than accountability—it will require increased public relations activities. It is important that the public relations activities be honest and continuous. Information programs cannot be put forth sporadically at decision-making times (elections) or transformed by glamorizing the spokesman and the message. Full and honest public relations in more and different ways will be required.

In summary, we noted the public relations significance of routine educational activities as well as special events. It is assumed that large school systems will make professional public relations help available for consultation and specialized public relations activities. Most of the public relations work will be done by educators serving as amateur public relations persons. The press, like education, is one of the basic institutions of a democracy and educators need to approach press relations in this context. We noted errors in public relations ranging from an apparent rejection of public relations as a legitimate concern to the embracing of public relations as an end in itself. Neither of these extremes is suitable to the present needs of schools and their communities. Throughout the chapter we have noted a vast and currently growing literature on the subject of public relations for schools.

Exercise 11.1
DIFFERENT STROKES

If you are working with colleagues in a course, each of you should independently prepare a brief news release or announcement dealing with the same set of facts but for different audiences. The facts can be those provided here or the actual details of a current happening in one of your local districts. The audiences should include:

Chamber of Commerce
School district employees
American Legion
Tax-savers association
Local AFL-CIO affiliate
Chapter of NAACP
Boosters' Club

Content. As noted, the content of the release could be topical or one of the following. (Use the usual who, what, why, when, where, how format. Be sure to list a contact person.)

1. *No Mill Stream?*

The board of education is placing a seven-mil increase in the operating levy on the ballot. It has been defeated twice before.

The money is pledged partially to raises for district employees and for urgent building maintenance.

If the levy is not successful, the district cannot operate for the full school year.

Three school closings are scheduled to economize in response to declining enrollment.

2. *Pot Luck*

Several drug-related incidents have occurred in and around a district secondary school. The principal proposes to cooperate with law enforcement agencies including legally sanctioned dog searches of lockers, use of informants, and criminal prosecution of users as well as pushers.

3. *Other Issues*

Directions. After the releases/announcements have been prepared, compare them for content, style, and tone. What concepts seem to have been observed in the design of the messages? What are the implications of this phenomenon for administrators?

SUGGESTED ACTIVITIES

1. Collect a number of letters to the editor that deal with education. Classify them by issue and by attitude, approving or disapproving, toward the schools. Try to find out how an editor decides which letters to print. Find out if a school administrator takes any action in response to criticism or suggestions offered in this manner.
2. Make a scrapbook of all school news published during a year. Classify articles in whatever way seems appropriate (e.g., sports, innovations, personalities, controversy, finance). Rank order the subjects according to number of articles in each.
3. Prepare a news release about a forthcoming educational event. Ask a public relations professional or a reporter to criticize your news release. Revise the release according to the suggestions offered, secure the necessary approval, and try to get your release published.
4. Attend an open house. Estimate the attendance of men, women, and children. Try to find out what aspect of the event has been most interesting to those present. If some children are involved in the program, find out how many visitors are related to the participating children. If no children are present, find out exactly how they were excluded. Note what the competition on television is for the time involved.

SUGGESTED READINGS

American Association of School Administrators. *Building Public Confidence in Our Schools.* Arlington, Va., 1983.

Armistead, Lew. *Building Confidence in Education: A Practical Approach for Principals.* Reston, Va.: National Association of Secondary School Principals, 1982.

Educational Communication Center. *The Public Relations Almanac for Educators, Volume 2.* Camp Hill, Pa., 1982.

Hilldrup, Robert P. *Improving School Public Relations.* Boston: Allyn & Bacon, 1982.

Kindred, Leslie W.; Bagin, Don; and Gallagher, Donald R. *The School and Community Relations.* 3rd ed. Englewood Cliffs, N.J.: Prentice-Hall, 1984, Part III.

Mayer, Frank. *Public Relations for School Personnel.* Midland, Mich.: Pendell Publishing Co., 1974.

National School Public Relations Association. *The Basic School PR Kit.* Arlington, Va., 1980. (Includes a variety of publications and materials. Contact the Association at 1801 N. Moore St., Arlington, Va. 22209.)

Ressig, Clinton. "Education's Bad Press." *Phi Delta Kappan* 57(4) (December 1975):272-73.

Unruh, Adolph, and Willier, Robert A. *Public Relations for Schools.* Belmont, Cal.: Fearon Publishers, 1974.

Walling, Donovan R. *Complete Book of School Public Relations.* West Nyack,N.Y.: Parker, 1982.

REFERENCES

American Association of School Administrators. "1982 Proposed AASA Platform and Resolutions." *School Administrator* 38(10) (November 1981):27-30.

_____ . Brochure: "1982 AASA/NASE Spring-Summer Seminars." Arlington, Va., 1982.

Anthony, Margaret. "How to Get Your School in the Limelight." *Executive Educator* 3(9) (September 1981):37-38.

Armistead, Lew. *Building Confidence in Education: A Practical Approach for Principals.* Reston, Va.: National Association of Secondary School Principals, 1982.

Bachman, Duane, Hamel, George F., and Kovalcik, Jerome G. *PR Programs for Small, Suburban, and Large Districts.* Arlington, Va.: National School Public Relations Association, 1980.

Bagin, Don; Grazian, Frank; and Harrison, Charles. *PR for School Board Members.* Arlington, Va.: American Association of School Administrators, 1976.

Bernstein, Jack. "Keep Cool but Do Not Freeze: Tips on Dealing with the Press." *Wall Street Journal,* May 17, 1982.

Bowers, Henry C. III. Personal letter, May 5, 1982.

Bowers, Henry C. III, and Law, Louise. "What Makes Educational News?" Unpublished study, James Madison University, Harrisonburg, Va., 1982. (Summarized in "Surprise: News Coverage Is Not All Terrible." *Executive Educator* 4[5] [May 1982]:8.)

Council for Basic Education. *The Schools and the Press: Occasional Paper Number Twenty-One.* Washington, D.C., 1974.

Hilldrup, Robert P. *Improving School Public Relations.* Boston: Allyn & Bacon, 1982.

Kennedy, Jack L. "Educating the Press to Provide Better Education Reporting." *Education Week* 2(1) (September 8, 1982):19.

Kindred, Leslie W.; Bagin, Don; and Gallagher, Donald R. *The School and Community Relations.* 3rd ed. Englewood Cliffs, N.J.: Prentice-Hall, 1984.

Krajewski, Robert. "A Superintendent Grills a Reporter." *American School Board Journal* 167(8) (August 1980):17-20.

Lindsay, Dianna M. "Making P.R. Everyone's Business—Especially Principals." *Ohio School Boards Journal* 26(6) (June 1982):20.

Magmer, Jeanne, with editorial assistance from Russell, Ronald. *Building-Level PR Programs.* Arlington, Va.: National School Public Relations Association, 1980.

Mayer, Frank. *Public Relations for School Personnel.* Midland, Mich.: Pendell Publishing Co., 1974.

Micklos, John, Jr. "Good News Is No News to Education Reporters." *Education Week* 1(32) (May 5, 1982):19.

National Association of Elementary School Principals. "Working With—Not Against—the Media." *Here's How* 1(1) (September 1982).

National Association of Secondary School Principals. "Building Public Confidence: Working with Media Develops Good News." *NASSP Newsletter,* February 1981, pp. 5-6.

National Education Association. Assorted slogans and bumper stickers, Washington, D.C., 1981.

National School Public Relations Association. *The Basic School PR Kit.* Arlington, Va., 1980.

_____ . "Educational Public Relations Standards for Programs for Professionals." Brochure. Arlington, Va., n.d.

"NSPRA Approves PR Syllabus." *AASA Professor* 5(1) (Summer 1982):1, 9-12.

Phi Delta Kappa. "Leadership Institute on Restoring Confidence in Public Education." Brochure. Bloomington, Ind., 1982.

"The School Public Relations Administrator." *ERS Circular* 3 (1971).

"Sultry, Sexy Voice Coos Facts of School Construction Plans." *Toledo Blade,* October 30, 1973.

"Surprise: News Coverage Is Not All Terrible." *Executive Educator* 4(5) (May 1982):8.

Thomas, Don. "Guidelines for Parents." One-page directive prepared by Salt Lake City Schools, Salt Lake City, Utah, 1982.

Tilden, Scott W. *Working with the Media.* Arlington, Va.: National School Public Relations Association, 1980.

Trump, John M. "Coast Is Clear for Developing School-Community Relations Program." *Ohio School Boards Journal* 26(6) (June 1982):19-20.

Unruh, Adolph, and Willier, Robert A. *Public Relations for Schools.* Belmont, Cal.: Fearon Publishers, 1974.

Van Dusen, Bruce B. "News-Media Relations: Telling It Like It Is." *School Administrator* 39(7) (July-August 1982):16-17.

12

ON CITIZEN PARTICIPATION

One who thinks about the relation of the school to the community which supports it will soon come upon questions of public policy which it would take an Einsteinian grasp of the calculus of felicity to answer.

(Willard Waller, *Sociology of Teaching*)

In 1973 Professor Arthur Foshay of Teachers College Columbia began an essay by noting: "One of the very rare new ideas in education is that the community should participate fully in the schools" (Foshay, 1973, p. 5). Although Foshay had a particular meaning of *participation* in mind—a learning community concept—he acknowledged that the ideal might be unattainable (p. 9). Today the ideal is even less attainable and there is evidence of a trend[1] toward a completely different kind of participation—a participation that is a contradiction in terms, a nonparticipation. Many parents are electing not to participate in public schools on any basis. They are removing their children with or without promised governmental assistance of tuition-tax credits and vouchers.

It is possible, of course, to reason that those leaving public schools are in the best sense seeking a learning community, but it is a particular kind of learning community much different from earlier concepts of community. Our discussion in Chapter 6 on special and

---

[1]Let me put this discussion in perspective by noting that in my first draft of this chapter I used the word *danger* instead of the word *trend*.

changing communities revealed some of the problems of administrators seeking to serve a myriad of "communities" in one school or one district. We should not be surprised to find many potential clients dissatisfied with administrators' efforts. The import of this phenomenon (abandonment of public schools) is that we are able to add to the short list of new ideas in education. For the first time in modern U.S. history, there is a sentiment to modify the core value of free public education for all. Whether this is primarily due to economic forces, government intervention, or loss of confidence can be debated elsewhere; the result is a new situation for educators—all educators.

It is too soon to predict with any certainty the new condition of education associated with current trends. Perhaps, the public schools will find a way to cope successfully with and serve the newly evident pluralism of communities; or perhaps the trend to alternative schools serving particular communities of interest will prevail. The only certainty now is that the consensus in public education is lost. The issue is not whether it can be recovered but whether a new consensus can be found. It is in this context that we consider ways of increasing citizen participation in education.

WHY CITIZEN PARTICIPATION?

The reader will have long since identified an assumption implied in all preceding chapters: that increased citizen participation in education is desirable. Practices that put people and communities at a distance or in the position of adversaries have been disparaged. Practices that open the schools, lessen the distance between education and communities, and support cooperative relationships have been approved.

The ideological and political basis for this assumption is well known. From this perspective, we can support increased citizen participation in education whether or not it can be established that the increase in citizen participation is accompanied by an increase in student achievement or, for that matter, in anything else. Although we hold this position, we recognize that it is not persuasive to educators in general nor to the organizations that represent groups of teachers, administrators, and even boards of education.

What is lacking to ensure the support of the professionals is empirical evidence, reliable data, to support the argument that citizen participation results in educational as well as political gains (see Ornstein, 1973). These data are not at hand, and, moreover, it will probably not be possible to collect and analyze them by present research methods and technology. There are suggestions that bringing the school and community closer together will permit educational improvements, but they are merely suggestions (see, e.g., Scribner and O'Shea, 1974). The correspondence between participation and improved student achievement is far from clear. It would be unpolitic as well as untrue for anyone to promise educational gains as a result of decentralization, community control, or increased citizen participation of any kind.

Davies (1981) provides a much-needed caveat for advocates of citizen participation. According to Davies:

There is an unfortunate and naive expectation that student achievement will be advanced by nearly any form of parent or citizen participation. . . . This way of thinking dooms parent participation to being judged a failure. (p. 95)

He notes further:

In fact, the most effective ways of discrediting the concept of citizen participation in education [are] to claim and seek to prove that it will have a profound impact on economic, social, and educational problems that stubbornly resist solutions. Having grandiose expectations that new forms of citizen participation will have sweeping results that can be convincingly and accurately measured guarantees that those new forms will fail. (p. 94)

Despite these disclaimers that citizen participation is not the miracle cure for educational maladies—a kind of broad spectrum antibiotic, a penicillin—there are certain benefits clearly associated with participation. A careful study by Salisbury (1980) took an interesting approach: he sought to measure and evaluate the impact of citizen participation on the participant. Noting first that participation is institution-specific, Salisbury concluded that some participants were changed. To report the findings accurately, we must emphasize that Salisbury makes it clear that he is speaking of only a fraction of the small population that became active participants. Thus, he can conclude that in a short period of time there will be only small changes but not trivial changes. "Spread over time and space these small changes in direction can build a very different kind of community, with participatory norms, self-confident citizens, and the enhanced mutual understanding and respect that so often accompanies active citizenship" (p. 200). Moreover, the changes may be profound for the individuals concerned.

Bowles' exploratory research (1981) found that the variables of school-community relations programs have virtually no impact on student achievement. However, his conclusion about models for school-community relations programs complements some of the studies reviewed in Chapter 3 (Stallworth, "Parent Involvement," 1982; Stallworth, "Identifying Barriers," 1982; Williams, 1982). Bowles concluded that there were perhaps four models for school-community relations programs:

1. If the desired outcome is public perception that a school has an effective program of school-community relations, then the school should communicate frequently and effectively.
2. If the desired outcome is increased student achievement, then the school should culminate its school-community relations activities in resolution and develop the problem-solving and conflict resolution skills of *all* its personnel.
3. If the desired outcome is a sense of institutional legitimacy by adults in the community, then frequent and effective communication should be the primary process effort.
4. If the desired outcome is change of macro public policy or practices (hypothetical), then participation should be the primary process effort.

More endorsement for participation is implied by Howey's report (1980) on successful schooling practices. One of six themes found by Howey to be associated with successful school practices was the quality of teacher-community relationships. This was more specifically identified as a consistent set of values between the faculty and the community and community support. In effective schools parents initiate a greater number of contacts with schools. Lezotte (1982) would support Howey's findings, as would Hill (1982).

One of the strongest research-based arguments—this one specifically for parent involvement—comes from Henderson (1982). In reviewing over thirty recent studies, Henderson concludes: "Parent participation, however defined, improves student achievement, however measured." These are strong words, indeed, but they are qualified somewhat in the accompanying review of studies. Henderson adds: "While we know that parents are central to the learning process and that many current programs work well, we are far from knowing what kind of parent involvement programs and processes work best. In fact, we are far from convincing many educators and parents, much less the Reagan administration, that it is necessary—and cost-effective" (p. 3).

Even though we have noted the optimistic reports of Henderson, Hill, Howey, Lezotte and others, we cannot, at this time, base our argument for citizen participation on gains in student achievement. Participation could even be irrelevant to achievement, although this possibility becomes more remote as studies accumulate. Despite this admission, we shall next consider additional means of encouraging citizen participation. Our rationale is that participation is part of the democratic ideology. It is needed to legitimate the schools. It makes new resources available to the schools. These considerations permit us to view participation as an end in itself while we await data to determine if it can be proven to be a means to facilitate student achievement.

PLANNING FOR CITIZEN PARTICIPATION

Rosener, in a brief but particularly important essay, makes the point that, although there are many problems associated with citizen participation, "Planning is the Achilles' heel of many citizen-participation programs. Insufficient time and analysis are devoted to planning, and, as a result, participation activities are selected arbitrarily" (1978, p. 109). To make a proper approach to planning, Rosener suggests that we answer the obvious, but nonetheless essential, questions of why, who, what, how, and when. Thinking first about the purposes of participation and then about what methods work best will avoid activities that may be under the control of educators but which ultimately satisfy no one.

Why

Logically, educators are almost compelled to begin any planning by considering the essential purpose to be served. None of them—none of us—has been spared the experience of lesson planning that begins with a statement of objectives and ends with an evaluation designed to ascertain, preferably by empirical data, whether or not and to what extent the objectives have been met. That question is third on Rosener's list of key questions: "Where do we wish the participation road to lead?" We have changed this question from "where" to "why." Rosener provides another set of questions to help us with our answer to "why." These are:

1. Is the participation intended to generate ideas?
2. Is it to identify attitudes?
3. Is it to disseminate information?
4. Is it to resolve some identified conflict?
5. Is it to measure opinion?
6. Is it to review a proposal?
7. Or is it merely to serve as a safety valve for pent up emotion? (p. 111)

The purposes of citizen participation will vary over time and at the same time. If readers will recall the types of participation identified in Chapter 3 on professional barriers, they can easily see how different purposes lead to different answers to all of the other questions.[2]

Who

The answer to the question "who" should be such that the citizen participation for which we are planning will be dictated by the purpose specified in our answer to the "why" question. Obviously, it must include all persons concerned with the effects, the planning, the implementation, and the participation. Readers are invited to make their own list of persons and groups who *might* be involved in the participation planned. We provide a start for a list of potential participants by providing examples of some of the more obvious groups:

Parents
Staff personnel (not teachers)
Community residents, not parents
Teachers
Chamber of Commerce
Scientific creationists
Others (don't forget other agencies and single-interest groups)

---

[2]The types of participation studied were school service, home learning, curriculum and instruction, and governance.

What (Functions)

Functions are essentially the answers to the second in the series of simple yet significant questions—"what." The complete question from Rosener is: "What are the specific functions we wish to have performed by this participation program?" (1978, p. 110).

Davies (1982, pp. 5-6) adapts the work of Windle and Cibulka (1981) to education in his answer to the functions question. These functions, phases of the policy process, are:

Authorizing
Enabling
Planning
Governing
Service-giving
Evaluating

Davies explains each with an example from education. *Enabling,* for example, means providing resources for a program, and Davies used the instance of "a parent association or local advisory group urging a school board to provide money to initiate or continue a school effectiveness project." Readers are asked to prepare their own list of functions by completing Table 12.1. The list of functions should be retained for use in an exercise that follows.

Table 12.1

**Incomplete, Prototypical List of Functions
of Citizen Participation in Education**

Function
1. Build support for schools.
2. Disseminate information about schools.
3. Measure opinions of citizens about an educational issue.
4. Solve or ameliorate a conflict.
5. Demonstrate the value of an educational practice.
6. Provide a means for concerned persons to be heard, to "let off steam," to have their say.
7. Establish priorities.
8. Demonstrate concern for meaningful participation in regard to an important decision.
9. Others.

Note: It is unmetric to stop at fewer than ten functions.

How

To answer "How should citizens be involved?" according to Rosener, one must consider timing, the kind and complexity of an issue, the quantity and quality of resources available, community characteristics, the political climate, as well as other factors (p. 114). Educators have been prolific in devising ways to answer the "how" question.(For a good example of techniques of involving citizens see Rich and Mattox, 1976).

Readers should experience little difficulty in generating a list of at least twenty techniques for citizen participation. We invite you now to make such a list by completing Table 12.2, which will also be most helpful for a subsequent exercise.

When

The timing of citizen participation activities is both an art and a science. Citizens are now sophisticated and can easily see through the sudden needs assessment timed to result in a report recommending an additional operating levy just in time to get it on the ballot. This may well be perceived as manipulation and, as such, be resented. It seems sensible that if citizens are to carry out the burdensome aspects of some service activity, they should participate early in the planning of the project.

Table 12.2

**Incomplete, Prototypical List of
Techniques of Citizen Participation in Education**

Techniques
1. Appointed advisory committee
2. Needs assessment
3. Open house
4. Telephone hot line
5. Attend PTA meeting
6. Volunteer playground supervision
7. Assist teacher (clerical, managerial)
8. Visit classrooms
9. Parent-teacher conference
10. Serve on a task force/committee
11. Others

Some questions of timing seem too trivial to mention, but perhaps the underlying concepts are worth identifying. Scheduling an important parent/citizen meeting in conflict with the current super-event on television is forcing some of our patrons to make a difficult choice. The underlying concept here is to recognize that citizens have multiple interests, and educators should avoid conflicting with these whenever possible—even at the price of occasional inconvenience to members of the educational family.

Techniques by Functions

We are now ready to apply the results of readers' creative efforts in completing Tables 12.1 and 12.2. Putting these data together in a matrix was suggested by Rosener who provided a list of fourteen functions by forty-three techniques at the end of her essay. That is your task in Exercise 12.1, Citizen Participation: Functions and Techniques.

Analysis of the matrix does not answer many questions about participation, but it does, at the very least, direct us to appropriate practices for each function. It forces educators to inquire as to the purpose of an activity before arranging it because it has long been a tool in our community relations kit. Too often we have relied on some practices (the ubiquitous open house) to serve functions for which they were ill suited. This could be a partial explanation of the apparent citizen apathy or lack of cooperation. Citizens may be quite appropriately apathetic or uncooperative about techniques that do not begin to deal with their particular concerns. To understand this phenomenon on a very practical level, consider these comments from a British study:

I no longer support the Parent Association because basically I don't like barbecues or cheese-and-wine functions. We are not motivated in terms of social contact with other parents, and barn dances . . . if it's going to be a social get-together, then we don't see any need for it. (Elliott et al., 1981, p. 112)

If an educator had sufficient lead time, it would be possible to move from the matrix to a more specific consideration of all techniques identified as being appropriate to deal with a given function. They could each be given a score on variables important to the educator. To suggest this procedure, assume that the function to be served is to disseminate information about schools. Four techniques in the portion

Exercise 12.1
CITIZEN PARTICIPATION FUNCTIONS AND TECHNIQUES

Directions. List the functions from Table 12.1 across the top and the techniques from Table 12.2 down the side. Then enter an X in each cell in your matrix where, in your opinion, the function will be served by the activity. We have entered the information for the first five functions and techniques as a sample.

Technique	Build support for schools	Disseminate information about schools	Measure opinions of citizens about an educational issue	Solve or ameliorate a conflict	Demonstrate the value of an educational practice	Be heard, let off steam	Establish priorities	Meaningful participation in important decision	Others
Appointed advisory Committee	X	X		X		X	X	X	X
Needs assessment				X					
Open house		X			X				
Telephone hot line			X		X				
Attend PTA meeting		X							
Volunteer playground supervision									
Assist teacher									
Visit classrooms									
Parent-teacher conference									
Task force/committee									
Others									

Table 12.3

Rating Techniques for Function:
Disseminating Information

	Criteria			
Technique	Cost	Feasibility	Probable Effect	Total
Advisory committee	4	4	5	13
Open house	5	5	2	12
Phone hot line	2	3	3	9
Attend PTA meeting	5	5	1	11

Note: If we were limited to only the techniques listed in Table 12.3, the choice of techniques would be the advisory committee. Obviously there are superior techniques to disseminate information, but of those listed the procedure favors advisory committees. There is a deceptive objectivity in assigning numerical ratings to criteria. Possibly this could be reduced by pooling the assessments of several persons. Readers might try this with their classmates. It should lead to a discussion about the different ratings given to the same technique by several persons.

of Exercise 12.1 completed as a sample were marked as contributing to that function. We would list all appropriate techniques and then rate them from 1 (poorest rating) to 5 (best rating) in each criterion, as in Table 12.3.

PARTICIPATION AND POWER

An element of any kind of participation, especially when we are considering groups, is power, influence, or control. A good way to consider how power may be involved in citizen participation is with Arnstein's "Ladder of Citizen Participation." (This source can be found in several places: Arnstein, 1969; Arnstein, 1971.) Arnstein describes eight levels of participation, ranging from no participation to complete citizen control. In Table 12.4 we attempt to apply his classifications to some types of citizen participation in education.

Table 12.4

**Arnstein's Ladder of Citizen
Participation and School Policy Formation**

Participation Level	Educational Equivalent
Citizen control	Free schools, complete community control
Delegated power	Community control of specific areas (e.g., personnel)
Partnership	Joint policy boards (Woodlawn Experimental Project)
Placation	Citizens on board of control (places usually allocated to representatives of groups on either community or central board of education)
Consultation	Local community hearings, surveys, needs assessment
Informing	Public relations practices, media, bulletins, letters
Therapy	Parent educational programs; recruitment of local leaders by paraprofessional salaries and socialization to educator norms.
Manipulation	Token advisory committees dominated by professionals or friends

Terms at the top of the table describe degrees of citizen power—citizen control, delegated power, and partnership. The central three levels describe degrees of token representation—placation, consultation, and informing. The lowest terms describe arrangements that permit no participation at all for citizens.

The educational equivalents that we provide as illustrations of Arnstein's levels need not always be limited to the level at which they appear in Table 12.4. The Woodlawn Experimental Project was identified as a "partnership" because community representatives shared power on a board with representatives of the schools. (Originally there were three partners: schools, community, and the University of Chicago. The university later released its places on the board to the community.) The recruitment of influential members of the community by giving them paraprofessional status was included as an example of therapy because that is one possible tactic open to educators. We do not imply that all paraprofessionals have been so recruited or even that the schools are seeking to do so. The example is the best we could conceive to show the meaning of *therapy* as a treatment of the citizen so as to cure him of wrong-headedness, that is, opposition to the policies of the educators. It also needs to be emphasized that the placement of a practice at a lower level is not an assessment of the usefulness of that practice. For example, needs assessment can be an example of token participation if that is the extent of citizen participation. When used in conjunction with other levels of citizen participation, needs assessment becomes a valuable, necessary practice in school-community relations. Table 12.4 refers only to the formal arrangements for participation.

Arnstein's typology was adapted by Cibulka and used in a study (1974) of district and school citizen advisory committees in Chicago between 1965 and 1970. Cibulka found the councils changing from consultation to informing to placation. When the pressure by the boards and the communities shifted to include their specifying how policy should be developed, the formal participation of citizens increased. Cibulka reasoned that this shift gave the boards more information, enabling them to hold administrators accountable for more formal participation. More importantly for our understanding of the phenomena of participation, Cibulka's study demonstrated that at no point was a high level of formal participation accomplished.

FORMS OF PARTICIPATION

Another excellent review of the characteristics of the usual types of citizen participation is *Citizen Organizations* by Yin et al. (1973). This is the report of a RAND Corporation study that "examines the possibilities for developing a viable and permanent institutional structure for citizen participation in government decision making, in the context of the programs of the Department of Health, Education, and Welfare" (p. v). The study was not aimed at *social* reform but at *administrative* reform to link citizen participation with the securing of specific services.

Participation Without Power

First the RAND study considered five forms of citizen participation that did not fulfill the study's criterion of giving power to citizens: volunteering, employment of paraprofessionals, grievance procedures, citizen surveys, and citizen evaluations. These forms should not be dropped from consideration because they can be used in conjunction with other modes of citizen participation.

As we mentioned in Chapter 9, it is common to use volunteers in schools. However, the report notes that "volunteers are usually not asked for and do not offer opinions about how programs should be organized, and they have at most little authority in the administration of routine activities" (p. 15). There are benefits for schools and for the volunteers in programs using volunteers but, used *alone,* volunteers do not bring power to citizens.

Paraprofessionals, especially in large numbers, may generate some small influence for citizens. Like volunteers, paraprofessionals may be effective in strengthening another form of participation that is capable of giving power to citizens.

Grievance procedures have the potential to reduce dissatisfaction and alienation for the complaining persons. Such procedures alone are not expected to increase the power of citizens. The usual routes for grievances are, first, to the school or agency involved, then to a representative (alderman, state legislator, congressman) or to the courts.

Citizen polls were considered in Chapter 8. It is possible that polls may collect individual opinions resulting in a broader, more powerful assessment than is possible by individuals acting alone. However, if no action need follow the poll, no power is changed. In any event polls are not likely to bring about important increases in citizen power over policies or practices in education. For polls to be important, educators must be convinced of the legitimacy of citizen views.

We have not discussed citizen evaluations—special program reviews conducted by teams dominated by citizens. In education, the closest thing to this has long been the survey. In evaluating schools, there are difficult technical issues that have tended to require professional assistance. There seems little interest in replacing professional surveyors by citizen-evaluators. If this mode of participation becomes an important tactic in changing power relations, it will probably be a result of the employment of professionals known to be of a certain persuasion to conduct the survey. We have all seen surveys whose goals of either firing or whitewashing the superintendent have been only partially concealed.

We turn next to a form of citizen participation that does seem to have the potential of enhancing citizen power: the citizen organization of boards and committees.

Participation That Enhances Power

Boards and committees can be classified by the level of authority that devolves to citizens. A governing board, at one extreme, determines policies, selects (and dismisses or rejects) personnel, approves budgets, and evaluates the quality of the service (education) provided. An advisory committee, at the other extreme, may serve only as a forum for the project staff to tell citizens about their program. Between these poles are committees of limited authority that have one or two limited responsibilities. The most important distinction is, however, between boards and committees (p. 25).

Studies of boards and committees support the conclusion that these forms of participation have an impact on the conduct of local public activities and services (p. 31). Nevertheless, participation on boards or committees is not likely to increase generalized trust in government. Moreover, bystanders—citizens who are not on boards or committees—are not likely to increase their trust because they can observe other citizens participating in government programs (p. 35).

The positive finding for participation was in the sense of having some effect on government actions: "a higher level of political participation is consistently associated with an increased sense of efficacy" (p. 36). This effect was not necessarily found in regard to participation in local school associations. Yin et al. conclude that "political participation generally is related to a general sense of political efficacy, but participation in local organizations may be related only to a sense of efficacy in regard to the specific program or activity" (p. 39).

PARTICIPATION BY INDIVIDUAL PARENTS

Because our emphasis is on groups of citizens we do not mean that educators have found the most effective ways of relating to individuals. Failures in this area are almost invisible unless they are so cumulative or so blatant that they cannot be ignored. Parent participation has been considered via their interest groups in Chapter 4 and directly and indirectly in all of the chapters dealing with practices of school-community interaction. Often, however, the preceding discussions have concentrated on involving citizens as a class. Conceivably, in the best of all possible worlds attention to the group needs would concurrently remove irritants to individuals. Since this is not a perfect world, educators will need to devise procedures for receiving and dealing with particular, personal problems of one or only a few citizens whether or not new forms of participation are adopted for the public in general.

The Enlightened Adversary Tactic

This parent-centered approach implicitly assumes an adversary relationship between parents and educators. The orientation is conveyed clearly in an early section of Ellen Lurie's book, *How to Change the Schools: A Parent's Action Handbook on How to Fight the System:*

My book is not the least bit intellectual; it is neither objective nor dispassionate. It is specific about the things I, and many of my fellow parents, hate most about the school system. And it suggests very tangible things other parents can do to try to change things. (1970, p. 8)

Lurie alerts her readers to abuses committed by schools and furnishes what is, in effect, a manual of tactics, to battle "the real enemy: the school system" (p. 266). Educators should read Lurie carefully—not to protect themselves against attack, but to gain a new perspective on their activities.

In most cases, Lurie's charges are well founded. If educators find that their own schools feature some of the deplorable practices she castigates, they would be well advised to take the lead in making changes—not to beat critics to the punch, but because it is the sensible, humane action required by the situation.

In the same genre as Lurie's *Handbook* is *The Third Side of the Desk* by Hannah Hess (1973). This is another guide for parents and has the subtitle *How to Change the Schools.* It is based on the case history of P.S. 84 in New York. Hess deals as much with curriculum and teaching methods as with confrontation tactics. Her goal is a more humane, child-supportive education regardless of the governance model that exists in the system: "to me, community control is only a tool to get good education. It is not an end in itself" (p. 271). If they cannot read the entire book, educators will certainly wish to study the "Screening Committee Questions" used to select a prospective principal (p. 260).

Although they have the same audience as Lurie and Hess in mind and the same purpose, Weinberg and Weinberg (1979) extend the adversary approach to new limits. To help educators see themselves as others may see them, we share this paragraph from their preface:

Teachers and administrators treat parents condescendingly or with contempt, handling the parents as they handle the child, high-handedly manipulating them out of their rights. Intellectually inferior, militant teachers have a ready arsenal for intimidating children and parents alike, in order to conceal teacher misbehavior and academic incompetence. This intimidation is intentional because of the educator's own concealed fears that parents might discover how inadequate teachers and schools are. (p. ix)

The Weinbergs then create vicious strawmen educators (e.g., Ms. Cana Handle, Dona Gottime, Ura Lyre, Reta Liate), who are then dealt with in a series of anecdotes. Unfortunately for the purposes of parent participation, the extreme hostility evident throughout their study makes it ill suited as a guide to behavior with real-life educators, who, whatever their faults, are rarely card-carrying monsters.

Legalistic Approaches

A more legalistic approach is taken by Freedom Through Equality, Inc., which assumes that, through existing rules and regulations, parents can make the schools respond. The slogan is: "Know Your Rights. See That Your Children Get the Education They Deserve" (1972, p. 1). The chapter headings of the publication, *A Handbook for Parents: Make the Public Schools Work for You,* suggest the scope of advice:

How to Assert Your Rights
How Your Child Can and Cannot Be Disciplined
What Schools and Classes Should Your Child Attend
Make Sure Educators Know You
School Records
Transportation
What There Is To Learn at School
Assistance Available to Needy Children
Title I Programs
Overcrowding and School Redistricting
Parent Groups and Community Organizations

Parents are advised that principals should be their first and strongest pressure point.

Principals are free to make many important decisions without going through the school board. They are close to teachers and students. They are responsible for knowing what is happening in their school and must be able to account for it to the school board. But you should not let them forget that their first duty is to the children in the school. (ibid.)

After reviewing a handbook such as this, educators may well wish to prepare one themselves if there is none available. One way to respond to the demand for accountability is to delineate guidelines of reciprocal responsibility similar to those set down in *A Handbook for Parents.*

Rational-Democratic Approaches

Rioux et al. (1980) provide another well-reasoned, data-based resource for parents, as does Davies (1976). His *Schools Where Parents Make a Difference* is a collection of successful case studies of democratic participation. In contrast to adversarial advisers Davies believes: "Schools need change, the change that only school-community alliances bring" (p. 9). Another perspective on individual parent participation is provided by writers such as Berger (1981), who seek to strengthen the partnership between professionals and parents. Berger identifies six role orientations for parents: spectators, accessory volunteers, volunteer resources, employed resources, policymakers, and teachers of their own children. Morrison (1978) stresses the role of the family. His definition of parent involvement is: "a process of actualizing the potential of parents; of helping parents discover their strengths, potentialities, and talents; and of using them for the benefit of themselves and the family" (p. 22). Buskin's *Parent Power* (1975) was another reasoned attempt to aid parents in relating to schools, but time has eroded the usefulness of Buskin's ideas. These sources are only samples of an extensive and growing literature on individual parent participation in education.

Governmental Publications

In our opinion, some of the best advice and information for *both parents and educators* can be found in governmental documents. For example, the handbook of the Texas Advisory Committee to the U.S. Commission on Civil Rights, *Working with Your School* (1977), is a superior reference for leaders in schools and communities. Particular sections on "How to Influence School Decisions" and "Dealing with People in the Education Pyramid" should be available to all persons interested in school-community relations.

Another governmental publication, *Working with Schools: A Parents' Handbook,* issued by the Division of Education, U.S. Office of Education (Pfeil, 1980) should be made readily available to any interested parents *after being circulated throughout the professional staff.* We close this discussion of individual parental involvement with a checklist (Exhibit 12.2) from this *Handbook.* Notice the built-in progression from observation through service and participation to advocacy, if needed.

Exhibit 12.2

Checklist: Parental Involvement

Personal Evaluation

1. Do I attend parent meetings?
2. Do I volunteer my services at my child's school?
3. Do I read newsletters and/or notes from the school?
4. Do I visit my child's classroom other than at conference time?
5. Do I know if my school or school district has a parent advisory council (PAC)?
6. Have I attended a PAC meeting?
7. Do I discuss my child's school with:
    Other parents?
    My child's teacher?
    The principal?
    Other administrators?
8. Do I know what role parents have in planning, carrying out, and reviewing the instructional program at my child's school?
9. Am I involved in such activities?
10. Do I know how to make a complaint about my child's school?
    Do I discuss the problem first with the person(s) most directly involved?
    If we cannot resolve the problem, do I talk with other appropriate school officials and/or parent groups? (Pfeil, 1980, p. 42)

ADVISORY COUNCILS

Almost certainly the most salient element in the new relationships between schools and their communities is the advisory council. Much of the concern is because it invariably gets at some redistribution or sharing of power. Some of the concern is due to the ambiguity of purposes and the attendant absence of identified constraints. Certainly, the professional literature has caught up with this new development in general, but the changes identified in previous chapters have again created situations new to educators. Councils with federal regulations specifying their roles as a condition of funding for some programs proliferated.[3] Paradoxically, Gittell (1980) concluded that the type of participation mandated by the government ultimately worked to the detriment of meaningful citizen participation: "In fact, advocates of citizen participation have more reason to despair now than they did ten years ago" (p. 241). Her argument is that the organizations have become service-delivery-oriented at the expense of "those who actively seek a redistribution of power throughout the system" (ibid). More moderate observers of the development of advisory councils disagree with this pessimistic assessment. (See esp. Smith, 1981; see also Jackson, 1980.) We must all acknowledge that the social dynamics are significantly different from what they were in the late 1960s and early 1970s.

Now, four states (California, Florida, Hawaii, and South Carolina) have mandates for parent participation in schools. A publication (Zerchykov and Davies, 1980) describes work in California, Florida, and South Carolina. All three states have created independent state-wide networks to foster citizen participation. Their activities focus on advisory committees but also explore other ways people can work with schools. The role of the state-level independent group is believed to be highly related to advisory committee effectiveness (Harris, 1982). All of these states have guidelines and prototype materials for the different levels of school advisory councils. (See, e.g., Dade County Public Schools, 1981.)

Individual schools and school districts have also prepared resource materials on school councils. Donald Thomas, superintendent of Salt Lake City Schools, is a prolific contributor to this literature. The *Shared Governance Training Manual* for the Salt Lake City District (1981) explains in detail the necessary constraints on shared governance, which are identified as education law, board of education policies, budget, and ethics. This seems necessary advice to all concerned to avoid seeming to invent after-the-fact roadblocks to some proposed plan of action and to avoid waste of everyone's time and effort.

Because of the variety of advisory committees and the ready

---

[3]Note that this requirement for Title I ESEA programs was removed during the Reagan administration: "Under the Education Consolidation and Improvement Act a district will no longer be required to have Parent Advisory Councils, but may continue those councils if it wishes to do so" (U.S. Department of Education, Office of Planning, Budget, and Evaluation, 1981, Section A, Subsection 1, p. 7). This is an additional instance of the influence of legislatures discussed in Chapter 7.

availability of publications, we will not attempt a comprehensive presentation. From the perspective of our readers such committees are only one piece of the mosaic of school-community relations, albeit an important piece. We shall, however, draw primarily on one source (Mann, 1973) supplemented by a checklist review from Pfeil (1980).

Mann maintains that shared control has three characteristics:

1. the regular opportunity for community participation in a comprehensive range of policy matter;
2. the inclusion of all relevant points of view; and
3. the probability that the community's participation will have an effect on school policy. (p. 5)

He takes up three different ways of selecting members for school-related groups: appointment, election, and a combination of appointment and election. He does not recommend appointment except for the unusual situation of selecting an ad hoc group to plan a better method of selection. He believes that appointed groups—no matter who does the appointing—will not be perceived as representative groups.

Elections are the preferred method of selecting citizen members for the committee or board. Any adult residing in the school district would be eligible to vote and all would be eligible to run for election except persons employed by the school. Proper notice of the election should be made well in advance by different media (e.g., announcements, leaflets, telephone). Candidates should be nominated by petitions requiring only a few signatures and all should run at large except in some high school districts where such an arrangement would leave some areas unrepresented (pp. 18-20).

Elections should be held at the school during a time that is convenient for most people. Mann suggests the night of the school open house. He would have the election held over a thirty-six-hour period to make it easier for voters to get to the polling place. Ballots would be secret and available in all relevant languages. Proof of residence (no minimum time limit) would be required and voters sign a list before they vote. A prompt, *public* counting of ballots is important. Candidates getting the most votes are elected (p. 21).

Combined election and appointment has the potential of insuring broad representation. For example, half the seats on a committee could be assigned to community organizations. The organizations could then elect or appoint their representatives according to their own policies. The other seats on the committee would be filled by an election of candidates at large as described above. The potential flaw in the combined election and appointment procedure is that it is possible that the organizations could double their influence by working to secure the election of additional members of their group. Clearly, the methods used to elect members of the committee have great influence on the sort of committee resulting from the process (p. 23).

Authority of School-Community Groups

Mann begins his discussion of the activities of school-community groups with the assumption that neither total professional control nor total community control is possible. Principals in cooperation with the school-community group should consider five factors that help determine the role of the group:

> The interests and abilities of the neighborhood group itself.
> Other possible factors (teachers' unions, the central board, community action groups, and so on).
> Legal restraints (federal, state, and local laws, regulations, guidelines, contracts, and so on).
> The estimated effects of the involvement on achieving the school's goals.
> The availability of the means and opportunity to influence decisions. (p. 28)

Areas of concern to school-community groups include curriculum policy, budget policy, personnel, and student concerns. The involvement of the school-community group should be at the policy level, not at the level of day-to-day operating decisions. The extent of involvement is developmental and varies from one area to another. Intensity and scope of involvement in any one issue is a matter for continuing, mutual resolution. If no compromise can be arranged, the principal may have to invoke his legal authority to prevail. This resort to legal authority should be avoided whenever possible because it can have serious and debilitating consequences on school-community relations.

Organization of the School-Community Group

An odd-numbered group of between nine and fifteen members is suggested. The creation and distribution of clear bylaws can help prevent misunderstandings. Meetings should be planned on a schedule related to the timing of school decisions. The agenda should be conspicuously posted and circulated before meetings. With rare exceptions, all meetings should be public.

Mann calls attention to the need to provide information and training to both community and school faculty. Staff anxiety can be lessened when teachers participate in the public planning of the involvement procedures. Citizen representatives need orientations to school policy as well as practice in working together to arrive at group decisions. Finally, it would be especially helpful if the school-community group could meet with early success. This requires attention to a local issue of real importance but of manageable proportions rather than a major reform in educational practice. When the group achieves a success, it should be commended and publicized by the principal (1973, p. 53).

The checklist, Evaluating Parent Advisory Councils, from *Working with Schools: A Parent's Handbook,* provides an overview of issues to be considered when establishing or working with an advisory council.

Exhibit 12.3
Evaluating Parent Advisory Councils

Membership
1. How many members are on the council?
2. How were they selected?
3. Are they representative of the parents in the district or school?
4. Are parents who are not members involved in council activities?

Meetings
1. Does the council have regularly scheduled meetings?
2. When? Where?
3. Are the meetings well publicized in advance and open to the public?
4. Do parents other than council members have an opportunity to speak at meetings?
5. Are council decisions and/or recommendations sent to all parents?

Training
1. Is there a training program for members of the parent advisory council?
2. What does it involve?
3. Do council members have basic information about the organizational structure of the local school district?
    Names and phone numbers of administrators?
    The basic curriculum in the district or school?
    Special programs that are available within the school(s)?

Activities

1. Is there a written statement of the responsibilities of the parent advisory council?
2. Have both administrators and council members agreed to the statement?
3. Has the council been involved in the following activities:
   Identifying the needs of children in the school or district?
   Establishing a list of educational priorities?
   Reviewing proposals for new programs?
   Planning new programs or changes in existing programs?
   Reviewing Textbooks and/or tests being considered for use in the school?
   Evaluating school programs?
4. Does the council invoke other parents in school activities?
5. Has the council established a complaint procedure for parents?

Support

1. Are funds available to cover parent council expenses, such as mailing, supply, and clerical costs?
2. Is space made available for meetings at times that are convenient to parents?
3. Do council members receive all the information they need to fulfill their responsibilities?
4. Does the principal (or superintendent) seriously consider the recommendations of the council?
5. Is there a staff member assigned as a liaison to the council? (Pfeil, 1980, pp. 43-44)

NEED FOR BALANCE

To this point we have been examining ways of increasing citizen participation in school activities. Reasons for this emphasis have been reiterated in several places throughout the book. An additional reason is that, in general, throughout the entire nation, citizens do not have adequate access or influence to affect educational policies and practices.

Although the prevailing condition justifies the stress on increasing participation, it is necessary to acknowledge that, obviously, this is not universally true. There are certainly situations where school-community relations are ideal. There are also certainly situations where there is too much citizen participation in school activities! For this reason, it is necessary to consider the problem of securing and retaining an appropriate balance between community participation and professional autonomy.

An excellent, theoretical conceptualization of the need for balance in the relationship between schools and communities was provided by Eugene Litwak and Henry Meyer. They identified at least three points of view among educators concerning the importance of the community in meeting school objectives: "closed door," "open door," and "balanced" (1974, pp. 4-6).

The "closed door" point of view holds that community involvement is extraneous and possibly harmful to the education of the students. This is the bureaucratic position widely held in European school systems. A community relations program for those who believe in this way would attempt to keep a maximum distance between schools and communities. Educators of this belief would reason that parents and others (including aides and volunteers) could only interfere with the effectiveness of the professionals.

"Open door" advocates believe that schools are only one of many educational institutions affecting students. Moreover, they assume that motivation for learning arises from the everyday, out-of-school lives of students. This is the position once ascribed to "progressive educators" and now held by many who favor a liberal, pupil-centered education. Community relations for these educators would lessen the distance between school and community and encourage closer contact.

The "balanced" position recognizes some merit in both of the other positions. Educators of the "balanced" persuasion acknowledge that sometimes schools and communities are so close that professional performance suffers and sometimes they are so far apart that they may be working against each other. These educators believe that there is an optimal social distance between the extremes of intimacy and isolation. Community relations for these educators would be designed to achieve an optimum balance. In a community of immigrants who fear and distrust the school, the need would be to close the distance between school and the community. In "Pill Hill," where a majority of professional, affluent parents intervene too often and too closely in school affairs, the need would be to increase the distance. In a community with both kinds of parents, the need would be to decrease and increase distance at the same time according to the group concerned—immigrants or professionals. The "balanced" position assumes that cooperation between expert professionals and others in the community is necessary.

Linking Mechanisms for Schools

Maintaining the appropriate balance is largely a function of linking mechanisms. These mechanisms may or may not be viewed by the schools as deliberate community relations tactics. Litwak and Meyer identify eight practices that seem to relate schools to their communities. The linking mechanisms are: detached worker, opinion leader, settlement house, auxiliary voluntary agency, common messenger, mass media, formal authority, and delegated function (Litwak and Meyer, 1974, pp. 16-18).

Detached worker. The detached worker is a professional person sent to the community to develop a more trusting relationship. Some school-community coordinators serve in this manner. School nurses, social workers, and parent partners represent this approach. Teachers and principals who visit the homes of their students may be operating to the same effect as detached workers.

Opinion leader. In this linking mechanism, the educator uses the influence of the natural leaders of the community. It is hoped that gaining the support of the key leader will cause him to deliver the support of his group. Some bond issue or millage campaign strategies rely heavily on this approach.

Settlement house. This mechanism provides facilities and professional staff in the community. The staff can influence parents and others to support school objectives and to lessen the social distance. Community school programs and, to some extent, lighted schoolhouse programs are examples of this tactic.

Auxiliary voluntary agency. This linking mechanism brings together educators and members of the community. The familiar PTA or mothers' club are good examples of auxiliary voluntary agencies. Usually the officers of the voluntary agency are not educators.

Common messenger. In this mechanism, persons who are members of both the community and the school are used as messengers. They can communicate both ways. Examples are students, paid aides, volunteers, and members of local boards or committees.

Mass media. This mechanism includes the typical media described in Chapter 10 on public relations: bulletins, newspapers, radio, television, posters, and so on.

Formal authority. This is the authority of law or tradition that requires members of the community to conform to school requirements.

Principals have this kind of authority. Attendance officers may also use delegated formal authority.

Delegated function. This mechanism delegates a responsibility to another organization that, in turn, links itself to the school community. The other organization may be a social agency or a medical agency.

The selection of which linking mechanisms to use is based on the goals of the school (to increase or decrease social distance) and principles of communication. (These principles are: initiative, intensity, focused expertise, and scope. Since their definitions are not essential to the development of the argument, they are not explained here. Any communications principles could be used. But see Litwak and Meyer, 1974, pp. 19-25.) Table 12.5 gives an overview of the utility of the eight linking mechanisms for two major positions on school-community relations. It is adapted and abridged from Litwak and Meyer, who included the third position, "balanced," which is omitted from Table 12.5. To generate the missing data on "balanced" school-community relations, readers need only restate the information provided in the other two columns. For example, the linking mechanism of detached worker is *very high* for closing social distance and *very low* for creating or increasing social distance. The missing "balanced" column would read: "very high when distance is to be decreased (e.g., when the community is hostile); very low when distance is to be increased (e.g., when the community is too involved)" (p. 27).

Table 12.5

Comparative Usefulness of Linking Mechanisms Used by Schools

Linking Mechanism	Estimated Usefulness to	
	Close Social Distance	Create or Maintain Social Distance
Detached worker	Very high	Very low
Opinion leader	Potentially moderate	Very low
Settlement house	High, potentially very high when community is friendly	Very low
Voluntary association	Moderate, potentially very high when community is friendly	Moderate
Common messenger	Low	High
Mass media	Low	High
Formal authority	Very low	Very high

There are, of course, other linking mechanisms used by schools. It should also be evident that linking mechanisms—as we noted for public relations practices—cannot make a difference if the substance of the educational program in the schools is inadequate or not congruent with community goals.

Linking Mechanisms for Communities

Although most of our readers are more concerned with the use of linking mechanisms from the educator's perspective, the reciprocal nature of school-community relations requires attention to linking mechanisms by which the community attempts to influence the school. Some of the mechanisms are similar but there are important differences. Among the linking mechanisms available to the community are: advocate bureaucracy, strategic influencers, voluntary associations, mass media, ad hoc demonstrations, sustained collective action, common messenger, and individual ad hoc contact (pp. 35-40).

Advocate bureaucracy. The community may seek to use one bureaucracy to change another. Sometimes pressure groups (discussed in Chapter 4) serve this purpose. The intervention of the ACLU on behalf of the rights of married students to participate in extracurricular activities and of the NAACP to remove racial bias from curriculum materials are examples of advocate bureaucracies. Law firms who bring suits against school systems and even newspaper "action lines" that investigate citizen complaints are also examples.

Strategic influencers. This mechanism consists of using the support of an important, powerful person on behalf of the community objective. The influential person may be within the school system or outside it. Securing the support of the governor for a decentralization plan is an easy example. Persuading the curriculum director or an assistant superintendent of the need to revise certain materials is going "over the head" of the principal to bring additional influence to bear on a community objective.

Voluntary associations. We have noted the role of the PTA as a possible school-community linking mechanism. Clearly, it can, and does, work both ways, school to community and community to school. Independent "Save Our Schools" types of organizations are other examples of voluntary associations acting to accomplish community goals.

Mass media. The media are not available on a regular basis but can be used to add to the impact of demonstrations or meetings or by creating newsworthy events. The tactic of serving as an information source to a sympathetic reporter is well known to more affluent, suburban critics of the schools. Reporters rely on such sources and are willing to cooperate and protect the identity of the news source if this should be necessary. Often the best access to mass media may be through an advocate bureaucracy, as discussed above.

Ad hoc demonstrations. This approach is often used in conjunction with the mass media to gain additional support for a community objective. Picketing, boycotts, marches, sit-ins are all examples of demonstrations. It is difficult, even for the initiators, to control the outcomes of demonstrations.

Sustained collective action. This mechanism resembles demonstrations, but is really a more sustained collective action against the school or school system to be changed. In addition to publicizing the community cause, this approach may cause economic damage—the loss of state aid due to sustained student boycotts. A strong organization is needed to support the strikes, boycotts, and other tactics characteristic of sustained collective action.

Common messenger. As mentioned above in the discussion of school linking mechanisms, a common messenger belongs to both the school and the community group. Some common messengers are employees, ranging from teachers (high powered) to crossing guards (low powered). Volunteers, board members, and students are all common messengers. An innovative use of common messengers is found in the Palo Alto, California, School-Community Input Team (SCIT). The SCITs, used to augment educational planning, are made up of citizens, parents, staff, and students (see Palo Alto Unified School District, 1973).

Individual ad hoc contact. This mechanism refers to all of the individual parent contacts to complain, get information, inform schools, or for any other purpose. It has been discussed to a large extent in a section above, "Participation by Individual Parents."

An analysis of the community-initiated linking mechanisms by principles of communication helps determine which ones are most appropriate in a particular set of circumstances. Although examples of this analysis are supplied by Litwak and Meyer, readers are cautioned that, "with our present state of knowledge, the development of a community program to affect school-community relations will involve complex assessments, value judgments, and much trial and error" (1974, p. 50).

Although the balance theory is untested, it has much to offer educators seeking a rationale to support their school-community relations activities. The logic is compelling even though we may never be able to design a study that will provide a sound empirical base. Many subjective analyses can be made by educators. Certainly, at least in the area of school-community relations, we will never know anything if knowing comes only from the controlled research models of psychologists and statisticians. Educators, especially school administrators, will need to employ other ways of knowing (see March, 1973, pp. 49-54).

SUMMARY

In this final chapter we identified a persuasive rationale for citizen participation in education. A logical approach to planning for such participation was delineated, including a matching of functions with techniques and some suggestions for deciding which techniques are most appropriate. Forms of participation were identified according to the amount of power associated with each form. Different kinds of participation were presented in a kind of ladder of increasing levels of citizen involvement. Boards were found to be more powerful modes of participation than committees. Some kinds of participation such as volunteer service were said to be without increased power for the participant. One manual designed to give specific help to educators seeking to establish school advisory committees was reviewed in some detail.

A separate discussion of participation by individual parents was necessary to avoid giving the impression that advisory bodies of any type could ever substitute for the essentially private, individual relationships between the parents of students and the educators of those students. The need for a balance between citizen participation and professional autonomy was acknowledged, and activities to increase and decrease the involvement of the community were identified.

In this entire discussion of schools and communities in transition we have established the need for improved school-community relations and have described and demonstrated methods of proven effectiveness. The present context of the public schools demands creative change in the relations between educators and their communities. It has been our purpose to stimulate that creativity in readers who are destined to provide the leadership essential to ensuring that the transition referred to in our title, *School-Community Relations in Transition,* is from the present unsure state to an improved, more harmonious condition.

SUGGESTED ACTIVITIES

1. Investigate the degree of citizen participation in school policies at a local or subdistrict level. Place the school or subdistrict participation arrangement on Arnstein's Ladder of Citizen Participation. Explain why you believe your placement is correct.
2. Three benefits are said to come from parent involvement:
   a. Parents are able to complement the work of education by becoming informed by their involvement.
   b. Education will be reformed by the presence of external observers. Educators will become more accountable. Parents may suggest changes.
   c. Citizens will enjoy the democratic right of participation.
   Make a list of the kinds of evidence you would seek to determine whether these intended benefits were being achieved. Then make a similar list of the major "costs" of parent involvement (for example, some loss of professional autonomy). Then note the kinds of evidence you would seek to determine whether these costs were being incurred.
3. Try to discover the best known, most vigorous critic of the schools in your district. Ask several educators for nominations. When you have identified the critic, analyze his tactics. Compare them with those advised by Lurie in *How to Change the Schools* or with Hess's suggestions in *The Third Side of the Desk.*
4. Identify a school that would be considered "closed door" using Litwak and Meyer's concept of balance in citizen participation. Make a list of all the linking mechanisms used by the school. Do the same for a school that would be considered "open door." Compare the lists of linking mechanisms.
5. Identify a school or a school district that has groups of clients that are:
   too distant from the school in terms of social climate, and
   too close, too involved in school activities.
   Try to discover if the school discriminates between the two groups in their community relations practices.
6. Think about education ten years from now. Prepare two scenarios, one assuming public schools can accommodate pluralistic communities and the other assuming the trend toward many separate systems prevails.
7. Visit an advisory council. Identify each separate transaction, create categories, assign each transaction to a category, and tabulate the results. Based on this one observation, what tentative hypothesis would seem worth pursuing concerning the nature of council activities?

SUGGESTED READINGS

Carrillo, Tony. "Making Your Council Work." *Citizen Action in Education* 6(1) (March 1979): 8, 10.

Clarke-Stewart, K. Alison. "Parent Education in the 1970s." *Educational Evaluation and Policy Analysis* (6) (November-December 1981):47-58.

Davies, Don, and Zerchykov, Ross. *Citizen Participation in Education: Annotated Bibliography.* 2nd ed. Boston: Institute for Responsive Education, 1978.

Fernandez, Happy. *Parents Organizing to Improve Schools.* Columbia, Md.: National Committee for Citizens in Education, 1976.

Fisher, Allen. "Advisory Committees—Does Anybody Want Their Advice?" *Educational Leadership* 37(3) (December 1979):254-55.

Hall, Burnis, Jr., and Barnwell, Eleanor I. "Working with Community Advisory Councils: Key to Success in Urban Schools." *Phi Delta Kappan* 63(7) (March 1982):491-92.

Holcomb, John H. "Don't Let Advisers Run Your Schools." *American School Board Journal* 169 (April 1982):39-40.

Litwak, Eugene, and Rothman, Jack. "The Impact of Organizational Structure and Linkage on Agency Programs and Services." In *Strategies of Community Organization.* 3rd ed. Ed. Fred Cox, John Erlich, Jack Rothman, and John Tropmans. Itasca, Ill.: Peacock Publishers, 1979, pp. 249-62.

Mann, Dale. "Political Representation and Urban Advisory Councils." *Teachers College Record* 75(3) (November 1977):379-97.

Moyer, Kerry L. "Four Steps to Effective Community Involvement." *Educational Leadership* 39(4) (January 1982):285-87.

Rowell, J. Cy. "The Five Rights of Parents." *Phi Delta Kappan* 62(6) (February 1981):441-43.

Saxe, Richard W., and Gish, Elmer. "Public Participation in Educational Policy Making." In *The Changing Politics of Education: Prospects for the 1980s.* Ed. Edith Mosher and Jennings Waggoner, Jr. Berkeley: McCutchan Publishing Corp., 1978, pp. 194-200.

Sinclair, Robert L. *A Two-Way Street: Home-School Cooperation in Curriculum Decision-making.* Boston: Institute for Responsive Education, 1980.

Stanton, Jim, and Zerchykov, Ross, et al. *Overcoming Barriers to School Council Effectiveness.* Boston: Institute for Responsive Education, 1979.

REFERENCES

Arnstein, Sherry R. "A Ladder of Citizen Participation." *Journal of the American Institute of Planners* 35 (July 1969):216-24.

———. "Eight Rungs on the Ladder of Citizen Participation." In *Citizen Participation: Effecting Community Change.* Ed. Edgar S. Cahn and Barry A. Passett. New York: Praeger, 1971.

———. "Maximum Feasible Manipulation." *Public Administration Review* 32 (special issue) (September 1972):377-90.

Berger, Eugenia H. *Parents as Partners in Education: The School and Home Working Together.* St. Louis: C. V. Mosby Co., 1981.

Bowles, B. Dean. "School-Community Relations, Community Support, and Student Achievement: A Summary of Findings." Mimeographed review of studies at the University of Wisconsin, Madison Research and Development Center for Individualized Schooling, 1981.

Buskin, Martin. *Parent Power.* New York: Walker and Co., 1975.

Cibulka, James G. "Measuring Formal Citizenship in Educational Programs." *Division Generator* 4(2) (March 1974):4-12.

Dade County Public Schools, Department of Community Relations. *Recommended (Revised) Guidelines for the Organization and Operation of Citizen Advisory Committees.* Miami, 1981.

Davies, Don. "Citizen Participation in Decision-Making in the Schools." In *Communities and Their Schools.* Ed. Don Davies. New York: McGraw-Hill, 1981, pp. 83-120.

_____. "Citizen Participation and School Effectiveness." Paper prepared for the Alaska Effective Schooling Project Design Conference, February 1982.

_____. ed. *Schools Where Parents Make a Difference.* Boston: Institute for Responsive Education, 1976.

Elliott, John; Bridges, David; Ebbutt, Dave; Gibson, Rex; and Nias, Jennifer. *School Accountability.* London: Grant McIntyre Ltd., 1981.

Foshay, Arthur W. "The Problem of Community." In *New Views of School and Community.* Ed. Julie Rash and Patricia Markun. Washington, D.C.: National Association of Elementary School Principals, 1973, pp. 4-9.

Freedom Through Equality, Inc. *A Handbook for Parents: Make the Public Schools Work for You.* Milwaukee, 1972.

Gittell, Marilyn. *Limits to Citizen Participation: The Decline of Community Organizations.* Beverly Hills, Cal.: Sage Publications, 1980.

Harris, Marshall A., director, Flordia Education Council. Personal letter, February 11, 1982.

Henderson, Anne T. "Parent Involvement: Does It Improve Student Achievement?" *Citizen Action in Education* 9(1) (June 1982):3.

Hess, Hannah S. *The Third Side of the Desk.* New York: Scribner's, 1973.

Hill, Jack. "A School Which Makes a Difference." *Citizen Action in Education* 9(1) (June 1982):8-9.

Howey, Kenneth R. *Successful Schooling Practices: Perceptions of a Total School Faculty.* Report ETT-30-7. San Francisco: Far West Laboratory for Educational Research and Development, 1980.

Jackson, Barbara L. "Federal Intervention and New Governance Structures." In *Communities and Their Schools.* Ed. Don Davies. New York: McGraw-Hill, 1980, pp. 145-88.

Lezotte, Lawrence. "Overview of Effective School Research." *Citizen Action in Education* 9(1) (June 1982):1, 10-11.

Litwak, Eugene, and Meyer, Henry J. *School, Family, and Neighborhood: The Theory and Practice of School-Community Relations.* New York: Columbia University Press, 1974.

Lurie, Ellen. *How to Change the Schools: A Parent's Action Handbook on How to Fight the System.* New York: Random House, 1970.

Mann, Dale. *A Principal's Handbook for Shared Control in Urban Community Schools.* New York: Teachers College, Columbia University, 1973.

March, James G. "Analytical Skills and the University Training of Educational Administrators." Seventh Annual Walter D. Cocking Memorial Lecture given at the National Conference of Professors of Educational Administration, Bellingham, Wash., August 16, 1973.

Morrison, George S. *Parent Involvement in the Home, School, and Community.* Columbus, Ohio: Charles E. Merrill, 1978.

Ornstein, Allan. "Research on Decentralization." *Phi Delta Kappan* 54(9) (May 1973):610-14.

Palo Alto Unified School District. "The School/Community Input Team as a Social Invention." Palo Alto, Cal., 1973.

Pfeil, Mary Pat (U.S. Office of Education). *Working with Schools: A Parents' Handbook.* Washington, D.C.: U.S. Government Printing Office, ED Publications no. 79-07109, 1980.

Rich, Dorothy, and Mattox, Beverly. *101 Activities for Building More Effective School-Community Involvement.* Washington, D.C.: Home and School Institute, Trinity College, 1976.

Rioux, William et al. *You Can Improve Your Child's School: Practical Answers to Questions Parents Ask Most About Their Schools.* New York: Simon & Schuster, 1980.

Rosener, Judy B. "Matching Method to Purpose: The Challenges of Planning Citizen-Participation Activities." In *Citizen Participation in America.* Ed. Stuart Langton. Lexington, Mass.: Lexington Books, 1978, pp. 109-22.

Salisbury, Robert H. *Citizen Participation in the Public Schools.* Lexington, Mass.: Lexington Books, 1980.

Salt Lake City School District, Office of Volunteers and Public Information. *Shared Governance Training Manual.* Salt Lake City, 1981.

Scribner, Jay D., and O'Shea, David. "Political Developments in Urban School Districts." In *Uses of the Sociology of Education: The Seventy-Third Yearbook of the National Society for the Study of Education.* Ed. C. Wayne Gordon. Chicago: University of Chicago Press, 1974.

Smith, Bruce L. R. "Community Control Revisited." *Journal of Community Action* (1) (September/October 1981):34-36.

Stallworth, John T. "Parent Involvement at the Elementary School Level: A Survey of Teachers, Executive Summary of a Report." Austin, Tex.: Southwest Educational Development Laboratory, 1982.

————. "Identifying Barriers to Parent Involvement in the School: A Survey of Educators." Paper presented at American Educational Research Association Meeting, New York, March 1982.

Texas Advisory Committee to the U.S. Commission on Civil Rights. *Working with Your School.* Washington, D.C.: U.S. Government Printing Office, 1977.

U.S. Department of Education, Office of Planning, Budget, and Evaluation. *Annual Evaluation Report.* Vol. 2. Fiscal Year 1981. Mimeo. Washington, D.C., 1981.

Weinberg, Richard L., and Weinberg, Lynn G. *Parent Prerogatives: How to Handle Teacher Misbehaviors and Other School Disorders.* Chicago: Nelson-Hall, 1979.

Williams, David L., Jr. "Parent Involvement at the Elementary School Level: A Survey of Principals, Executive Summary." Austin, Tex.: Southwest Educational Development Laboratory, 1982.

Windle, Charles, and Cibulka, James G. "A Framework for Understanding Participation in Community Mental Health Services." *Community Mental Health Journal* 17(1) (Spring 1981):4-18.

Yin, Robert K., Lucas, William A., Szanton, Peter L., and Spindler, J. Andrew. *Citizen Organizations: Increasing Client Control over Services.* Santa Monica, Cal.: RAND Corporation, 1973.

Zerchykov, Ross, and Davies, Don, with Chrispeels, Janet. *Leading the Way: State Mandates for School Advisory Councils in California, Florida and South Carolina.* Boston: Institute for Responsive Education, 1980.

NAME INDEX

SUBJECT INDEX